TOWN AND HINTERLAND IN CENTRAL JAVA

TOWN AND HINTERLAND IN CENTRAL JAVA

The Banjarnegara productionstructure in regional perspective

Wouter de Jong
Institute for Urban and Regional and Research/INRO-TNO
Delft, The Netherlands
Frank van Steenbergen
Ministery of Development Cooperation, The Netherlands

GADJAH MADA UNIVERSITY PRESS
1987

277.31.10.87

Printed in Indonesia by:
GADJAH MADA UNIVERSITY PRESS
8609205–C1E

ISBN 979–420–077–8

PREFACE

In 1830 Dipayuda, ruler of the regency Banjar-Watulumbu, asked the Dutch Colonial Government to be allowed to have a new court built south of the Serayu River. He felt that his present residence north the Serayu was too isolated. When the river flooded, a recurrent problem, communications became impossible. Soon as he was permitted, Dipayuda had a site prepared south of the Serayu. A hill was leveled to provide a flat piece of land; as a sign of power two *waringin* trees were planted; a *Kabupaten* building and a home for the Dutch Assistent Resident were erected; some roads were laid: the stretch of land had become a regents seat. Until today this fact, at August 22nd, is commemorated. Every year there is a party at the *Kabupaten* building, and festivities are held in the town. Dipayuda is not forgotten either. The grave of Banjarnegara's founder, some miles west of town, is neatly maintained. A lane, connecting central square and main market, is named after Dipayuda. And kin relations, linking present town inhabitants with the founding father are minitually sought out.

To the traveller present day Banjarnegara appears the eye of the storm. The highbeat life, that characterizes Java's cities, seems unknown to ostensibly lethargic Banjarnegara, though it is not too far away. Banjarnegara is located on the east west provincial road from Magelang to Purwokerto. All trough island traffic on Java uses the arteries along the north and southcoast, thus circumventing Banjarnegara. Town dwellers whether affectionally or with discontent, speak of Banjarnegara as *Kota Pensiun* or *Kota Sepi*

(Pensioner Town or Quiet Town). Is Banjarnegara a *Kota Pensiun*? Why did we research this town?

Recent literature on spatial planning emphasizes the role of small towns in the process of regional and national development. Towns are supposed to act as intermediates between countryside and big cities, where economic and bureaucratic decision making is concentrated. The increased attention for the function of small towns in development is linked to many phenomena; the excessive growth of metropoles, the failure of big city centered development policy, the neglect of rural resources. In a way it has become a very fashionable subject. But planning concepts are not always realistic however, and empirical evidence on the present functioning of small towns lags behind regional planning notions.

The Section Developing Countries of the Utrecht State University Geographical Department started a research programme to help filling this gap. Since several years, small urban centres and their hinterland are studied in Mali, West Africa. To broaden insight on the subject a second Small Town Research Programme was started in Indonesia, an area totally different from Mali. The reasons to take Indonesia, in particular the Upper Serayu Valley region in Central Java, can be summarized as follows:

— The relatively unique settlement pattern of Java. For a developing country primacy is low in Indonesia, which means that a comparatively high percentage of the urban population lives in medium—and small—sized towns.
— The lack of recent empirical research into the socio-economic structure and regional functioning of small urban centres in Indonesia.
— Established and fruitful contacts between the Universitas Gadjah Mada, Yogyakarta and the State University of Utrecht, that led to the willingness of the former to parttake in the programme.
— Wide research experience in Indonesia of the Geographical Department, Section Developing Countries, especially in rural areas in the Upper Serayu Valley region, which results could be used in the new project.

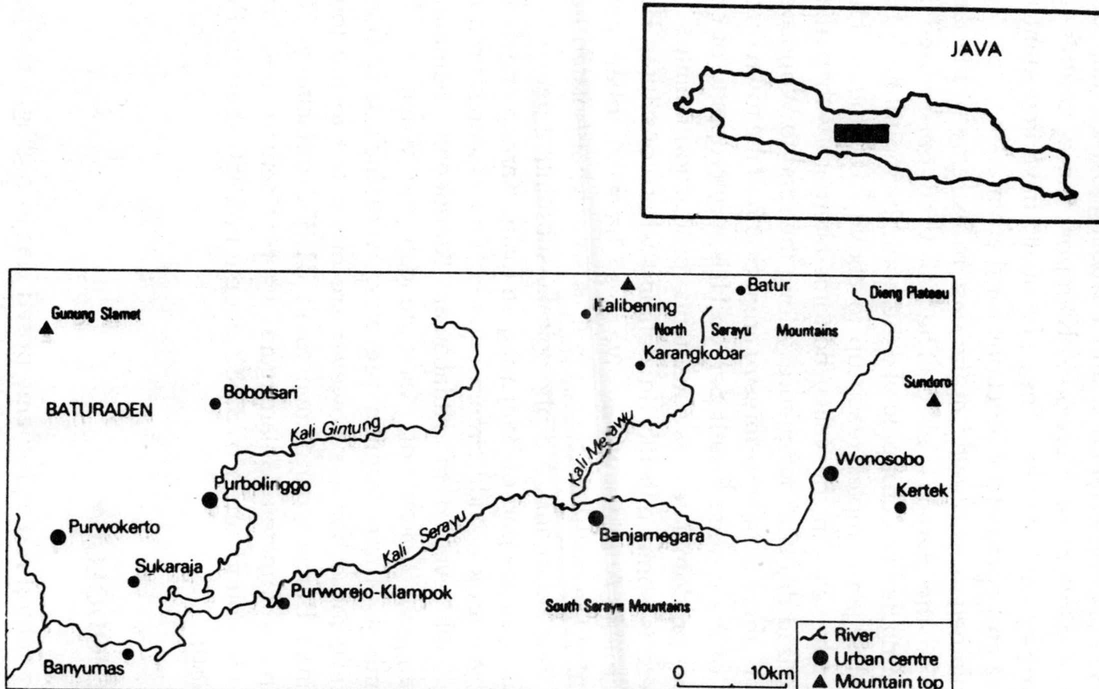

MAP OF URBAN CENTRES IN THE SERAYU VALLEY REGION (taken from US Army Map 1944)

Map 0.1. Serayu Valley Region

Banjarnegara was the first town to be explored in this programme (January—June 1983). Follow up was planned in Wonosobo, Purworejo-Klampok and Purbolinggo (see map 0.1). With the exception of Purworejo-Klampok these centres are *kabupaten* (regency) capitals. They potentially have important administrative and commercial functions for the hinterland.

Banjarnegara is situated at the eastern extreme of the large depression in the Serayu Valley. The valley bottom is used for technically irrigated rice cropping. To the north the mountains of the Dieng-Jembangan complex reach up to above 2100 meter. Here rainfed paddy fields in the valley bottoms alternate with partially commercialized dry land agriculture. Along the road to Wonosobo, east of town, there is an agro-forestry area. South of the town on the poor soils of the eroded South Serayu Hills, dry cropping of corn and cassave predominates, as subsistence production mainly.

There is some difficulty in defining what constitutes Banjarnegara town. Administratively five *desa* have an urban status (*kelurahan*). One of these, Sokonandi, is somewhat isolated from the other four *kelurahan*. Morphologically substantive parts of two rural status *desa* are part of Banjarnegara town; Karangtengah and Wangon. We took a wide circumscription. Our research area encompassed all seven *desa;* Kutabanjar, Krandegan, Semarang, Parakancanggah, Sokonandi, Karangtengah and Wangon. Thus some hamlets, where farming prevales, were included. Socio-economically these hamlets however are orientated to the town. Thus defined Banjarnegara town totals 31,352 inhabitants. The population of *kabupaten* Banjarnegara, whereof Banjarnegara is the capital town, counts up to 673,582 people in 1980 (Sensus Penduduk 1980).

0.1. METHODOLOGY

The central research theme posed was to highlight the position of Banjarnegara as a regional centre. The study aimed at collecting information on the town's production structure with regard to its position in the hinterland. The following research objectives were stated:

1. To determine the position of Banjarnegara in the urban system and the area served by the town's institutions and enterprises.
2. To determine the range of town based enterprises, their sectoral composition and interlinking and management characteristics.
3. To investigate the intraregional and interregional economic relationships of town based enterprises, with special regard to the importance of Banjarnegara enterprises for the marketing and processing of regional primary and secondary surplusses.

It should be understood that as small town production structure was a crucial issue, key entity in our study was the private enterprise. It is defined as: "autonomously operating units of organization, consisting of one or more persons who are more or less permanently engaged in the production and/or trade of goods and/or services for the reason of making profit".

In order to reach the stated research objectives, a first step was to compile statistics from government institutions in town. At a later date this procedure was repeated with a more purposeful attitude. Major sources were: *Bappeda Tingkat 2*, *Kantor Statistik*, *Kantor Kecamatan*, *Dinas Perindustrian*, *Dinas Perdagangan*, *Dinas Peternakan*, *Dinas Pertanian*, *F.B.S.I.*, *D.P.U.* and banks in the town. Though these statistics contained valuable information, no registration of enterprises at these institutions could suffice as a sampling frame. Neither could we use the Population Census of 1980 as a point of departure, for, contrary to previous censuses a question into the people's profession—indirectly an indication of type of enterprise—was not included. Therefore we decided to carry out a count ourselves. Compromising between accuracy and time constraints, we chose the method of visiting the head of each *Rukun Tetangga* (neighbourhood). In the public administration of Indonesia the *Rukun Tetangga* is the smallest unit. In Banjarnegara such neighbourhoods contained 50 households on average. Secrets are few in a small inert town like Banjarnegara, and a head of a

Rukun Tetangga is well-acquainted with most activities of the inhabitants of his neighbourhood. A drawback of this method of registrating was that Banjarnegara based enterprises, whose head lived elsewhere, were excluded from the count on enterprises.

A clustered sample was taken from the count to select the enterprises to be interviewed. Per type of enterprise taken, for instance jeweller, contractor, *tempe* processor, we selected at random. Not all types of enterprises were equally represented, a few branches were concentrated upon to come closer to the stated objects, to wit: trade in primary commodities and cattle trade, for this should shed a light on the third research objective; retail trade; *toko, warong, pasar* traders and itinerant traders, for this provides work to many and it might be seen how Banjarnegara's hinterland is served by it; construction, the boom sector; and industry, which is often proposed as a solution for all sort of things. For reasons of comparison we surveyed a number of enterprises outside the key branches. It should be noted that one major employer in town was excluded from analysis: agriculture. While the government institutions, not being enterprises, were excluded from this part of the analysis, though frequently treated as contextial information.

The 186 questionnaires provide the main body of information. They often served as a starting point for a lenghty talk. Besides, data from the questionnaires were supplemented by some 15 in-depth interviews with well informed businessmen.

On the town's main market three counts were made, posing some elementary questions. These three counts partially corrected the drawback of the Count of Enterprises, for at the *pasar* many non-urbanites have settled their enterprise. Some rural markets were visited too, notably *pasar* Kalibening, *pasar* Karangkobar, *pasar* Wanadadi, *pasar* Purworejo-Klampok, *pasar* Mandiraja and *pasar* Tunggoro. Market officials at these markets were interviewed on commodity flows and origin of traders. Knowledge on livestock trade was completed by two non-systematic *pasar* surveys at *pasar* Petambakan together with visits to responsible *Dinas Peternakan* officials.

Finally some information on Banjarnegara's past was traced

by conversations with long-established entrepreneurs and a former regent. Back in the Netherlands historical data were gathered by reading reports from the colonial bureaucracy, notably the Mindere Welvaartverslagen and the Memorie van Overgave. The Rijksarchief in Den Haag was visited to consult the archives of the Serajoedal Stoomtram Maatschappy (further on reterred to as SDS) and the Ministerie van Kolonien.

Though we put our name to this thesis we should acknowledge the people, without whom the work on this thesis would never have met an end:

Pak & Bu Timoek Siddharta, for their hospitality; Diederike de Jong-Pel for her care and assistance; R. Hermawan Setiabudi and Budiyanto, friends and helpers indeed; Milan Titus and Jan Palte, experts on Java; Bupati Drs. H. Winarna Surya Adisubrata, Pak Cirno, Bu Paulus and other Bappeda Tingkat II employees for their cooperation; the Geography Department of the Universitas Gadjah Mada for the sponsorship; and all those Banjarnegara entrepreneurs whom we honoured with a visit, but troubled with our questions.

CONTENTS

Chapter 1

INTRODUCTION

The growth of primate cities in Southeast Asia is a well documented phenomenon. Although Southeast Asia is one of the least urbanized parts of the world, population figures of its major cities have soared to astonishing proportions. Indonesia is no stranger in this company. Jakarta's population doubles every 15 years and had reached 6.5 million in 1980. This metropolitan growth is linked with migration from the countryside as well as sustained by natural increase. Two processes seem to be at work here: employment opportunities in the countryside dwindle, while population increase goes on unabatedly. New agricultural techniques are introduced to the cost of often marginal employment. Consider for instance the spreading change in rice harvesting methods; village women using *ani-ani* knives harvesting stalk by stalk are replaced by hired labourgangs using sickles (Collier 1978). Even large scale, capitalintensive agricultural undertakings endure harsh competition; deteriorating terms of trade are challenging their position too. Non-agricultural activities are also under pressure, both in the countryside and in the regional centres, for competition of big city-based enterprises has loomed up, both in secondary and trade activities. In some branches the take-over of small-scale activities has already been completed.

On the other hand migrants are lured to big cities, where a wide range of jobs is offered. For Jakarta it has been shown that most migrants find employment in the informal sector (Sethuraman 1976). It has been stated that the size of the informal sector in metropoles like Jakarta is correlated with the number and size of large scale industries and government departments, the so-called formal sector. This correlation partly depending on the expectations of would-be migrants to eventually find a formal sector job. The suggestion however, that these formal job opportunities would directly attract migrants to Jakarta is denied. Most migrants would never quality for a formal job. Another type of migrants takes up living in big urban centres for the facilities offered in these places, most important of all being education.

Underneath these processes is the concentration of development investments in a few metropolitan centres. This tendency—whether spontaneous or induced—was justified by spatial conceptualizations of economic growth theories like Perroux' pole de croissance and Hirschmann's trickle down notions. Adherents of such concepts have argued that development efforts should be concentrated so as to give rise to savings on infrastructure and transport costs for the enterprises. These so-called urbanization and conurbation economies should tempt other industries to settle in the growth pole to make use of the forward and backward linkags thus created more easily. These notions have heavily indluenced development policy, implemented by third world governments and international aid agencies. An example of such concentrated investment in Indonesia: during the seventies Jakarta absorbed 60% of all foreign investments in Indonesia and 26% of all private Indonesian investment, while government expenditure was twice as high in Jakarta compared to the highest provincial figures. Though expanding fast, Jakarta contained only 4% of the Indonesian population (Rondinelli 1983).

Once a certain level of development is reached, and an innovative centre has come into being, it is perceived that growth should spread and intraregional differences as well as differences between city and countryside would flatten out. The type of activity considered most fit to trigger off growth and succeeding spread was the import substitution industry. Earnings from primary export were channeled into this sector. Import substitution, however, turned out to be unfit as a solid base for the national economy, as it was quite limited in its prospects, due to a lack of investment capacity and marketing opportunities. The capital funding sector suffered from low product prices, while on the other hand demand for manufactured products remained low and concentrated. After the first and easy stage of consumer good import substitution, Indonesia was confused at how to continue its industrialization policy. Several avenues are proposed like starting capital goods industries, upgrading agricultural export products or exporting consumer goods.

By this time it has become clear however that the growth pole policy as outlined above is a misfit. Although the concept of concentration of investments still has many supporters, new ideas have emerged. Critics of growth pole policy state that, apart from its basic weakness of concentrating on economic growth instead of welfare and employment, growth pole policy has had some other serious drawbacks. It caused metropoles to expand to multimillion city jungles. Even worse, the preference it implied led to a neglect of living circumstances in the countryside and of social services in general. Spread of development turned out to be wishful thinking only. A new development paradigm was opted for.

Amidst these criticisms and due to a concommitant rise of regional planning, attention for small towns was born. Previously small towns had only been thought of as centres for the public administration and locations for social facilities. It was now sensed that small towns might offer an alternative, acceptable to both urban-oriented and rural-oriented development strategists. However, beyond these expectations vision was blank. As Kartahardja (1979) did put it: "In the planning of settlement patterns in Repelita III, as well as in other conceptions, the development of settlement conceptions are mentioned, such as 'regionalization', 'Jabotabek', the development of new centres, etc. Many of these conceptions are not well prepared and cannot be used as a practical guidance for the development of settlements". McTaggart & Stormont (1975) have indicated that in devicing town plans, Indonesian planners have often taken refuge to western concepts like zoning for instance, without stating what measures should be taken. Salient examples of copying western concepts in devicing regional plans can be read in Giebbels (1983) and van Roozestraaten (1983), treating the metropolitan area's Jakarta and Bandung area respectively. Spatial planning concepts appointing a role to small towns as satellites similar to those used in comparable Dutch plans underly the proposed regional urban structures. This criticism also applies to the *Rencana Induk Kota*, 20 year master plans that are to be prepared for all *kabupaten* capitals.

Nevertheless a first step has been taken into the establishment of small town and rural-centered regional planning, by installing *Bappeda* planning councils in all *kabupaten*, that coordinate regional development planning with an eye to town development (Soegiyoko & Sugiyanto 1975).

Below in chapter two, four concepts are outlined on which the planned development of small urban centres might be modelled. What kind of production structure suits each concept is explained as well. Though not very explicit, in the scarce literature on small town development relevant to Indonesia, similar concepts are revealed, whether seperately or in combination. A synopsis of small town trends ends this chapter 2; it is a first test to the feasibility of these concepts. Chapter 3 serves the same purpose, sketching Javanese small town social structure, and helps interpreting findings on the Banjarnegara production structure. The results of the research activities are the subject of chapter 5 to 14. Before these empirical chapters however a model is detailed as an instrument with which the production structure of the regional centre can be analyzed.

Chapter 5 then gives an introduction to Banjarnegara town and *kabupaten* Banjarnegara. In the succeeding chapters several branches within the production structure of Banjarnegara town, centre of *kabupaten* Banjarnegara, will be reviewed: chapter 6 focuses on ambulant and market trade, the latter at the physical core of Banjarnegara town; chapter 7 is on retail trade too; *toko* and *warong* are dealt with; in chapter 8 the town limits are exceeded as it reviews how the marketing of fruit, vegetables and rice is organized from village to town and on; chapter 9 documents livestock trade, partly marketing as well; chapter 10 is outside the sphere of trade, discussing the construction branch; chapter 11 treats industry and as a bonus chapter 12 is on service enterprises. Chapter 13 and 14 are the concluding chapters. Chapter 13 returns to the analytic model of the production structure and sees how the results from the seperate branches fit in with assumptions posed in chapter 4. Chapter 14 finally evaluates how the Banjarnegara production structure as explored in chapter 5 to 12 compares to the different small town concepts, treated in chapter 2.

Chapter 2

SMALL TOWN CONCEPTS AND TRENDS

In the introduction we noticed a lack of vision, at least a lack of uniformity, considering the future of small towns. Despite bright predictments, there is paucity of insight. In this chapter we will try to distinguish four concpets dealing with small town development and show the consequences these concepts imply on the urban production structure. In literature on planning often two or more of these concepts are propagated in an interlinked way. For reasons of clarity, however, we discuss them seperately. Beforehand we would like to note that spatial planning such as opting for small town development is meaningless, unless supported by or supporting other policies. Even more, planning in general is mostly confined to creating opportunities. Whether goals will be reached is not determined by the quality of planning only, though it may help.

After outlining the four concepts, there will be a preliminary review, confronting them with empirical evidence from small towns as is known from literature.

2.1 THE CONCEPTS

2.1.1 Small towns as propulsive growth centres

A number of authors, faced by the excesses of metropolitan

growth have translated growth pole theory in opting for secondary growth centres. It is felt that in metropoles congestion is on the verge of overtaking economies of agglomeration. The concept of a growth pole is not abolished, it is only located in other places not to put further pressure on the overcrowded cities, like Jakarta, Bandung, Medan and Surabaya. Lo and Salih (1978) introduced the concept of urban efficiency with regard to agglomeration economies. Their point is that these econimics fail to work beyond a certain city size, though the city might continue to grow. They advocate a line of policy of both redirecting metropolitan growth to middle-sized cities and stimulating lower level towns to grow into this efficient size class. By having propulsive growth centres in other parts of the country, regional inequalities might diminish too. Soegiyoko & Sugiyanto (1975) have conceived of such a 'centres of growth' network.

The sort of activity associated with this concept are large scale industries with high labour productivity and high potential to interlink with other acitivities. Such industries need a well-developed physical and institutional infrastructure. Their existence might mean the presence of a trained labour force and high quality commercial services, whether in-firm or not. It will attract other companies to the growth pole, subsidiairy as well as independent enterprises (Rondinelli & Ruddle 1978). To facilitate spread to the hinterland the complex should develop functional relations with agriculture and rural home industries (Hansen 1978, 1981). Regional physical and human resources have to form the base of the main industry. Often agro-based industries are thought of a propelling, in small town centres of growth. But mineral resources, hydro-power plants and existing artisanal skills might be a point of departure as well (Rondinelli 1983).

2.1.2 Small towns as absorptive growth centres

Elaborating the growth centre concept, some authors emphasize the aspect of the redirection and diminishing of migration streams. It is felt that small towns might compete with a larger city as a place of domicile for would-be migrants, provided sufficient labour opportunities are offered (Watts 1962, Rondinelli & Ruddle 1978, v. Rozestraaten 1983). Presuming that is, that the search for a living is the dominant motive for such a migration. Small towns do have some amenities to offer, compared to metropoles, namely a more informal and easy going atmosphere, which might help in the search for a job, and low costs of living. Generally speaking, small towns are less familiar with such problems as lack of living space and a burdened infrastructure.

If small towns are to redirect the metropole-ward migration flow and attract rural migrants as well as urbanites, labour absorptive activities should be encouraged within the small town production structure. This might entail large scale labour intensive enterprises, but more often small scale industry is thought of (Lo & Salih 1976). What is labelled the informal sector comes to the fore—in chapter 4 we will opt for a more convenient term—: low-capital, local-resource enterprises, that are managable without high-tech skills. They should however offer a minimum renumeration that justifies quitting your rural job and not trying for Jakarta, Surabaya or somewhere else.

This type of labour absorption is in line with current practice, for—as Sethuraman (1976) showed for Jakarta—most migrants tend to find work in small scale trade, transport or industry. Such labour intensive, small scale activities in small towns will differ in character from those in metropoles. In places like Jakarta, abundant purchasing power exists, supported by the salaries of factory workers and government officials. Besides small scale industry products might be ordered by metropolitan large scale enterprises. In this way a large body of informal trade, services and industries is sustained. In small towns, though local pockets of wealth, there is no such complex to address at. Informal sector activities—next to petty trade and services—should be directed at upgrading regional primary produce or substituting large scale manufactured goods.

As discrimination of informal activities and competition from large scale industry are nation-wide, a policy that intends to give breath to informal job opportunities in small towns should be nationwide as well. On a local level the development of skills and the use of locally produced goods should be stimulated. Finally it should be noticed that such an employment program in small towns will not always incur a growth of their poplation figures. Road communications in most Javanese regions are nowadays that up to standard that commuting from the villages in possible.

2.1.3 Small towns serving accelerated rural development

Instead of being focal points of growth, one might conceive of small towns, geared to speeding up rural development. This small town concept is frequently repeated in regional planning. It regained popularity with Friedmann & Douglas' (1976) challenging 'agropolitan district' idea. A country should be split up in 'single, integrated, self-governing districts', as they put it. This requires that each district should have sufficient autonomy and economic resources to plan and carry out its own development. A decentralization of decision-making and concommitant landreform are considered crucial steps by the authors. Not every spatial theorist and certainly not every planner is as demanding as that. Still strong integration between town and region is a necessary thing, to be guaranteed at least by good transport communications (Taylor 1978, Stohr 1981).

The sort of urban enterprise associated with this concept is linked up with rural, especially agricultural production. In the first place, it entails government extension services and private enterprises distributing inputs like high yielding seeds, fertilizer, insecticides, tools. Secondly, it includes enterprises that take account of marketing or processing agricultural produce. Next, rural non-agricultural enterpr es should be equiped with tools and raw materials too and marketing and processing of the home industry products might be taken care of in regional centres as well. Both large scale and smal scale urban enterprises might be considered in these respects, the most important thing not being size, but their subsidiairy and beneficial role.

One can imagine that these supporting activities do not meet standards of efficiency when dispersed over a region. Because of the volume of input necessary to sustain an agro-processing plant for instance, its best locus might be in a regional centre. The same holds true, although in a lesser degree, for trade and service activities.

2.1.4 Small towns as service centres

The needs of both town and village population are addressed at in the service centre concept. Though in the past not explicitly dealing with small towns, the notion of spread of services has a long history. Hospitals and schools as well as extension offices are regarded as pawns in the development game since prewar colonial times. Facilities are unevenly spread in developing countries, they are rather concentrated in the larger cities. For reasons of justice public facilities, like education and health care, ought to be accessible to all citizens, including those living on the countryside. In many instances inspired by central place theory, interpreted normativily, small towns are thought efficient locations for such services (UN-ESCAP 1978, Rondinelli & Ruddle 1978). A good transport network is a prerequisite. As it is possible to plan public facilities, equal access seems an attainable target. In case of those private enterprises that function as service facilities, like stores, repairshops, printing industry or public transport companies, steering their settling and growth is less easily manipulated.

This service centre concept resembles the previous rural motor concept. It differs in dealing with the whole range of enterprises serving consumers, be they other enterprises or private persons, living on the countryside or in the town. For the services they offer, it is supposed there is no rural match. The concept of rural motor is narrowed towards assisting productive activities only.
motor, on the other hand is narrowed towards assisting productive activities only.

This brief discussion of small town concepts does not pay tribute to combinations of concepts, often urged for. Cross-overs between service centre and rural motor, or absorptive growth pole and rural motor are met. As several authors have pointed out, the functions outlined seem to correlate to town size. For instance: propulsive growth pole potential will be more developed in larger towns, because of the larger pool of skilled labour and managerial abilities and the larger opportunities for interindustrial linkages and subsidiairy services to develop (Rondinelli 1983). Another example is given by Lo & Salih (1976), who point out that smaller towns are more apt to act as agropolises, while middle sized towns can become absorptive growth poles. Rondinelli emphasizes in this respect that especially secondary centres are large pools of indigenous skills and industry, already oriented towards labourintensive activities.

From chapter 5 on, dealing with the Banjarnegara situation we will therefore not limit our attention to small town production structure and contacts with hinterland only, but look at inter urban relations as well. Before seeing how the concepts apply to Banjarnegara town however, we will point at some trends presently going on in Indonesia, that contrast the course of events suggested in the four concepts.

2.2 CONTEMPORARY TRENDS RELEVANT TO SMALL TOWNS

Looking at urban growth rates (see table 2.1) the small town bracket (20.000—100.000 inhabitants) turns out to be growing fast. Though the percentages supports optimism on small town development, the picture of reality is deceptive however. Besides stagnancy in the medium size class, the heterogenity of small towns prohibits an easy generalization. Small towns include bureaucratic centres, extraction and frontier towns and suburbs. Especially within lower size categories, towns diverge in outlook as they might be dominated by one function (Cohen, English & Brookfield 1978).

In Indonesia small town growth should be largely attributed to frontier and extraction towns outside Java. Apart from a few satellites of larger conurbations, most Javanese towns are of the bureaucratic centre type and their growth seldom exceeds natural population increase. Banjarnegara serves as an example in this respect. Birth rates exceeded death rates with 2.2% in the *kabupaten*. *Kecamatan* Banjarnegara (which includes more than the town population only) grew slightly more: 2.70% annually in 1976—1980. Still of all *kecamatan* in *kabupaten* Banjarnegara none grew as fast as *kecamatan* Banjarnegara. See table 2.2. As population all over the *kabupaten* grew only at 1.50%, this hints at a rural exodus. It also hints at Banjarnegara's shortfall as an absorptive growth pole.

Table 2.1 Urban growth in Indonesia to town size-class

	Indonesia		Central Java	
City size	1930—60	1960—71	1930—60	1960—71
> 500,000	4.8	3.7	2.7	2.5
100—500,000	4.1	2.4	2.4	1.1
50—100,000	3.3	3.2	2.1	3.3
20—50,000	2.9	2.2	1.7	2.4

Source: Blankhart (1980).

Table 2.2 Annual population growth in *kabupaten* Banjarnegara (1976—1980) per *kecamatan*

Banjarnegara	2.70%	Purw.Klampok	1.03%	Karangkobar	2.62%
Sigaluh	2.66%	Susukan	1.71%	Punggelan	2.47%
Madukara	0.53%	Mandiraja	1.32%	Pejawaran	2.43%
Bawang	1.08%	Purwonegoro	1.47%	Batur	—0.13%
Banjarmangu	0,65%	Rakit	1.34%	Kalibening	0.42%
Wonodadi	0.16%	Pagentan	1.85%	Wanayasa	1.75%
		Total kabupaten	1.50%		

Source: Banjarnegara Dalam Angka 1980.

Probably Watts' (1962) argument is valid for Banjarnegara. In his study on Tanggerang, Watts postulated that for the Tanggerang villager, who takes his leavings, the extra trouble of moving to Jakarta, instead of settling in the regional centre, is futile, considering the better job prospects offered in the metropole. Of course Tanggerang is only half an hour train ride from the capital, but Banjarnegara has good traffic connections with big urban centres on Java too. Every day two busses depart to Jakarta for instance.

From a number of small town studies—a scarce commodity in the Indonesian context—we shortly highlight some observations that comment on the small town concepts formulated. We already quoted Watts who, studying Tanggerang town, saw it falling short in absorbing rural migrants from *kabupaten* Tanggerang, despite its potential: a well developed infrastructure and nearby Jakarta's urbanization and conurbation economies without the congestion and overpopulation. He could not foretell that nowadays Tanggerang is projected as an absorptive growth centre again; as a satellite in the Greater Jakarta Agglomeration, it is supposed to attract Jakarta's overflowing population and migrants heading for the capital (Giebbels 1983).

In the fifties anthropologist Lesley Palmier (1960) studied two towns at the western end of the Serayu Valley Region: Purwokerto and Banyumas. Purwokerto, a medium-sized town, by then it can be indicated from Palmier's study, resembled a propulsive growth pole. It had a large Chinese population and showed dynamism as both an industry and a trade centre. Later population growth has affirmed so: Purwokerto has grown steadily and it is the only town in the Serayu Valley that counts more than 100,000 inhabitants (Milone 1966; Titus, de Jong & v. Steenbergen 1986).

Propulsive growth had no hold in Banyumas, according to Palmier. Apart from traditional industries, like batik and handicrafts, no sizeable industries could prosper in this small town, at one time an important government centre. The same holds true for Kota Gede, near Yogyakarta city, according to Nakamura (1976). Despite its being called Java's sole industrial town, Kudus did not seem to be much of a propulsive growth pole either. Castles' (1967) analysis of this small town throws doubt on the local spin-off of the town's main industry. Raw materials for the town's wide-spread clove sigarette factories were purchased outside the region. Generated capital is largely invested in enterprises located elsewhere or spent on consumptive purposes. Remarkably this town is nowadays making a second start. New industries, producing electronic articles promise to have better chances in propelling economic growth. Şalatiga's 2000 employee textile mill is another enclave within a small town production structure (*Universitas* Satya Wacana 1977). This raises the question whether a town does have to have more than 100,000 inhabitants to be a propulsive growth pole?

2.3 TRADE CIRCUITS AND TOWN DEVELOPMENT

Another trend casts doubt upon the viability of the small town concepts of rural motor and absorptive growth pole. Grant Anderson (1980) and Mai (1983) both indicate that many small town jobs in regional trade have disappeared. Regional produce being incorporated in the national circuit is at the base of this process.

Basically one might discern between three trade circuits: the local circuit, the regional circuit and the national circuit. More levels might be imagined, but on a small town level the proposed division is easily tractable and suffices for our analytic purposes. The local circuit is confined to trade within the *desa* or between neighbouring *desa*, mainly between producer-consumers or between producer-traders. Commodities handled through the entire region move in the regional circuit, often passing the regional centre or organized by urban based traders, though not necessarily so, as Chandler (1981) showed for the sales of clothing in Central Java. She found a substantive inter-*desa* regional trade organized through *desa* based businessmen. In the Javanese context this means that in the regional circuit commodities move between different *kecamatan*. When regional production surplusses exist the national circuit comes into play. In the national circuit, there is exchange between different parts of the country. Quite often big city merchants have a pivot role in this trade.

Now the way the several circuits are interlinked should be shown. There are two models: hierarchy or by-pass. In diagram 2.1 these are drawn. In the hierarchy model, the local, regional and national circuits are chains in the commodity flow: traders at the national circuit buy from traders at the regional circuit, who have bought from traders at the local circuit, whom producers have even-

Diagram 2.1 Interlinkage of trade circuits: some models.

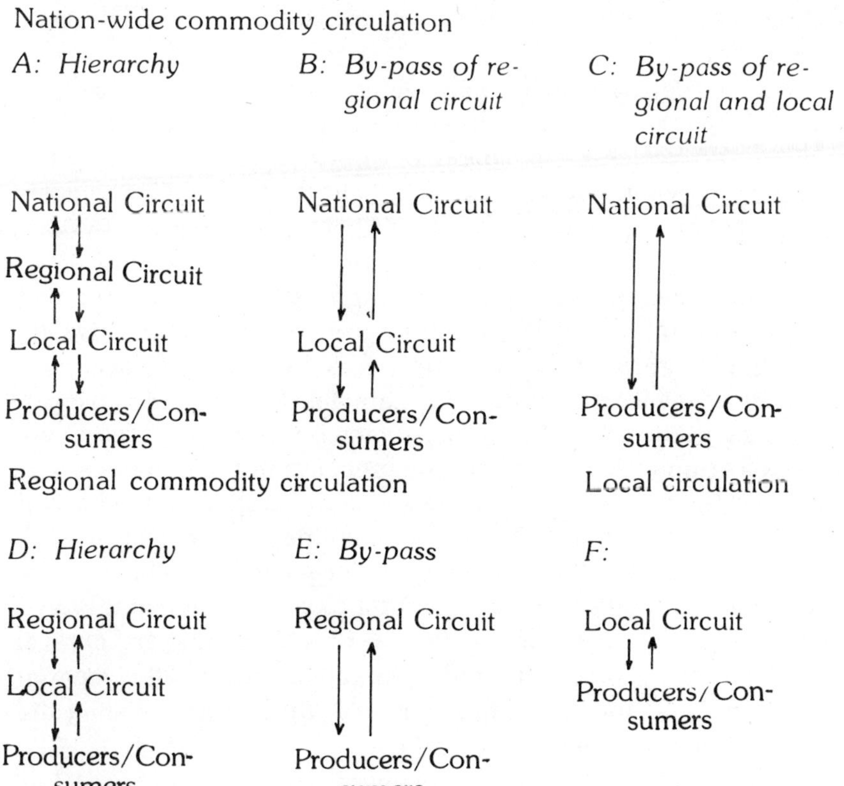

tually sold to. This example refers to the upward movement of goods. In the by-pass model circuits are skipped. The most extreme form is a merchant purchasing from producers and exporting the merchandise out of the region (model C).

This example depicts products, that have a nation-wide circulation. Other products have a local or regional range only. There is a correlation between circulation range, and thus circuits possibly involved, and scale of production. One might expect a large scale of production to infer large surplusses. To sell all produce from large scale manufacturing or agriculture, marketing has to have a national range. Small scale industry or peasant cash cropping, on the other hand, will have their products bulked and retailed within the region or *desa*, unless there is a complex of small scale producers, specializing in the same product.

Sofar outlined, a balance seems to exist in the scheme of things. However, there is a tension between nation-wide circulation and regional circulation of commodities, enhancing the possibility of regional and local circuits being by-passed. This point is highly relevant for small towns. We will illustrate so.

As agricultural commercialization is spreading on Java, surplusses grow. Accomodated by improved road networks, big merchants from large cities penetrate the countryside and dealing with farmers directly, buy up entire harvests at once. As these merchants offer advance payments, they are able to compete with local, low capital traders. Besides, as these merchants, having bought the crop, will arrange the job of harvesting (*tebasan*), the farmer can circumvent his obligation of having fellow villagers share in the harvest (Carlier 1980, Palte et al 1981). Local and regional circuits are by-passed this way. In other instances the local circuit retains its share when city merchants purchase at rural markets. Sometimes even enterprising local traders, often rich farmers (Nibbering & Schrevel 1981), disposing of larger funds of capital, take up the *tebasan* working method too and export directly, thus short-circuiting the regional circuit from below.

This tube-like system of agricultural marketing means a blow to regional centres, especially the function of the *pasar* is undermined. From Dewey's (1962) study on an East Javanese market, one might infer that by the time she conducted her survey commodities went up and down a hierarchy of *pasar*. Why have the *pasar* lost their function of connecting village and metropole? Next to the preference for the *tebasan* harvesting arrangement, Grant Anderson (1980) mentions a number of reasons. There is a need for quick transport of perishable goods that is certainly not met by the physically neglected, low efficiency *pasar* system. Penetration of the countryside was facilitated by an increase in transport services since the start of the seventies. A number of lowest level *pasar* have already closed down, giving rise to circular causation. To this Mai (1983) adds the influence of state marketing boards, especially the *K.U.D.* So there is a tension between regional and national circuit, leading to non-*pasar* trade overtaking *pasar* trade.

The distribution of factory-produced goods also has repercussions on the regional circuit. The fierce competition suffered by the local petty industries means that their output, that was bulked and marketed within the region, is replaced by products imported to the region. Bulking of these commodities disappears; regional circuit now confines to distributing factory-produced goods and even this function is under attack. Rural shops and market traders retailing factory goods often get supplied directly from travelling traders originating from the larger cities (Mai 1983). Mai describes another example of by-pass in retail trade: the selling of seafish in Minahasa, Sulawesi, which distribution is organized by a cooperative, that supplies village posts directly, thus eroding the intermediate function of towns.

Though one should not get the idea that all local and regional trade is on the verge of being absorbed in national networks, we now look at the consequences of this trend towards national incorporation.

In the first place, the by-pass which is facilitated by this incorporation means a loss of jobs in the local and regional trade circuits. Small scale trade is one of the largest informal employers and the by-passing of regional centres in the sphere of marketing has a grave backlash on the small towns' potential as an absorptive growth pole.

Secondly, there might be a circular causation effect. As small scale trade is obstructed in its development, small scale industry looses one of its major marketing outlets. This enlarges the troubles small scale industry faces to survive under the competition of large scale manufacturing. Thirdly, the regional industries, that are often supplied raw materials by regional primary producers, have to compete with prices paid for by big city merchants. This accounts not always competition for the same products, but also and maybe more often, competition for labour and land, A commercializing peasant applies his efforts to some crops only, with high yields and prices, while crops forming an input to small-scale industries are apt to be neglected. The tight relation between peasant and petty commodity producer—a.o. suggested by Armstrong & McGee (1968)—is endangered by rural commercialization and concurrent large scale marketing. In general, town-based agro-industries loose their grip on the countryside. The rural motor function of the small town is dismantled in the process of national incorporation. Quite significantly Friedmann & Douglass (1976) correlated the rural motor concept with a plea for a certain degree of regional self-reliance.

These adverse effects might be counterbalanced, if prices for the majority of farmers would rise. A marketing structure nearing monopsomy by a few merchants however is not favourable in this respect (Grant Anderson 1980). As unequal trading partners come into play the opportunities for a transfer of surplus increase, as Santos (1976) has shown for fruit trade in Peru. An early Serayu Region case might exemplify such trends. A few Chinese traders, controlling tobacco trade in Batur, could bully tobacco growing peasants having no marketing alternative at the first half of this century (Palte et al 1981). A situation of unlimited competition, on the other hand, guarantees that manipulation has no hold. By-pass or hierarchy and its consequences for the producer, is a tangible subject however; other outhors have pointed to the fact that the involuted *pasar* trading apparatus increased prices for consumers and lowered prices at the farmgate.

Chapter 3

CONNOTATIONS ON JAVANESE SMALL TOWN SOCIAL STRUCTURE

In this chapter we briefly sketch a Javanese small town social structure. As this subject was outside the main focus of our research, paying heed to it serves to see whether the small town concepts documented in chapter 2 are realistic or not. Too often socio-cultural conditions are not considered in planning for development. In this chapter was will draw on studies by Palmier (1960), Geertz (1963, 1965) and Castles (1967) mainly. Their analyses are rendered up to date with observations from Banjarnegara. Chapter 3 is split in four paragraphs; the first three paragraphs each deal with one major social fraction within the small town society. The fourth summarizes the relevance of the sociological considerations on the planning concepts.

3.1 PRIYAYI

If there is one class to be associated with small towns on Java and, according to Geertz (1963) with their stagnancy, it is the *priyayi*. Most Javanese towns originate as centres of administrative control and only few of them have been able to become more than that. Hence an administrative elite has always made up a large part of the small town population, and as a regency capital Banjarnegara is no exception to this rule.

The contents of local bureaucratic order changed in the course of time, but will not be understood without looking at its roots. *Priyayi* is a central concept in understanding the behaviour of local government officials. It is a term that used to be reserved for those of noble descent.

Before the Dutch settled in Java and conquered the whole of it after the Diponegoro war, Java was dissected in a host of feodalities only loosily interlinked. Communications were poor by then. Sutherland (1979) has described the precolonial system of feudal gentry ruling over peasantry as "...hierarchically organized officials with wide and generalized powers, loose definitions of duties, a strong emphasis on rank differentials, while relationships were personal and often arbitrary". The rule of the *priyayi* was legitimized by metaphysical notions as the *priyayi* were believed to have transcendental powers and they were held responsible for the trade-off between good and evil in society.

The Dutch suprapower introduced itself by demanding loyalty from the *priyayi* rulers. Mindful of the like over like principle, the Dutch—apart from consolidating it—did not interfere at the local bureaucratic level, their sole interest being to receive commodities desired for (Burger 1975).

Priyayi independence however was diminished. They lost their flexibility and ability to deal with local forces (Palmier 1960). From a ruling caste they were gradually transformed into a corps of civil servants. Their janus-faced position was a difficult one for they had to obey the colonial bureaucracy (*Binnenlands Bestuur*) as well as retain their traditional authority (Schrieke 1957). To upkeep their status—a lifestyle that has been qualified as lavish—renumerations from the Dutch were hardly sufficient and other sources of income were adapted. Moreover, in the course of the 20th century the small town *priyayi* definitely lost their economic base, i.e. traditional rights to labour and land, making their position even less fortunate. Favouritism and sycophancy became keywords in gaining position within the *priyayi* corps.

When after 1920 education among *priyayi* took a flight, ambitious native officials were quickly frustrated in their endeavour to modernize administration. Sutherland (1979) sums up *Binnenlands Bestuur* intolerancy as: "no innovation, no creative political response to social and economic change could be tolerated by colonial dogma". During this period the term *priyayi* became also subject to inflation. As the lower echelons of the civil corps grew and as non-governmental white collar jobs arose, the *priyayi* changed into an open class, many new civil servants inventing noble predecessors. The contours of present day small town bureaucracy became already visible.

After the Japanese occupation and the turmoil of the independence struggle the role of the local bureaucracy changed. Their prestige was damaged and their loyalty to the Indonesian state was being questioned. Especially since many retained their loyalty to the Dutch even till the late fourties. Many remarkable instances exist of continuity in keeping office under Dutch, Japanese and Indonesian government, but the *priyayi's* claims of being the natural local level rulers were not shielded anymore.

In the turbulent and uncertain period following independence, political leaders tried to gain support by installing followers in the administrative corps, thus creating their own bureaucratic factions. Meaning a first step towards a steady growing bureaucracy, it did not ameliorate efficiency. While wages dropped, in the sixties, inflation rose, and economic insecurity was widespread, a civil servant's post was still attractive, giving access to bureaucratic power. The wage situation temporarily improved in the seventies, while the growth in number of officials was halted.

Nowadays bureaucratic behaviour still sticks to a tradition rooted in the past. Due to the enormous extent of the administrative corps, its elements of low initiative, obsession with status, the importance of personal relations, and preference for general education have influenced Javanese small town society heavily. Although the *priyayi* status, of old attached to office jobs is grossly inflated, still many youth, as we could observe in Banjarnegara, aspire to become a government official.

The dislike of manual labour is another element of the *priyayi* tradition, and as Palmier (1960) describes, it is very difficult for families of *priyayi* status to search an income outside the white-collar jobs. In Palmier's Banyumas case, the production of fine *batik*-cloth is one of the very few occupations their status allowed. Even in such a job one has to pretend it to be a secondary income.

Nowadays the situation has slightly changed, as many officials, forced by low wages and high expenditures seek a secondary income opportunity. In Banjarnegara for instance the occurrence of small enterprises financed by civil servants and managed by their family members is widespread. In higher ranks some take occupations in construction companies, as president of the board for instance, letting their influence and information in the administration. It seldom leads to them starting and managing enterprises, status still being an impediment to economically enterprising behaviour.

3.2 THE QUEST FOR THE INDIGENEOUS ENTREPRENEUR

If the *priyayi* civil servants middle class generally despised business initiatives, then who were to bear the brunt of the onset to development? In the past authors looking at town economies have often concentrated on what type of individuals could be identified as entrepreneurs or at least whether a certain category of enterprising people would have the right ambition and capability to set the wheel in motion. It was felt that economic live was dictated and contained by the chinese minority and this unfortunate situation would not end unless an indigeneous middle class got the opportunity. Both Geertz (1963) and Castles (1967) conceived of the pious muslim businessmen (*santri*) as the pivots in this process, pointing at their religious motivation, their commercial know-how and access to interregional trade networks. *Santri* are a distinct group within the small town social structure. Their origins are at Java's northcoast, which is the stronghold of devout Islam, as opposed to the syncretist *abangan* that concentrated in inland territories mainly. In the twenties *santri's* settled in small towns after having been itenerant traders for a long time (Geertz 1965). Most of them started retail shops or small factories.

Geertz (1963) stresses the importance of such indigeneous entrepreneurs: "the central problem the leaders in development face are organizational" and "It is the ability and originality to organize a range of diverse economic activities—store or small factory—that most distinguishes a Modjokuto entrepreneur from his non-innovative bazaar-trader fellows, not wealth, not education or even drive."

Geertz' negative view on the bazaar sector is contradicted by Sethuraman (1976) and van Dijk (1982) who, impressed by their entrepreneurial spirit also ascribe a—limited—role for the very small scale enterprises in employment creation and who argue for support given to the informal enterprises, like credit facilities and management courses. It has been argued too that this very small scale sector has an important social function; for example in garbage disposal or in providing cheap transport (Versnel 1983).

Most *'wong cilik'* find a living in occupations like small scale trading, services and home-industry, especially foodprocessing. Geertz (1965) states that this mass of small people originate from villages settling down in small town *kampongs* or from lower class migrants that came in from other towns. Of course these people fulfil another role than can be expected from a dynamic middle class. But when conditions allow them to and competition from big industry is not to harsh, some of them could develop into entrepreneurs.

However some authors rightly remarked that by concentrating on individual enterprises only—even when one pays sufficient attention to their interactions with other enterprises—one overlooks that conditions external to enterprises set out limits on profitability. Brunsveld (1983) e.g. noted that within the *tahu-tempe* processing sector in the Jakarta region the major problems did not stem from characteristics of the enterprises, but were caused by local conditions like fresh water supply or waste disposal. Forbes (1981) points at external conditions on a more abstract plane, indicating the gloomy prospects of the petty commodity sector—in spite of their entrepreneurial spirit—as they can only accommodate to niches left by capitalist producers in Indonesia's economy.

Even the class that in the sixties has often been recognized as the indigeneous entrepreneurs—the muslim merchant bourgeoisie—has not been able to fulfil these expectations, and external conditions played an important role in this respect. Competition from Chinese and a new type of businessman coming to the fore, are issues in this respect.

Robison (1978) in an article on modern day elites in Indonesia has analysed the emergence of a non-entrepreneurial bourgeoisie that has its—temporary—power base in the bureaucracy. These bureaucatic capitalists have gained richness by handing out licences and government contracts and by participating in joint ventures with chinese or foreign businessmen. Apart from this elite, another elite has emerged which Robinson calls clientelist. This includes only some of the *santri's* and entails all people who, though not office holding themselves, by affiliating with the bureaucrats were able to prosper.

This clientelist middle class' most valuable resources are social know-how and connections, not technical skill, labour ethos or marketing acumen (Roepke 1974). Features well known from the *priyayi* culture outlined earlier. Bureaucracy's tightening grip on economic climate impedes entrepreneurial dynamism. Robison's analyses could well be adapted to the small town circumstances of Banjarnegara, of old an administrative centre. As we described in the previous paragraph, civil servants set up small scale enterprises—using their access to bank loans—and participate in larger ones. The bureaucrats have come to play a major rule by handing out licences and contracts to a clientelist middle class, e.g. using their newly gained task of allocating *Inpres*-funds to contractor companies. This will be illustrated further in the chapter dealing with the construction sector.

3.3 CHINESE BUSINESSMEN

In his essay on the Kudus clove cigarette industry Castles (1967) notes how Chinese businessmen increase their market share to the cost of *santri* entrepreneurs. Castles attributes the Chinese success over the *santri* to a number of factors. The Chinese manage to tie their most labourious workers by offering better labour conditions. They also have entry to an all Indonesia distribution network and borrowing money is easier for them because of their in-group solidarity. The absence of religious restrictions facilitates doing business and in general they are more responsive to giving their enterprise a legal status, thus avoiding inheritance troubles. Geertz (1963) has added some personal traits like the Chinese saving behaviour and their greater business insight. So in most towns trade and industry are dominated by the Chinese. Tan (1965) shows for the Chinese in the town of Sukabumi that most of them find employment in these sectors, a majority of them heading their own enterprise. This accounts particularly those recently immigrated.

From some economic branches, it seems however, Chinese have withdrawn completely. Agricultural marketing is the best example. In Banjarnegara e.g. trade in tobacco, copra and other cash crops was organized by Chinese traders before Independence. As Chinese were compelled to give up living in the countryside, these sectors have slipped out of their hands. They have reverted to industry, transport, wholesale and retail trade in the towns. In Banjarnegara too most *toko* are chinese owned, as is the town's only manufacturing plant, the coconut oil factory.

Chinese however, were never an acceptable alternative to indigeneous entrepreneurs, as their group is not an open one. The community has been called 'inward looking' and Chinese relate mostly to Chinese in other towns. Within Banjarnegara especially the *totok* part is tied by kinship relations. Some of the Chinese frequently congregate for a *hwe*, a chinese version of the rotating credit system. Chinese number only few in Banjarnegara, but their alloofness and wealth is a source of discontent for Javanese. Big anti-chinese riots occurred in 1965 and 1980, when chinese stores were ransacked.

In official policy Chinese are still being discriminated to the favour of *pribumi* Javanese entrepreneurs, who are awarded government contracts. This affirms a pattern described by Palmier (1960): Chinese businessmen dependent on Chinese in especially the private sector while Javanese entrepreneurs, though sometimes only chinese dummies, depend on public contracts. With regard to the construction sector, a major scene for such interactions, this describes especially the situation at *kabupaten* level, for nationwide and provincial projects are still often handled by chinese companies.

3.4 THE IMPACT

Now what is the impact of this briefly sketched structure on the concepts outlined in chapter 2?

Firstly, it is frequently put that by strengthening executive and administrative power all sorts of problems in development might be solved (Program Kerja Bupati 1983). Given these socio-cultural traits, it is doubtful, however, whether strengthening local bureaucracy or broadening its warrants per se will improve the small towns' role as a service centre. Neither would such a move of necessity be functional to supporting the other concepts. On the contrary it might even mean a harass to the small town enterprising society as they are further subjugated to rules, interpreted freely. On the other hand it should be mentioned that the local *priyayi* elite's regular and sometimes high (added) income creates sufficient demand for luxury items for retail shops to exist. Moreover the powerful position and regular salaries of especialy high ranking officials enables them to buy on instalments. For the same reason they are qualified to receive all kinds of formal loans. This money is often invested in a small industry or retail store.

Secondly the dead-end street the *pribumi* entrepreneur is in was noted, and the unacceptability of the chinese businessmen as 'leaders in development'. Moreover, as chinese play a leading role in the town's economy, chances of creating a propulsive growth pole are diminished. As has been noted the chinese community is mainly inter-urban oriented and they have their own networks for supplying goods and channeling investments. In this way the development of regional backward and forward linkages is barred and the cumulative causation of investments, a concept central to growth pole development, will be denied.

Chapter 4

ANALYZING URBAN PRODUCTION STRUCTURES: A MODEL

The main focus of this thesis is on the small town production structure. In chapter 2—3 we summed up how this production structure was conceived from different angles. We also indicated some drawbacks of these perceptions.

This chapter is meant as a point of reference in analyzing the production structure of Banjarnegara and the way its enterprises are related with rural activities. In order to structure the diversity and complexity of the whole gamut of urban enterprises we devised a model that will be outlined in paragraph 4.1. In the following paragraphs we will go into detail on how enterprises of similar and distinct category interact. Concludingly some remarks will be made on the domain of the model. A more extended treatment of the model is given in Titus, de Jong & v Steenbergen (1986).

4.1 OUTLINING A MODEL

Banjarnegara town's richest inhabitant—admitted so by most town dwellers—owned a number of companies: In the company that had a monopoly to distribute kerosene to Banjarnegara, Wonosobo and part of Purwokerto regency, he held an 80%

majority participation. By *Pertamina* he was granted the the right to run the only petrol-pump, both in *kabupaten* Banjarnegara and *kabupaten* Wonosobo. Besides he had obtained an agency from the state logistic depot (*DOLOG*) to wholesale refined sugar. Last but not least, as the town's biggest Javanese contractor, he took care of most large-scale construction projects in the *kabupaten*. Between this man, a vivid example of a clientelist entrepreneur, and a peddler or a *tempe*-processor, there is a world of difference, not only in terms of income, but in terms of management as well. These extremes constitute the borders of a whole spectre of urban undertakings. Discussing the small town production structure, one cannot avoid structuring and generalizing in this diverse world of enterprises.

When analyzing urban production structure in third world countries an important theme is the coexistence and confrontation of capitalist and pre-capitalist modes of production. Production modes can be recognized by certain characteristics of enterprise-management (to be called *structuring characteristics*). Central to the capitalist mode are: commercial orientation, the employment of wage labour, division of labour, intensive use of capital, segregation of management and ownership. Pre-capitalist structuring characteristics e.g. are the use of family-labour, blending of productive and consumptive spendings, no division of labour, the prevalence of non-monetary economic relationships. Usually enterprises are marked by a mix of capitalist and pre-capitalist elements. Van Dijk (1982) did show this for small scale enterprises in Salatiga. As a result of incomplete capitalist penetration enterprises working fully within the capitalist mode of production are as scarce as those working fully within the pre-capitalist mode. The way pre-capitalist structuring characteristics, like the use of family labour, persist, is not to be taken as a token of traditionalism. A management that holds to pre-capitalist values, while structured along capitalist lines may often be the most functional in a third world context (Dike 1979).

Confrontation between modes of production is multi-facetted. Generally however it is manifest in three ways. There is confrontation as all enterprises have to operate in a context that has its terms ultimately set by world capitalism. It must be noted here, that degree of capitalist penetration must not be interpreted ideologically or normatively. Next, there is confrontation between enterprises in the way of competition between pre-dominantly capitalist and pre-dominantly pre-capitalist enterprises. Finally confrontation can be signalled within enterprises, as many enterprises work in an increasingly capitalist mode. Therefore it is possible to classify enterprises in a continuum-like way on base of the number of capitalist structuring characteristics instead of on dichotomous criteria.

Studying functional relations between production activities demands however, that one starts from tangible types of enterprises, instead of modes of production. Such an approach is necessary as data are only available for enterprises as a whole, whereas structuring characteristics of both modes of production occur side by side within one enterprise. A tracing of commodity flows and transfer of surplus between production modes is therefore bound to fail.

To cope with the issue of linkages between enterprises, we opt for a division to type of enterprise within the urban economy. This distinction is made on base of *form characteristics*, that can be easily identified, like scale of production or status of registration. Criteria like these are used in census and industrial counts as well. The model outlined in diagram 4.1 therefore discerns a small scale petty commodity sector from a large scale corporate sector within the urban subsystem. Although each sector has its roots in one mode of production, it has its off-shoots in the opposite one. So within each sector it is possible to classify enterprises, continuum-lik according to the number of capitalist/pre-capitalist structuring characteristics. A similar distinction is repeated in the rural subsystem. Identical to the urban corporate versus petty commodity distincition, a commercial sector is discriminated from a peasant sector. Summarizing it is supposed that most small scale enterprises belonging to peasant or petty commodity sector are dominated by the pre-capitalist mode of production, while the same applies for corporate and commercial sector vis-a-vis the capitalist mode of production.

Diagram 4.1 A model of regional production structure

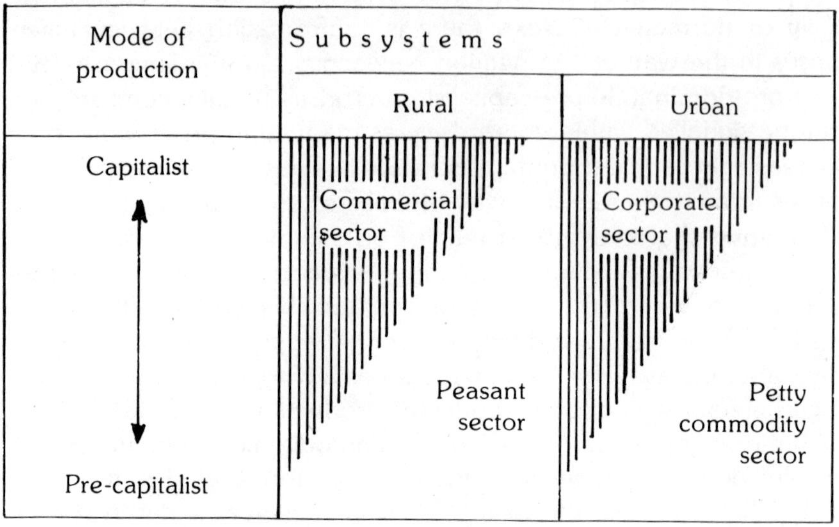

For the enterprises that we surveyed in Banjarnegara town such correlation stands out from table 4.1, in which the number of indicators of capitalist mode of production is set out against a form characteristic, being average monthly turnover.

From this table it can be seen that as the scale of enterprises rises, the number of capitalist characteristics rises too. This tendency is valid for averages only, because the extremes are deviating strongly. Obviously there are many examples where a large scale

Table 4.1 Number of indicators of capitalist mode of production by monthly turnovers for Banjarnegara enterprises (in Rp 1000)

	0	1	2	3	4	5	6
lowest	20	2	3	16	20	426	230
median	82	162	160	423	3166	2852	63033
highest	186	100013	102040	156298	1005078	152719	125837

combines with few capitalist elements, as well as the other way around. This suggests that the process of capitalist penetration—considered as the capitalist mode of production driving out or transforming pre-capitalist modes—is not a smooth and homogeneous process. Probably it is not even an unilinear process. In chapter 6—14, when seperate branches of the small town economy are treated in extenso, we will tentatively shed light on these questions.

The indicators used for delineating corporate sector from petty commodity sector are stated in table 4.2. This table also states what characteristics operationalize capitalist and pre-capitalist mode of production in our analysis. These are not the only operationalizations possible. In distilling petty commodity sector from corporate sector, status of registration or level of technology might be suggested as alternative indicators. To us a precondition for an adequate operationalization however, is its compatibility to different branches within the urban production structure. Status of registration would not suffice then, for in industry, construction and trade respectively, different departments using different standards take up the enlistment. Technology does not match the criterion of compatibility either. Level of technology might discriminate between industries, but technology in industry is of a kind different to trade (see table 4.3). Moreover, pluriformity of technology among trade enterprises is limited. Hence, instead of registration or technology, we took a multiple scale indicator. Scale of production is a prime form characteristic. It is necessary to have a multiple indicator for if one would rely on one indicator, like number of persons employed for instance, this indicator would be significant in construction, but it would not be so in trade, for even big trading ventures involve very few employees. Only additional indicators, like turnover, solve this problem.

Table 4.2 Operationalizations of form characteristics and structuring characteristics

FORM CHARACTERISTICS	
CORPORATE SECTOR	PETTY COMMODITY SECTOR
— Monthly turn-over more than Rp 5.000.000	— Monthly turn-over less than Rp 5.000.000
or	and
— Volume of capital goods over Rp 5,000,000	— Volume of capital goods below Rp 5.000.000
or	and
— 10 or more employees on pay-list	— Less than 10 employees on pay-list
STRUCTURING CHARACTERISTICS	
CAPITALIST MODE	PRE-CAPITALIST MODE
— Head of enterprise is engaged with sales and organization at the most	— Head of enterprise is engaged in all lines of work
— Wage workers employed	— No wage workers employed
— No family labour employed	— Family labour employed
— All inputs purchased	— Some inputs from home production or own farm
— Value of capital goods surpasses Rp 250,000 per person engaged	— Value of capital goods does not surpass Rp 250,000 per person engaged
— Using formal or informal credit	— Only private money used
— Extra money would be invested in undertaking	— Extra money would be spent consumptively

Table 4.3 Technology in trade and industry compared with scale

Montly turnover (Rp 1000)	<100		100—1,000		1,000—10,000		>10,000	
Capital goods used	Tra	Ind	Tra	Ind	Tra	Ind	Tra	Ind
Light tools and display devices	12.2	19.3	2.1	18.7	15.9	6.0	5.3	—
Heavy tools and mech. equipment	1.5	5.4	6.3	16.9	7.9	7.8	3.7	—
Machinery	1.0	—	—	3.6	—	6.0	—	1.8
Transport equipment	2.6	0.6	4.2	3.6	7.4	7.3	4.3	2.4

4.2 INTERSECTORAL RELATIONS

The way that seperate sectors of the regional economy are interrelated might be shown using the scheme outlined in diagram 4.2. We think it more appropriate dealing with relations between enterprises only and skip the relations between societal classes that are associated with a certain type of employment in a certain type of enterprise.

Though this latter strand of theory is very useful in tracing society's inequalities, from an analytical point of view it tends to ambiguity. Since, first of all, type of employment is incongruent to social class. Secondary income opportunities can illustrate this point. For households depending on divergent sources of income it would be hard to relegate, as a corrolary, one family to different social classes. The number of persons and households that derives income from more than one source is substantial. In the Banjarnegara sample, for instance, it turns out that 37% of the heads of corporate sector enterprises supply their income by earnings from agriculture or a government job. For the petty commodity sector, the figure is 31% (see table 4.4).

Table 4.4 Source of secondary income per sector (in %)

	Heads of enterprises receiving additional income from:				Family members receiving additional income:	
	agri-culture	civil service[1)]	wage labour	other enter-prise	yes	no
corporate	22	15	—	24	87	13
petty com	26	5	2	11	94	6

1) Including pensioners

Now how to delimit a class of petty commodity producers or a class of capitalist producers or a class of government employees? Moreover, it is deceptive to have relations between people that hold a job in distinct sectors equated with intersectoral relations, as is common use in social anthropology and neo-marxist writings.

Forbes (1981) for instance took factory proletariat being supplied household necessities by petty commodity producers as an example of relations between corporate/capitalist sector and petty commodity sector. We think this goes too far. The ambiguity can be shown in the defining of the class of proletarians. Who are the proletarians? Does it concern those people working for a wage or the people that have lost access to means of production: the final result of proletarianization? These are two different definitions; a lot of factory workers are not proletarianized. They are temporary migrants or, especially in small towns, commuters; both them and members of their household might still be engaged in agriculture. Such is for instance reported by Castles (1967) of the *kretek*-factory workers in Kudus and by Universitas Satya Wacana (1977) of Salatiga's textile mill. To this we add Banjarnegara's coconut-oil factory, where most wage labourers have taken up additional jobs, like tilling a plot of

Diagram 4.2 Intersectoral relations between petty commodity, corporate, peasant and commercial sector

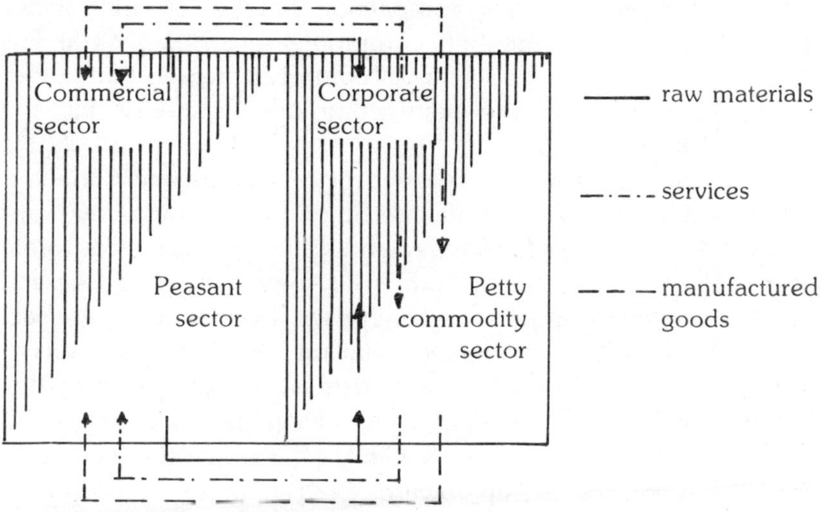

land or maintaining a fish-pond.

For this reason we concentrate on relations between enterprises only. The simplified chart of diagram 4.2, to be tested in the next chapters might be something to depart from. Assumptions like those by Armstrong & McGee (1968) and Missen (1972) should be adapted.

Armstrong & McGee and Missen have stated that the petty commodity sector is closely linked to the peasant sector, by which it is supplied its major raw materials and trading commodities. Penny & Ginting (1980) have reported how commercialization of home-compound tree crops coincided with an increase in local small scale trading. On the other hand a shrinking of peasant production will have repercussions on the petty commodity sector. There may be many reasons for such a shrinking: agriculture might be organized in a large scale manner and peasant surplus farming be replaced with commercialized monocropping. This enables corporate sector merchants to take over from petty traders, resulting in a by-pass of local trading networks, a theme that was already dwelt upon in chapter 2.

Such short-circuiting of the petty commodity sector is one specimen of the all pervading competition that the corporate sector is supposed to exert on the petty commodity sector. In general, it is accepted that the corporate sector will control all markets that render attractive profits, while the petty commodity sector is left the crumbs.

Capitalist penetration however might also engender the survival of petty commodity producers. Some petty commodity branches exist due to machinery devised and distributed by the corporate sector. Take for instance the numerous fotocopiers and freezers, that are exploited by small scale enterprises. Besides corporate sector enterprises use petty traders for retailing manufactured goods or subcontract orders to small scale industries, usually on terms dictated by corporate sector enterprises, giving rise to a transfer of surplus (Forbes 1981). Lebrun & Gerry (1975) fear that such subcontracting might be a step towards petty commodity producers loosing control of their means of production and being swallowed by corporate sector enterprises.

One should however not get the impression that as time grows all petty commodity producers will disappear or become subjugated to corporate companies. Dick (1978) described how *prahu*-sailors withstood competition of big marine transport companies, being a prove of the viability of intermediate forms of organization and technology. In fact they face their harshest competition from informally operated motorvessels. To this we add that in Banjarnegara one-freezer icecream home producers were able to compete with ice factories on the ice cream market and that these corporate enterprises were brought to the brink of bankruptcy. Nevertheless the general trend is not in favour of petty commodity producers. In the manufacturing industry of Indonesia, McCawley & Tait (1979) depict a large scale sector, that grew rash in 1970—1977, outpacing small scale and cottage industries. Dapice & Snodgrass (1979), using different statistical data, sketch a comparatively stagnant large scale sector while small scale manufacturing—in employment figures—grew fast but involutionary, as its marketing domain is limited.

Now returning to the interlacing of peasant and petty commodity sector, the intricacy of the regional economy can be shown. When the small town petty commodity sector is diminished consequential upon corporate sector competition, this will have a backlash on the peasant sector, for it is deprived of a major marketing outlet and a major supplier of farming inputs. Like other statements in these paragraphs, these are postulations and chapter 5—14 will investigate how they apply to the Banjarnegara reality.

4.3 INTRASECTORAL RELATIONS

In the past decades it has become very habitue to attack Boeke's dualistic theory on neglecting the relations that exist between the seperate sectors of the economy. Though Mourmans (1981) has noticed that this is not paying tribute to Boeke's comments on the subject, it certainly shows the shift that has taken place in development publications. Concentrating within the urban context on the interlacing of corporate and petty commodity sector and even stating that survival of petty producers is to a large extent determined by this interlacing, should however, not deflect attention from the way enterprises within the same sector interact.

Geertz (1963) described the *bazaar* economy as being: "based on the independent activities of a set of highly competitive traders who relate to one another mainly by means of an incredible volume of ad hoc acts of exchange. Although such an economy has the advantage that it employs vast numbers of people on a marginal or near marginal level of living, it has the disadvantage that it turns even the established businessmen away from an interest in reducing costs and developing markets...". These often quoted lines exemplify three things that are mentioned frequently as typifying the petty commodity sector: intricate deliverance relations, huge competition and its absorbing vast numbers of people. With regard to the latter, the growth of the petty commodity sector is often dated to start in the first part of this century. Peluso (1982) for instance quotes women traders who state that before 1930 entrance to petty trade was priviliged to those inheriting commercial skills from their mothers, whereas nowadays this 'branch is considered open to everyone. High competition between petty commodity sector enterprises seems related to such unlimited access. Breman (1976), on the other hand, has pointed at seclusion mechanisms that react to such employment pressure. In some branches to start operating the new entrants should have the approval of the ones already in the metier. In Banjarnegara groups of own account workers protect their work in this way, especially in small scale services like *pasar* porters, *manols* on the minibus terminal and petty cattle brokers.

Whether seclusion mechanisms are effective or not, one thing should be noted, competition within the petty commodity sector is considered to be of a kind different from the competition between petty commodity sector and corporate sector. Contrary to the latter, the first kind is usually not conceived to coincide with the disappearance of the weakest actor in the process, and is even considered an expression of the increasing number of small scale enterprises and the high labour absorptive character of the sector.

Above mentioned state of affairs might incorrectly hint at a unilinear process of ongoing fragmentation being typical for the petty commodity sector. Kahn (1975) in a study on blacksmithing in West Sumatra however showed how there can be cyclic fluctuation within petty commodity production. Periods of prevalence of independent small scale units of production alternate with periods of integration of smithies towards larger scale production entities. The most recent period of integration was after the rebellions of 1958 when import of steelware into West Sumatra came to a standstill and the smithies got organized into 'factory' type of enterprises.

The growth of small scale enterprises into medium sized ones, even on the brim of entering the corporate sector, is a constant theme by those who explore the prospects of the petty commodity sector (Missen 1972, Lebrun & Gerry 1975). The Banjarnegara *kabupaten* government seems eager to engender the integration of petty enterprises into larger units too. In fact getting them to be members of cooperations seems in concreto to be its only vision for the petty producers (Program Kerja Bupati 1983).

Finally we should pause at corporate sector intrasectoral relations. This unfortunately is a subject that has hardly been explored. Sometimes the imitative behaviour of some corporate sector entrepreneurs is pointed at. This behaviour is probably related to the fact that many people with proper finances are not entrepreneurs pur sang but should be called investers, putting their money in an undertaking, that has proven to be safe. In Banjarnegara this would mean buying a minibus or a truck and let it out or start a contracting firm. Most likely such non-innovating behaviour is part and parcel of bureaucrats and clientelist businessmen making up the small town middle class (Muhaimin 1983).

4 4 THE REGIONAL CONTEXT

The model given in diagram 4.2 might gave the false impression of being a regional model, summarizing all relations between regional centre and countryside. Rural-urban relations however are no longer determined at the regional level, if they ever were. The cash-crops from *kabupaten* Banjarnegara circulate in the national circuit. Manufactured goods from metropolitan centres are retailed through Banjarnegara's commercial network.

In the next chapters the extent of extraregional relations will be sought out. Assumptions on intersectoral relations will be examined too: How do corporate sector enterprises relate to petty commodity enterprises? Are they linked by mutual supply of commodities, subcontracting or does competition for similar market segments prevail?

Given these considerations and given the internal structure of small scale business, what perspectives are there for petty commodity enterprises? Are they the labour absorbers held for? Is the easy entry picture a valid one or is it confined to some parts of the petty commodity sector? Is joining a cooperation a feasible solution for problems met?

How do petty commodity sector enterprises relate to countryside activities, especially the peasant sector? Is it the peasants major marketing outlet and when peasant surplus production gets commercialized, is the petty entrepreneur an intermediary between peasant and corporate sector enterprise?

In answering these questions, it ought to be remembered is that our data base is town oriented. Though we gathered data on rural agricultural and non-agricultural activities and rural and inter urban trade too, our focus is on the small town enterprises. Such point of departure might distort one's view. An example: though the petty commodity sector's major supplier might be the peasant sector, one cannot infer that the peasant's major marketing outlet is the petty trader. For in absolute numbers the urban subsystem makes up for only a small portion of the regional population.

Apart from data on the small town production structure, additional data were compiled that should help putting the small town production structure in a proper framework. In the next chapter we will try to sketch Banjarnegara in its regional context. In chapter 6—12 that follow it, the themes of this chapter will be done with in the seperate branches of the small town economy: marketing of primary produce, cattle trade, retail trade, construction, industry and services. Chapter 13 is dedicated to a review of the Banjarnegara production structure in terms described in this chapter.

Chapter 5

AN OVERVIEW OF BANJARNEGARA TOWN AND REGION

Banjarnegara town, the object of this study, is one of the best conserved Javanese inland *kabupaten* towns. The large central square with the two *waringin* trees is still intact. Despite the devastations of the Independence Struggle when the frontline was near Banjarnegara, many buildings in town date from pre-1940. More important, even the past day pace of live seems preserved. The town does not have much employment to offer to its youngsters and many of them migrate to Jakarta or Semarang. To some degree, their departure is counterbalanced by a return flow of pensioneers. Though interesting to study for its own sake, Banjarnegara town cannot be studied in isolation of its hinterland or without reference to other urban centres in the Serayu Valley Region. This chapter, based on the scarce reliable historical and contemporary information available, intends to provide background data on Banjarnegara. It consists of three parts.

First a bri overview of the past of *kabupaten* Banjarnegara is given, of which Banjarnegara town is the capital town. Map 5.1 depicts the *kabupaten*. Paragraph 5.2 treats the evolution of the urban system of the Serayu Valley, and gives special consideration to present day Banjarnegara town. In the last paragraph the *kabupaten* is returned to, giving a short sketch of its economic activities.

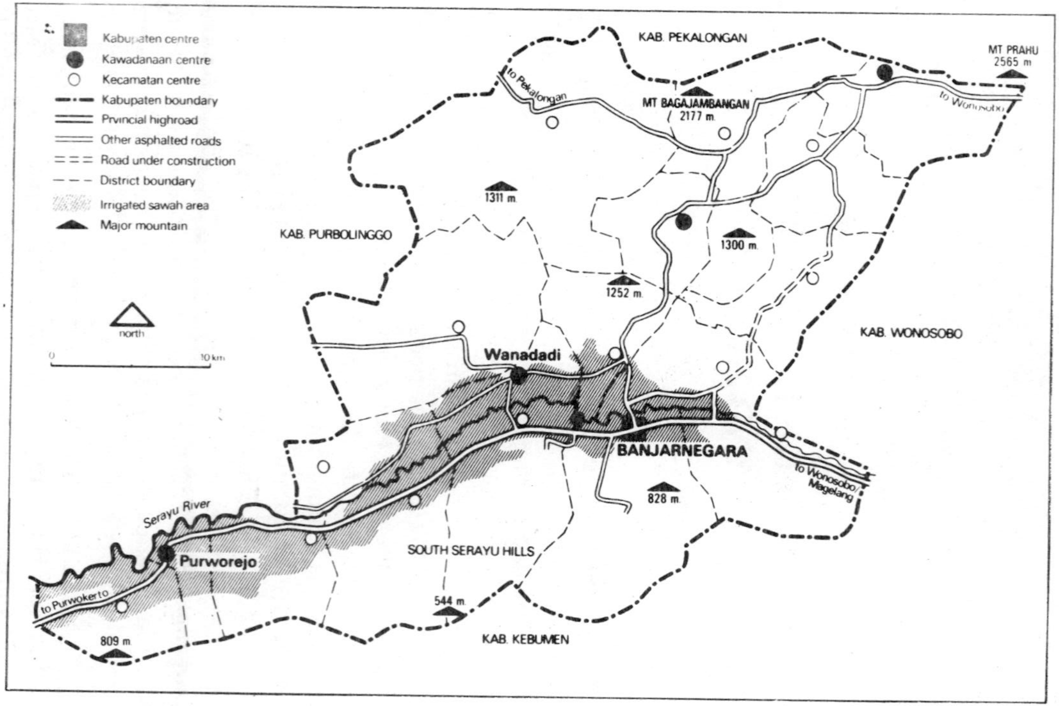

Map 5.1 Kabupaten Banjarnegara

5.1 A BRIEF ECONOMIC HISTORY

Like most towns in the Serayu Valley Region, Banjarnegara originates as an administrative centre. After the Diponegoro Insurrection (1830), Dipayuda, a regent from the dissolved regency Ayah near Kebumen, was transferred to the interior of Java, to the regency that was called Banjar-Watulembu by then. On his instigation and with the consent of the colonial bureaucracy, Banjarnegara town was built as his court on the fairly accessible plains south of the Serayu River. In those days the town must have hardly differed from a big village, except for the attributes of a regent's court, a central square and the dwellings of both regent and assistent-resident. The town's function at that time will have been limited to administration and tax-collecting, and some trade in surplusses from the predominantly subsistence economy. Commercialized production at that time was confined to the distant Batur District in the Northern Serayu Mountains, where tobacco cultivation had been introduced some decades before. Gradually however the regency became integrated in the colonial system. In the second half of the nineteenth century cashcropping of coffee, coconuts (to be turned into copra or oil) and fruit developed (Titus 1982). In this period many waste lands to the north and south of the Serayu River were populated and cleared for dry land agriculture mainly (Carlier 1980). It resulted in an expansion and densification of Banjarnegara town's service area. Communications nonetheless were poor between the different parts of what nowadays constitutes regency Banjarnegara. In comparison to the east-west throughfare to Banyumas, road connections within the regency were of an inferior quality, especially in the accidentated terrain north of the Serayu. It did not allow too much interaction between the lowland districts bordering the river and the Northern Serayu Mountain districts, especially beyond Karangkobar. Merchandise had to be transported by porter or on horseback or—in the planes of the valley bottom—by bull-cart. In those days Banjarnegara town's trade network was oriented eastwards, to the Central Javanese cities. On the other hand, from

Purworejo-Klampok onwards, the Serayu River could be used as a transport medium and most cargo in this district was headed west by *prahu* to Cilacap or back. Extraregional trade however was of a limited volume. Export products, next to the Batur tobacco, were cassave, fruits, groundnuts and coconuts or copra. In Banjarnegara town a couple of traders, from Chinese descent or originating from Yogyakarta, were engaged with it. Some other merchants had their domicile outside town; *desa* Mantrianom (*kecamatan* Bawang) housed four export traders. Still for the major part trade concerned local and regional circulation, which was focussed on the markets, of which *pasar* Banjarnegara had already become the biggest one in the *kabupaten* by then. Corn, rice, cassava and fruits were the main agricultural products traded on this market next to home-industrial goods: palmsugar, coconutoil, bambooproducts and metalworks (MWV 1907).

The accessibility of Purworejo-Klampok and the abundant *sawah* fields alongside the Serayu River had impelled a sugar factory to establish in this centre. In the western part of present day *kabupaten* Banjarnegara the factory had 10,000—15,000 ha planted with cane. Outside sugar production large scale farming and industry were absent to the vicinity of *kabupaten* Banjarnegara.

The sugar factory in Purworejo-Klampok induced a private railroad company, the Serajoedal Stoomtrammaatschappy, to include the town as a station in the narrow gauge network, that was constructed in the last decade of the nineteenth century. The Serajoedal Stoomtrammaatschappy (SDS) connected most towns in the Serayu Valley to the main interisland railroad lines at Maos and Purwokerto. Without too many extra costs the traject was extended from Purworejo-Klampok to Banjarnegara town (1898). It reverted the orientation of commercial activities in town and somehow strengthened its position as a break-of-bulk point for the, albeit not overwhelming, export of primary commodities and the import of salt, cloth and manufactures. Due to this competition of manufactured items an extensive secondary sector, based on local inputs and local demand, never had a chance to develop. Existing small industries activities like *batik* cloth-, leatherware-, metalware- and bambooprocessing endured hard competition; even between 1905—1929, which, with the exception of 1920—1924, was a period of comparative wealth in *kabupaten* Banjarnegara (SDS). In this period the production of commercial surplusses grew; cattle fattening in the uplands increased, as well as the cultivation of fruit and vegetables. The small town bureaucracy, part of it Dutch, expanded in these decades as well.

The 1929 krach and the subsequent world economic crisis of the thirties had a profound effect in the Serayu Region. The factory in Purworejo-Klampok was the first of the four sugar plants in the Serayu Valley to close down. It left a substantial number of peasants and land labourers in the lowland districts devoid of monetary income. The down years impeted some organized outmigration of rural poor from Banjarnegara to South Lampung (Sumatra). Some serious famines appeared in these years as well (Titus 1982).

5.2 URBAN CENTRES IN THE SERAYU VALLEY REGION

5.2.1 Evolution of the urban system

Considerable population sizes were never attained by urban centres in the Serayu Valley during the colonial period. In 1920 Banjarnegara town numbered 5,900 inhabitants. Its population size in 1930 is unknown, but will not have surpassed 10,000 inhabitants. At that time the town consisted of three *desa*, to with Kotabanjar, where Dipayuda had built his court, Krandegan and Semarang. Purwokerto town, counting a mere 33,000 inhabitants was the largest urban centre in the Serayu Valley in 1930, as table 5.1 demonstrates.

After Independence most towns in the Serayu Valley continued to grow slowly. In this period the number of public facilities centred in the towns augmented. New institutions on the plane of education,

Table 5.1 Population sizes of urban centres in the Serayu Valley Region (absolute numbers and index)

	1920	*1930*	*1961*	*1971*[1)]
Purwokerto	12584 (100)	33266 (264)	80556 (640)	94023 (747)
Purbolinggo	13810 (100)	16435 (119)	22698 (164)	24434 (177)
Wonosobo	7327 (100)	10701 (146)	16170 (221)	18757 (256)
Banjarnegara[2)]	5900 (100)	—	13351 (226)	16008 (271)
Urban Java *1000	2319 (100)	3549 (153)	10124 (437)	13728 (592)

1) Estimates on base of Sensus Penduduk, cf. Titus, de Jong & van Steenbergen (1984).
2) Banjarnegara 1920 figure taken from Encyclopaedie van Nederlandsch-Indië

Source: Milone (1966), Sensus Penduduk 1971.

health care and public administration were established in *kabupaten* centres like Wonosobo, Banjarnegara, Purbolinggo and Purwokerto (Milone 1966, Witton 1969). It caused the small town bureaucratic middle class to grow. This expansion might have caused an increased purchasing power in the small town, which enhanced the import trade of luxury items on its turn.

From 1970 onwards, the *kabupaten* centres experienced a second wave of institution building. The policy of strong and ultimate centralization wore down a little, and rising national oil revenues gave room for part of the budget to be channeled down to the *kabupaten* level. Civil servants' wages were raised and new offices were established. Funds were put at the disposal of local bureaucracies to be spent on infrastructural improvement, i.g. constructing roads, policlinics and primary schools. The allocation of this latter *Inpres* budget induced some to start as a contractor in the *kabupaten* centres. The (re)improvements on the road network, financed by *Inpres*, and the explosive growth in truck and minibus traffic reinforced the interlinkage between *kabupaten* centre and hinterland. On the other hand, however, this traffic disclosure enabled merchants from distant places to penetrate to the countryside, to the cost of local traders.

In the 70's a nation-wide programme was launched to improve the agricultural production, especially rice production, by introducing modern inputs like high yielding seeds, pesticides and fertilizers. This so-called *Bimas* programme increased production figures and raised the income of the rural population as a whole, though, as the polarization trend—observable in the Serayu Valley Lowlands already in the thirties—was reinforced by it, it benefited better-off farmers most of all (Titus 1982). In the dryland zone, this polarization trend is less pregnant; but marginalization is reported (Wolters 1983).

The increased production and the increased, though concentrated, rural income improved marketing and retailing opportunities for the small urban centres in the Serayu Valley. In marketing trade however traders in the small towns have to face competition by traders from out of the region. Retail trade seems to have suffered less from this extraregional competition. Especially Purwokerto, Purbolinggo and Wonosobo have thriving shopping facilities, that cannot be explained by the needs of the towns' population only.

Most towns in the Serayu Valley have grown, albeit at an all but dramatic velocity. Still the towns' growth outpaced population growth at the countryside. Purwokerto is the only urban centre in the Serayu Valley that grew rapidly. In 1971 its size had nearly tripled compared to 1930. Purwokerto by now has evoluted into a higher order centre to the towns in the Serayu Valley. In fact it is the only centre that has a municipality status (*kota administratip*). Located strategically on the north-south axis from Cirebon to Cilacap, it has the best traffic connections. Its wholesalers and industries have a hinterland, that stretches as far as Banjarnegara.

Kabupaten centres like Purbolinggo, Banjarnegara and Wonosobo are the next layer in the urban hierarchy. Public administration and trade determines their occupational structure to a marked degree as table 5.2 shows; industry does not add up to much in these towns. One will find most industry, agro-processing usually, dispersed to the countryside. Of the *kabupaten* centres, Purbolinggo has the best traffic connections, whereas Banjarnegara is least endowed, situated on the crossroads between the provincial road from Wonosobo to Purwokerto and the branch road up north to Karangkobar.

The third level in the urban system of the Serayu Valley concerns 10,000 people centres, like Sukaraja, Bobotsari, Banyumas, Kertek and Purworejo-Klampok. These are the centres of the now extinct administrative level of *kawedanan* (district). Some of these centres have a potential to expand, while others have stagnated, like Banyumas, the former seat of the residency. Finally, the bottom of the urban pyramid is made up of a number of *kecamatan* centres like Wanadadi, Karangkobar and Batur in *kabupaten* Banjarnegara or Garung in *kabupaten* Wonosobo, that hardly merit an urban classification. Such places however often locate a substantial central market, serving surrounding villages.

Table 5.2 Urban labour force to profession in kabupaten in the Serayu Valley 1971[1)]

	Purbolinggo	Banjarnegara	Wonosobo
Branch	%	%	%
Agriculture	7.0	5.6	1.8
Industry	13.2	5.4	7.7
Construction	2.9	2.6	1.3
Trade & transport	37.7	41.9	39.8
Services[2)]	35.9	43.4	45.3
Other activities	2.6	1.2	4.0

1) Labour force of all desa classified as urban in the kabupaten
2) Services include public administration.

Source: Sensus Penduduk 1971.

5.2.2 Banjarnegara town

At present Banjarnegara town consists of seven *desa*, to wit Kotabanjar, Krandegan, Semarang, Parakancanggah, Sokonandi, Wangon and Karangtengah. Map 5.2 is Banjarnegara's town plan. Five *desa* have a formal urban status; *desa* Karangtengah and *desa* Wangon however have a rural status, but should be included within the town limits, since a considerable part of these *desa* is morphologically and socio-economically integrated with the *desa*, that are formally classified as urban.

In *desa* Krandegan the commercial and bureaucratic activities are concentrated. Most government offices, the town's major market, as well as a minor market, the prime shopping street and two terminals for public transport are located in Krandegan. It contains most of the higher income residential quarters, with asphalt roads and sidewalks, populated by government officials and well-to-do businessmen. In addition Krandegan also includes some low income neighbourhoods, where most of the traders live. Besides, 80% of the few Chinese inhabitants of Banjarnegara live in this *desa*.

Desa Kotabanjar and *desa* Semarang are the other two core *desa*. In these *desa* contractors and export traders reside. The former desa, housing the mosque, is a typical *santri* area. Semarang and Kotabanjar do locate many shops too, clustered especially along the provincial highway.

Kampung make up the town's lower echelon living quarters. They are erected behind a facade of brick and concrete buildings in the town centre or in the desa outside the urban core. In these *kampung* roads are seldom metalled and a lot of the houses are wooden and bamboo constructs. Compound gardens and fishponds give some of these quarters a rural outlook. The basic activities of Banjarnegara town—commerce and administration—are not manifest in these neighbourhoods apart from the dwellings of petty traders and low-ranked civil servants.

Banjarnegara town has grown slowly in extent and popula-

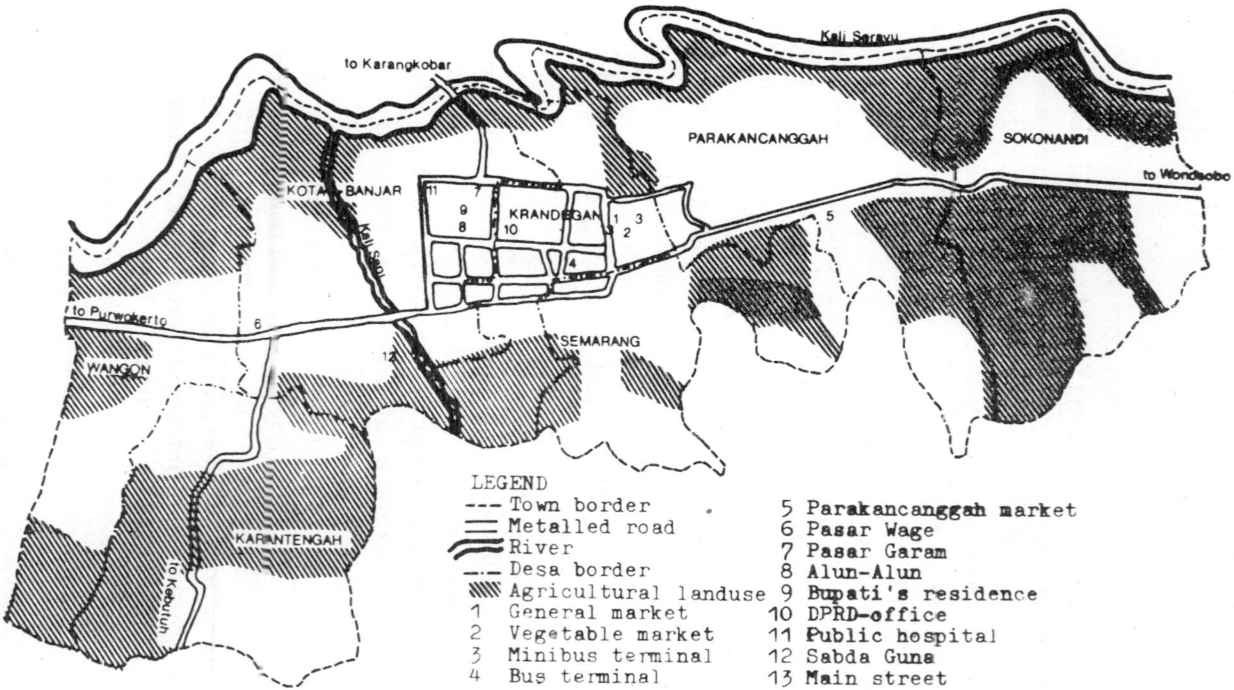

Source: Topographical Map 1912 updated with Peta Desa

Map 5.2 Town plan of Banjarnegara 1983.

tion. The town's recent expansions are the completion of cheap concrete houses for government officials in the eastern end of Sokonandi and next there is new building in Krandegan, south of the Serayu River, and in Kotabanjar in the Kali Palet area. In the 60's and the 70's population growth was below that of Java as a whole (2.5—3%, cf table 5.3). In the last few years of the 70's a somewhat higher growth is indicated: 2.80% (cf table 2.1), but these figures are less reliable for they are not based on census numbers. Growth rates for the *kabupaten* as a whole are definitely lower: 1.60%, implying to all probability an outmigration from *kabupaten* Banjarnegara. In no way do the figures suggest that Banjarnegara town intercepts many of the outmigrants. Labour opportunities in town might not allow so. Table 5.2 presented the 1971 occupational structure. For recent years, alas, only data from the Monografi Desa are at hand, which are very unreliable and leave a substantial portion of the people in the productive age groups unclassified. The Monografi Desa data are shown in table 5.4. The only conclusion that can be positively drawn from the data is that tertiary occupations prevale.

The predominance of the tertiary sector is evident too in the enumeration of enterprises per branch in Banjarnegara town, as presented in table 5.5. This table summarizes the results from the count on enterprises in February 1983. Combining this count with the results from the questionnaires, we estimate that 87% of the

Table 5.3 Population growth of Banjarnegara town

	1961		1971		1980
Population size	13,351		16,008		19,355 1)
Growth rate (%)		19.9		20.9	

1) Taking desa Kotabanjar, Krandegan and Semarang. If corrected for the change of administrative borders, the population size would be 26,845.

Source: Milone 1966, Sensus Penduduk 1971, 1980.

Table 5.4 Occupational structure of Banjarnegara town 1982[1)]

	Absolute	*Percentage*
Agriculture	1612	9.8
Secondary sector:		
Employer	613	3.7
Employee	623	3.8
Construction worker	1012	6.2
Trade	919	5.6
Transport	144	0.8
Administration	1383	8.4
Other incl. services	5776	35.2
Unclassified	4294	26.2

1) Population of 10 year and older, minus schoolgoing children

Source: Monografi Desa 1982.

Table 5.5 Number of enterprises to branch in Banjarnegara town February 1983

Agriculture	1287[1)]	Restaurants	143
Large scale industry	1	Transport	
Small scale industry		Minibus rent or driver	83
Building material industry	79	Becak driver	161
		Horsecart	29
Food industry & food-processors	267	Other	69
		Toko	149
Other industry & crafts	190	Warong	221
		Market & other trade	657
Construction		Services	252
Contractor	42		
Construction workers	533		
Repair	115		

1) Situation 1980: figure from Sensus Penduduk

Source: Count On Enterprises 1983, Sensus Penduduk 1980.

enterprises in Banjarnegara town (excluding farms) belongs to the petty commodity sector, while 13% is corporate sector. Noteworthy too is the considerable number of agricultural enterprises in Banjarnegara town. To the number of 1287 enterprises, poultry-farms and fishponds should be added.

Another big sector in Banjarnegara town is the government apparatus. As Banjarnegara town is a *kabupaten* centre, many government institutions have taken up quarters in Banjarnegara town. A lot of these institutions are meant to serve a population that surpasses the town's borders; there is the *kabupaten* government, three bank offices, thirteen highschools, a hospital and a host of departments. The next paragraph examines whether the rural population is actually served by Banjarnegara town's facilities. In addition to the kabupaten level institutions, Banjarnegara locates departments of lower administrative levels: notably the *kecamatan*, of which Banjarnegara is the centre, and *desa* offices.

5.2.3 The service area of Banjarnegara's public facilities

This paragraph reviews to what extent institutions in Banjarnegara town are utilized by people residing outside town, thereby testing the rationale behind the concentration of *kabupaten* level public services in the *kabupaten* centre. This brief evaluation is executed by tracing the origins of users at five of the town's institutes; students at the *S.M.A. Negeri* (public senior highscool), in-patients at the regional hospital and debtors at the three government banks in town. Map 5.3 a—c, taken from De Jong, Palte & Van Steenbergen (1983), presents the results. It shows that these facilities are first and foremost used by town-dwellers and people from adjacent *kecamatan*.

Map 5.3a depicts the *kecamatan* of origin of students in the first two classes at the *S.M.A. Negeri* in Banjarnegara town. There seven other senior highschools in the *kabupaten*, all of them private schools, of which three are located in the town as well. These private senior highschools however are said to be of lower quality

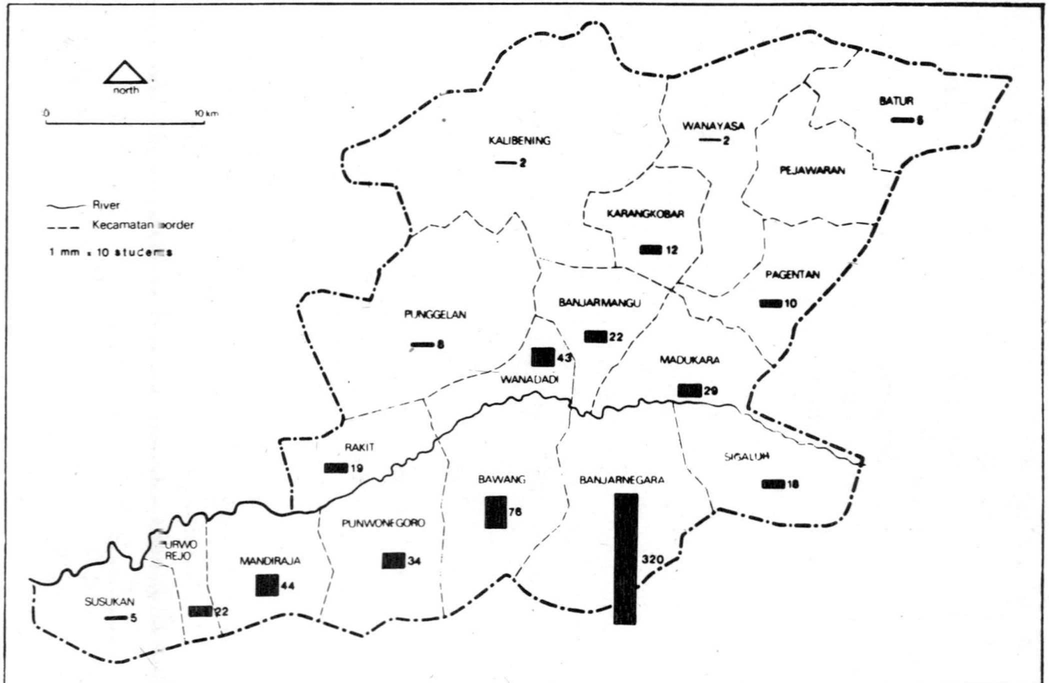

Map 5.3a Number of students per kecamatan of origin at the public SMA in Banjarnegara town

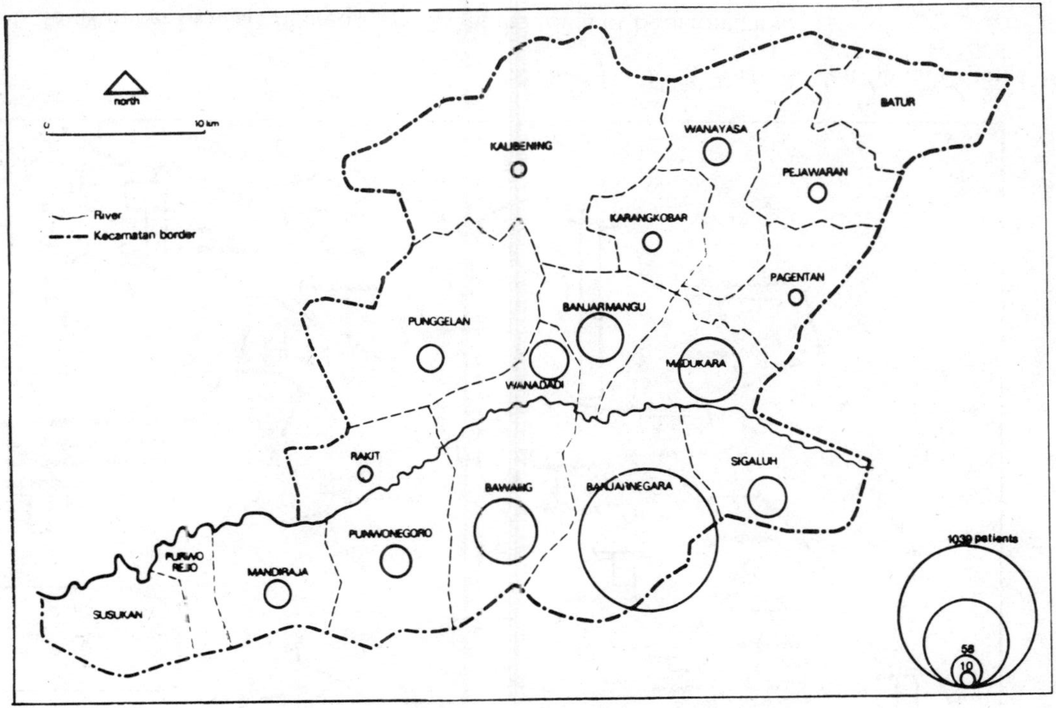

Map 5.3b The number of in-patients at the regional public hospital of Banjarnegara to region of origin.

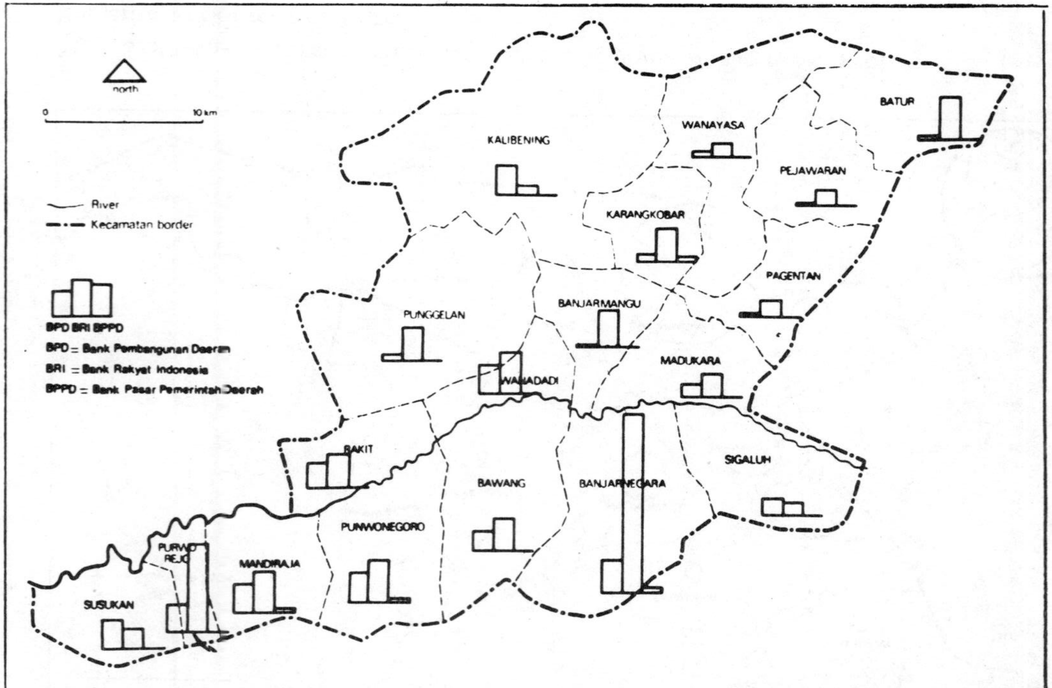

Source: De Jong, Palte & Van Steenbergen (1983).

Map 5.3c Number of users of credit facilities at the town of Banjarnegara to type of bank and region of origin

and higher expenses. To take only the public highschool is not an unrealistic indicator of school accessibility therefore. By far most students at the *S.M.A. Negeri* come from Banjarnegara town. A still substantial number of pupils originates from *kecamatan* along the provincial road and from *kecamatan* immediately north of town. Children from the mountainous northern subdistricts do not seem to frequent the public highschool in Banjarnegara town. Apart from accessibility, other impeding factors seem to be the low level of previous education and the poverty of the population of the northern districts. School entrance fees figure up to Rp 40,000 and board and lodging or alternatively transport expenses will be Rp 600—1000 daily.

A similar contracted area of origin is shown by the distribution of in-patients to subdistricts of origin at the regional hospital. Again, the majority of users comes from the town. The only alternative in the *kabupaten*, comparable to the Banjarnegara town hospital, is a catholic hospital in Purworejo-Klampok. A second private hospital in Bawang hardly comes up to the level of a clinic. Map 5.2b shows that especially in the peripheral *kecamatan* in the northern part of the *kabupaten* people are devoid of hospital care. Patients in these districts are served by *puskesmas* (community health centre) only.

With regard to the formal credit facilities, the situation is considerably brigther. Map 5.3c depicts the *kecamatan* of origin of debtors at the three government banks, that have an office in Banjarnegara town: the *B.R.I.*, the *B.P.D.*, and the *B.P.P.D. Kecamatan* Banjarnegara has the highest score, but the town's banking institutions do not fail to serve people beyond the town limits. Besides, both the *B.R.I.* and the *B.P.P.D.* have branch offices in *kecamatan* centres: the *B.P.P.D.*, the *pasar* bank, is open one day a week at six rural markets in the southern part of the *kabupaten*; the *B.R.I.* even has regular offices in every *kecamatan* centre, where loans can be obtained to a maximum amount of Rp 500,000 for agricultural purposes. The debtors at these *B.R.I.* branch offices are not included in map 5.3c.

Apart from agricultural credit schemes, the public credit facilities in Banjarnegara town are mostly used by big merchants, construction companies and transport enterprises (see table 5.6).

Table 5.6 Number of debtors and amount of debture to government banks in Banjarnegara town, per branch

	Number of debtors			*Amount of debture in Rp 1000*		
	BRI	*BPD*	*BPPD*	*BRI*	*BPD*	*BPPD*
Agriculture						
BIMAS	12559	—	—	171.532	—	—
Other	4571	188	—	751.557	132.557	—
Industry	—	262	4	—	207.505	13,300
Construction	18	—	—	316.011	—	—
Trade	1218	633	107	1.472.398	736.117	180,525
Transport	32	237	42	74.809	171.982	279,550
Civ. servant	1720	—	—	293.473	—	—
Services	17	—	—	82.589	—	—
Cooperatives	23	—	—	30.367	—	—
Other	47	242	—	100.864	221.924	—

Source: B.R.I., B.P.D., B.P.P.D. Banjarnegara.

In addition, civil servants, both active and retired, are an important category of clients at the banks.

5.3 KABUPATEN BANJARNEGARA

Kabupaten Banjarnegara is the major context, in which the economy of Banjarnegara town will be studied. For Banjarnegara is the capital town of the *kabupaten*, even though the hinterland of its public facilities covers only a limited part of it. *Kabupaten* Banjarnegara is presently among the poorest of Central Java. Its gross regional product per capita ranks second lowest within the province. Table 5.7 shows that the gross regional products of bordering *kabupaten* are higher, though Wonosobo is a minus area too.

Caused by a diversity in local physical conditions, *kabupaten* Banjarnegara shows a great variety in landuse (Palte et al 1981).

Table 5.7 Gross regional product and population figures of three kabupaten in the Serayu Valley

	Regional product per capita	*Population size*
Purbolinggo	Rp 60,225	679,290
Banjarnegara	Rp 39,543	678,083
Wonosobo	Rp 40,639	618,083

Source: Wonosobo Dalam Angka 1981, Banjarnegara Dalam Angka 1980, Purbolinggo Dalam Angka 1980.

Map 5.4 a—b and table 5.8 depict some of this variety. In the northern part the mountains of the Dieng-Jembangan complex reach up to 2000 meter. At the cool and high altitude areas in *kecamatan* Batur and Wanayasa, and to a lesser degree Karangkobar and Pejawaran, intensive cash-cropping of vegetables and tobacco is found, though the last crop has lost its pre-1940 importance. The same applies to cattle fattening, which is concentrated in the high and medium high altitude subdistricts. On the lower slopes of the northern districts, there is non-commercialized dryland cultivation of staple crops like maize and cassava, alternating with rain-fed sawah in the valley bottom. Alas, the area north of the Serayu River is very erosion-prone and in many villages landslides have removed the fertile topsoil. Some pockets of mixed gardens, a more stable ecological system, are found too, at medium high altitude: coffee, *salak*, oranges and other fruits are the products from these agroforestry systems. *Kecamatan* Sigaluh, to the east of Banjarnegara town, is an agroforestry area too.

The South Serayu Hills, to the south of the Serayu River, is the least endowed area. Agriculture on widespread infertile soils moves in a downward spirale. Commercialized and subsistence cassave cultivation prevales, for cassave is a crop, that is low in its demands, and thus suited to less fertile soils. As this crop, however,

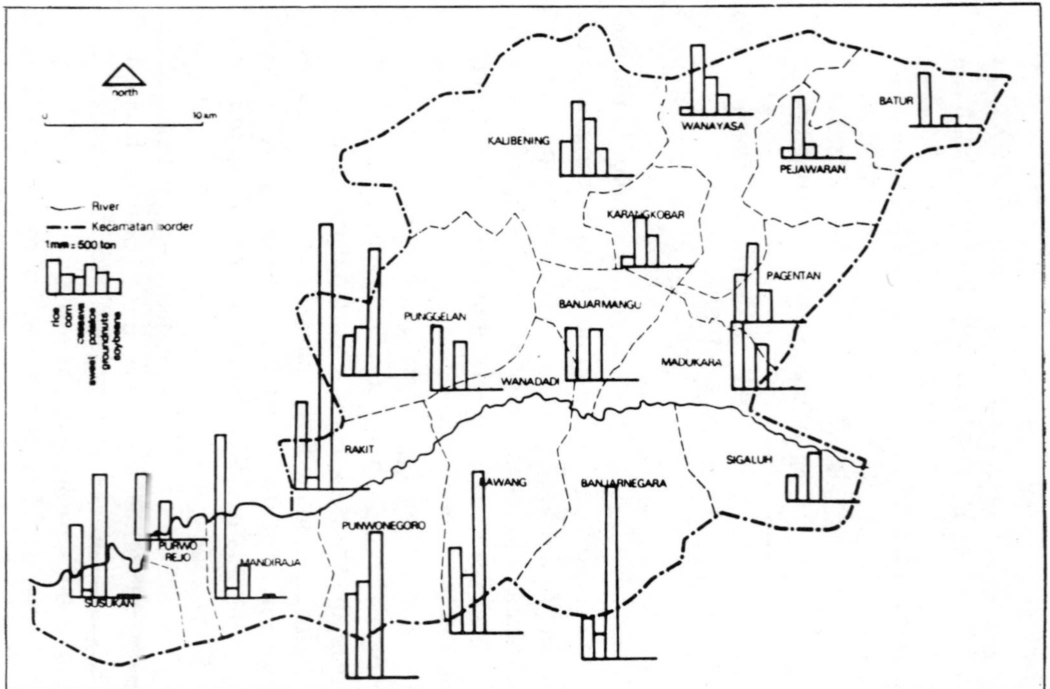

Source: Dinas Pertanian

Map 5.4a Production of main food crops to kecamatan in kabupaten Banjarnegara

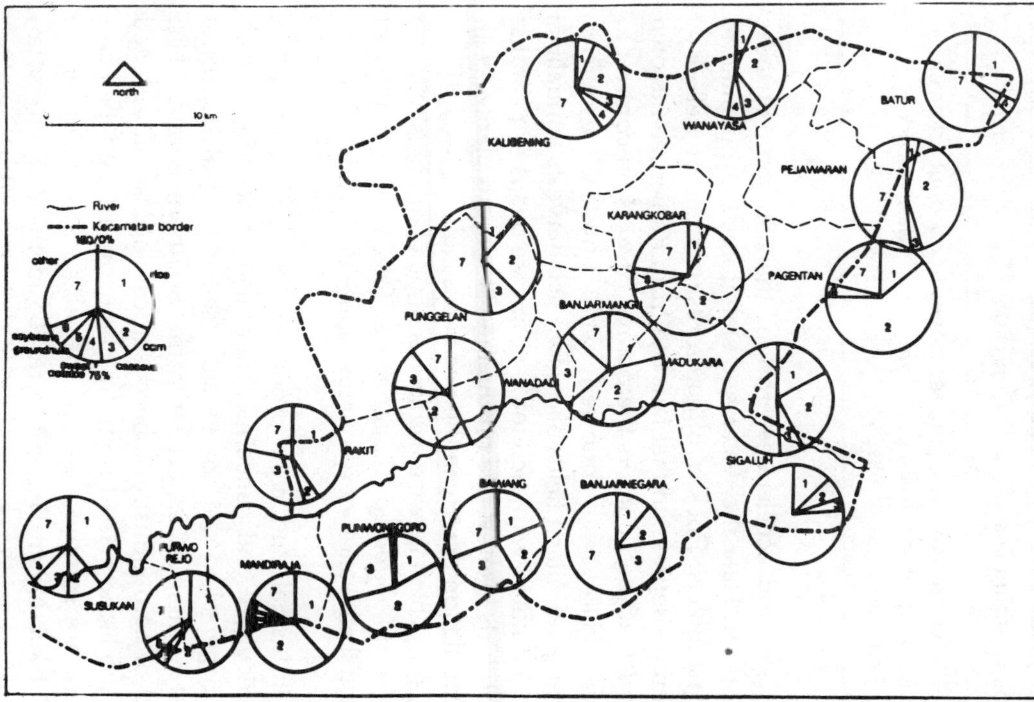

Source: Dinas Pertanian

Map 5.4b Main land use categories in Kabupaten Banjarnegara

Table 5.8 Main crops in kabupaten Banjarnegara

	Northern Mountains	*Central Depression*	*Southern Hills*
Crops	maize, tobacco, tea, quinine, vegetables, some rice, oranges.	rice, maize, cloves coffee, coconut, fruits.	coconut, cloves, cassava, rice

exhausts the soil and accelerates erosion, the condition of these ridges deteriorates. Near the watershed state forests are planted to bridle the worst effects. Pockets of agroforestry occur as well.

The central depression that fans out from Banjarnegara town onwards to the west and borders the Serayu River is, in contrast to the Southern Hills, well-endowed with physical resources. Technically irrigated *sawah* fields allow two rice harvests annually at most places, alternated with secondary crops like beans or peanuts. Village compounds in most rice producing villages are planted with tree crops. Population density in the rice belt is high: 800—1000 inhabitants per ha, which is twice as high as population density in the upland districts of *kabupaten* Banjarnegara. This density, combined with the unequal allocation of resources, brings about poverty in this area too.

Most industrial and craft production in the *kabupaten* is related to agriculture and concerns simple agro-processing, which explains its dispersal to the countryside (see map 5.5). Coconut sugar is most numerous, especially in the Southern Serayu Hills. Another kind of agro-industry, tobacco-processing, is concentrated in the Batur subdistrict. Apart from the ubiquitous home-type agro-industry, there are some pockets of specialized production at the countryside of *kabupaten* Banjarnegara. To mention the most important: bamboo-craft in *kecamatan* Mandiraja and Punggelan, woodcraft in this latter *kecamatan*, and copper-shops and forges in *kecamatan* Banjarmangu and Sigaluh respectively.

This primary and secondary production is partly reflected in

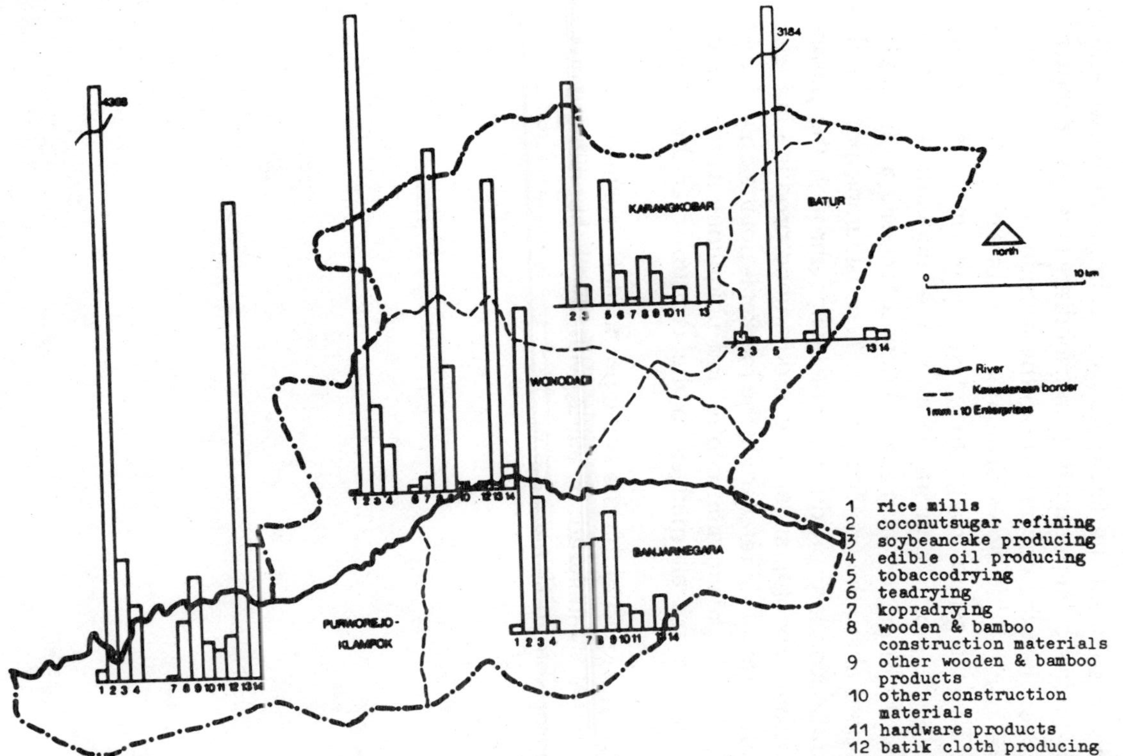

Source: Sensus Pertanian 1973

Map 5.5 Number of enterprises to kind in Banjarnegara

the trade flows at *pasar* in the *kecamatan* centres. In most *kecamatan* centres there is a *pasar* every five days. In addition there are markets in some of the larger villages. Commodity flows and trader movements at the *pasar* interlink subdistricts to one another and moreover, link the countryside to the outside world. Map 5.6 summarizes commodity flows at some *pasar* in *kabupaten* Banjarnegara. Two things are brought to the light by this map; the minor central role of *pasar* Banjarnegara in the network and the prevalence of distribution at these markets, especially at the well-accessible ones along the provincial road. A considerable portion of primary and secondary produce is not bulked through the *pasar* system; cassave, coconut sugar, rice and bamboo products are examples in this respect. In retail trade the market is not the only channel either, *toko* in *kecamatan* centre and ubiquitous *warong* and ambulant traders are alternatives to the consumer at the countryside.

In the next part of this thesis the production structure of Banjarnegara town is analyzed; it starts with the *kabupaten*'s chief market: *pasar kota* in Banjarnegara.

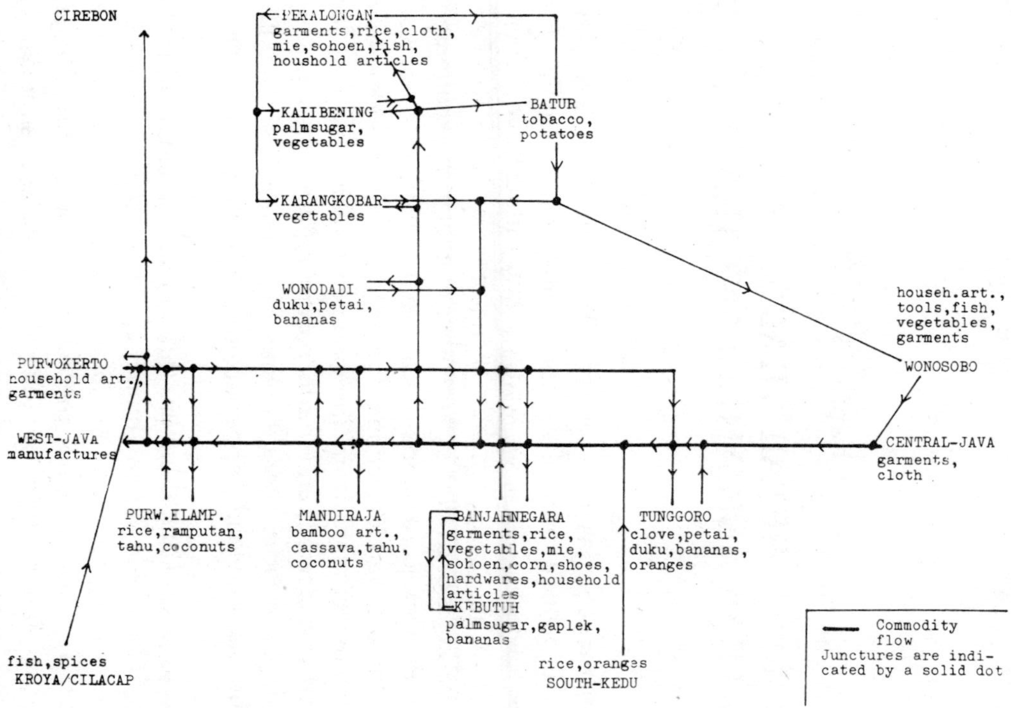

Source: Pasar Surveys

Map 5.6 Commodity flows in the kabupaten pasar system

Chapter 6

RETAIL TRADE: PASAR AND AMBULANT TRADE

Banjarnegara has two centres. One is the central square, founded by Dipayuda, tranquil except at public manifestations. The other is the town market, *pasar kota*, buzzing with activities; everyday more than 500 traders make a living at *pasar kota*. The Banjarnegara market is unrivalled by any other market in the *kabupaten*. In fact only Purworejo Klampok has a daily market too. *Pasar kota* consists of three seperate sections; the vegetable market seperated by the minibus terminal from the concrete building, where the general market is located, and thirdly *pasar* Ampera, where poultry and secondhand bicycles change owner. This market is situated just south of the main building, appendixed to it by numerous stalls in front.

Next to *pasar kota*, there are three minor general markets in Banjarnegara (see table 6.1 and map 5.2). These minor markets are located at some distance from the major town market, but near rural feederroads. The biggest minor market for example, *pasar* Wage, caters for rural *desa* south of the town and is situated, strategically near a node of *toko* in what once was the Chinese quarter. As is illustrated in table 6.2 in the next paragraph and will be returned upon in paragraph 8.2, turnover at these markets is strikingly lower

Table 6.1 Number of traders to merchandise at three minor markets in Banjarnegara town, February 5th 1983

	Pasar Wage (normal day)	*Pasar Garam (normal day)*	*Pasar Para-kancanggah (busy day)*
miscelleneous vegetables	21	11	14
soybean cakes	6	2	2
misc. foodstuff	3	5	4
biscuits	11	2	5
prepared food	12	3	3
fish	1	1	—
meat	2	—	—
househ. utensils	4	1	1
bananas	—	1	1
clothes and footware	1	1	1
tobacco	1	—	1
coconut sugar	4	—	—

Source: Pasar Surveys

than turnover of traders at *pasar kota.*

In the past the Banjarnegara market already was a major *pasar*. Reports written at the turn of the century mention that some imported manufactures were sold, but most trade concerned a local circulation of foodstuffs and home industrial products (SDS van Delden 1896, Mindere Welvaarts Verslagen 1907). Banjarnegara *pasar* catered for some transito flows too, mainly serving Wonosobo town. Banjarnegara had a daily market by then, though monday, tuesday and saturday were peak days. In 1918 a second market was established in the Chinese quarter, disappeared by now, *pasar* Wage being a remnant of it.

This chapter will treat *pasar* Banjarnegara anno 1983. It will concentrate upon the retail section at the general market. In the next chapters some other parts of the *pasar* trade will be dealt with, notably fruit, vegetable and rice trade, that merit special attention (chapter 8). This chapter will first outline how the general market is organized, and how this organization approaches institutionalization. The second paragraph will give an overview of relations within the branch, especially the position of the *pasar* as manifesting the regional circuit is depicted. The chapter will progress with a case study on trade in clothes. A final paragraph will have ambulant traders as its subject, closely linked with *pasar* trade.

6.1 PASAR KOTA: BAZAAR ECONOMY INSTITUTIONALIZED

At first sight, the internal division of the general *pasar* building seems illogical. Some rows are crowded with stalls and squatting traders displaying their wares alongside entrance ways. On the other hand virtually empty rows occur. It hints at the failure of the *pasar*'s spatial organization. The reason for this unbalanced division is the method followed at the allotment of stall space. In map 6.1 the division of the *pasar* to commodities traded is shown. Rows of stalls are assigned to certain sorts of traders, grouped to kind of merchandise. The rows that appear empty on the southside f.i. are used by fruit trades, and this is a seasonal business. Travelling and casual traders, like the *lebaran* clothes merchants, might use their places at the slack season of fruit supply. Still, though there is plenty of room in this part of the *pasar*, many non permanent traders will prefer to squat at the crowded northside, alongside the gangways and entrances. Trade hustles there, more people pass, attracted by the concentration of foodstuff stalls; the chance of good sales is higher. The gangway floors at the northside of the *pasar* are lined up with small scale traders, like palmsugar, fresh fish, *tempe, tahu* and tobacco sellers.

The *pasar* is often supposed to symbolize involutionary growth in an urban context. The absence of a developed organizational form, and as a corrolary a capacity to absorb a vast

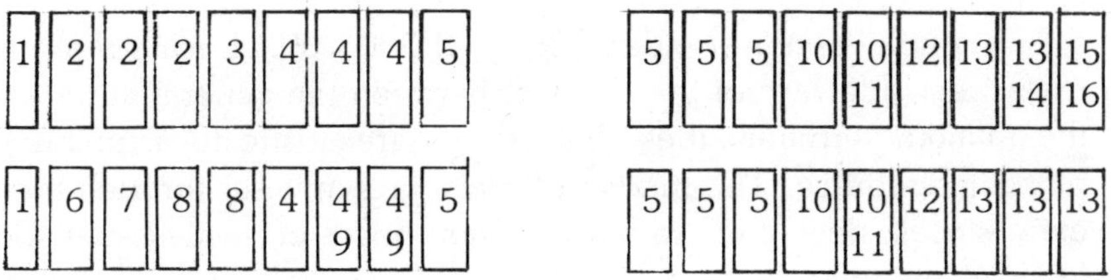

1 vegetables
2 miscellaneous foodstuffs
3 meat
4 rice
5 clothes
6 drugstores
7 cigarettes
8 non perishable foodstuff
9 cereals
10 household articles
11 bamboo products
12 tools
13 fruits
14 watchmakers
15 barbers
16 tobacco

Map 6.1 Overview of general pasar Banjarnegara

number of people, should have their climax in *pasar* commerce. Such is Geertz' (1963) description. In present day Banjarnegara institutionalization seems to be the trend at the general market however, not loosely defined tasks. At the general market officially row plots of 5 m^2 are hired from the market warden. All available plots are rented. When the *pasar* building was erected in 1978, a trader could buy an option for seven years of usage, that would cost Rp 100—500,000, depending on how strategically a plot was sited. Annual rent is low, a modest Rp 750—1250 per m^2. Besides, like everyone that manages a trading venture within a radius of 1.5 kilometer from the *pasar*, a pasar trader has to pay daily *bea* (market tax), Rp 20—40 per m^2. Interim selling of options to *pasar* plots is allowed, and it happens frequently, as can be observed, for many traders occupy more than 5 m^2, which could not have been acquired by the official procedure.

Little shops, called *kios*, surround the market place; they make up its side walls. They too can be hired from the market warden, at Rp 1750—2500 monthly. When the *pasar* was newly built, the entrance option was Rp 150—200,000, but nowadays selling one's option renders Rp 1—2,000,000. Located at the mainstreet sideways of the *pasar* or between the general *pasar* and the minibus terminal, these little shops are at the focal points of public intercourse. The market officials, grown wiser through these experiences, decided to raise the option prices of newly issued *kios* to the same level.

Caused by the high level of entrance fees for the fixed plots, trade in Banjarnegara's main market has become rather exclusive. Traders with small capital resources could not afford the initial option in 1978. The situation has even deteriorated since then, for underhand interim option prices are even higher, a situation ratified now by the option policy of the market officials. Thus small scale traders are restricted to gangway trade or have to try to find a place outside the *pasar* complex. This explains the difference in turnover, that table 6.2 depicts, between traders with a fixed place at *pasar kota* and those without. Strikingly, a number of traders that have a fixed place at *pasar kota* are of a corporate sector scale, in contrast to the generally accepted image of the petty *pasar* vendor. They also distinguish themselves by their slightly larger number of capitalist characteristics. Table 6.2 is a salient prove of the effect of plot allotment at the general market.

The institutionalization is not confined to the fixed places. Even gangway places at *pasar kota*, especially the most popular ones, are claimed. By non written agreement every gangway seller has a user's right to a place. Only sites unoccupied after eight o'clock in the morning are free. According to the market warden, trading in such claims has not developed yet, though it might be lucrative, for some of the floor sites have a very central location. All in all it is not that easy to start at *pasar kota*. The obstacle of high option prices and user's rights has reduced flexibility of the *pasar* system. Though skills needed (cf. table 6.3) do not suggest a high threshold, the average age of *pasar* enterprises, which is 14 years speaks a different language.

The traders at the Banjarnegara market are mostly town dwellers or originate from *desa* bordering town (see table 6.4). The

Table 6.2 Structuring and form characteristics and monthly turnover of pasar and ambulant traders

Type of enterprise	Sector	Number of cap. charac-teristics	Turnover in Rp
Pasar Kota: fixed place	Petty-Corporate	1—5	18,485,500
Pasar Kota: non fixed place	Petty	2—3	669,800
Minor pasar	Petty	2—3	136,500
Ambulant trader	Petty	2—3	441,000
Tukang kredit	Petty	2—4	475,000

Table 6.3 Experience and skills needed in pasar enterprises

Previous work experience		Stated skills needed	
Never worked before	10	No skills needed	1
Wage worker before	4	Learned by oneselve	20
Own account worker before	7	Learned at other enterprise	9
Headed own enterprise	9		

only exception is the vegetable section of the *pasar*, where plots are not as fixed as in the general market (see paragraph 8.2 as well). The urban core *desa*, Krandegan, Semarang, Parakancanggah and Kutabanjar count most traders. The other *desa*, Sokonandi, Wangon and Karangtengah are more rural and agricultural in outlook and orientation. Non farming activities like trader, government official and *toko* owner are less represented here.

Table 6.4 Origin of traders at Pasar Kota, at March 17th, May 9th and June 14th 1983

	19–3	9–5	14–6		19–3	9–5	14–6
Town:				Kec. Banjarnegara	52	61	86
Krandegan	100	120	133				
Semarang	75	67	72	Kaw. Banjarnegara	65	59	66
Par. canggah	80	81	82				
Kutabanjar	48	29	39	Kaw. Karangkobar	16	8	10
Sokonandi	18	23	18				
Karangtengah	12	9	10	Kaw. Batur	3	2	2
Wangon	5	2	7	Kaw. Wonodadi	31	27	24
				Kaw. Purw. Klampok	27	8	20
				Serayu Region	20	20	16
				Outside Serayu Region	17	12	14
Total town	338	331	361	Total non town	231	197	238

1) This table includes retail as well as wholesale traders, repairmen, barbers and foodstalls at the general pasar, vegetable pasar and pasar Ampera.
2) Kaw. means kawedanan, a now extinct administrative level between kabupaten and kecamatan.

Source: Pasar Surveys

6.2 PASAR KOTA: THE REGIONAL CIRCUIT

Goods and services offered at the *pasar kota* mainly concern basic needs. Traders in foodstuffs and clothes constitute the major categories, as can be made up from table 6.5. Some seasonal fluctuation can be read from this table too, though it only covers a period of three months. The number of fruit sellers and buyers ranges with regional supply, while the extent of clothes trade

Table 6.5 Number of traders at Pasar Kota according to kind of commodity traded at March 17th, May 9th and June 14th 1983

	17–3	9–5	14–6		17–3	9–5	14–6
Miscellaneous vegetables	48	47	45	Meat	6	13	12
Petai	12	1	1	Palmsugar	5	9	6
Salak	12	17	11	Tobacco & cigarettes	28	31	22
Bananas	15	8	16	Confection & footware	76	103	117
Peanuts	12	9	12	Drugstores	13	19	26
Miscellaneous Spices & nuts	10	14	6	Household			
Rice & corn	13	23	22	Bamboo products	11	9	9
Non perishable foodstuffs	61	63	61	Tools & ironware	19	21	16
Biscuits	31	24	38	Gold & jewelry	3	2	2
Prepared food	15	39	23	Watchmaker	11	10	9
Dried and fresh fish	15	14	14	Barber	6	9	11
				Tailor	8	10	7
				Others	—	15	16

Source: Pasar Surveys

expands enormously, shortly before and during *lebaran* (in 1983 from medio June to medio July), the muslim fasting month, when virtually everybody buys a new pair of clothes or gets one.

Despite most commodities being of the foodstuff and manufactured product species, products put up for sale at the Banjarnegara market show an impressive range. In this paragraph we intend to survey the role of the general market in commodity circulation.

From table 6.6 it can be seen that 60% of traders at pasar Banjarnegara trades in products, that originate from within the *kabupaten*. This commerce consists of products from agriculture and home industry. The output of the latter industry traded at *pasar*

Table 6.6 Number of traders to origin of major commodity sold at Pasar Kota, March 19th 1983

Product origins from:	*Agriculture*	*Home industry*	*Manufacturing*
Kabupaten Banjarnegara	186	118	—
Serayu Region	17	21	4
Outside Serayu Region	17	12	118

Source: Pasar Surveys

Banjarnegara concerns *tahu*, *tempe*, *krupuk*, *kecap*, snacks and, outside the sphere of the small scale food industry: bamboo products and copper utensils. It signals an unequal commodity exchange; for all manufactured products—with high added value— have to be imported to Banjarnegara. Traders selling such imported manufactures number 24%. The correlation between scale of production and circulation range, commented upon in paragraph 2.1, is confirmed on micro level. From table 6.6 it might be seen too that commodity exchange within the Serayu Valley does not add up to much. This is probably a reflection of the lack of differentation of production structure between the seperate *kabupaten* in the Serayu Valley Region. It makes one believe that there is a potential for local industry to develop; competing manufactured products, that are imported to the region through *pasar* and *toko* trade. Chapter 11 wil labour on this theme.

For most commodities traded at the Banjarnegara market, several chains are involved before they reach the small town *pasar*. A small fraction of only 6% of the traders at the *pasar kota* are producers themselves, most of them Banjarnegara town food-processors. Traders that handle produce from the *kabupaten* usually buy these from intermediate traders, village *bakul* that transport their wares to the town or, not so frequent, are met at the countryside. A 12% minority of *pasar kota* traders go to producers in kabupaten

Banjarnegara to purchase their merchandise.

For manufactured products there is a different situation. In this respect Banjarnegara *pasar* traders, like the *toko* as will be shown in chapter 7, represent the regional circuit in a national commodity circulation. Some traders (20% of all traders) might go and fetch the merchandise somewhere in Indonesia. Even more common is it for such transaction to take place at the *pasar* itself; traders are served by wholesaling or factory agents, that tour Central Javanese *pasar*.

Table 6.7 Traders at Pasar Kota, March 17th 1983: product's origin and location where merchandise was bought

Banjarnegara Town		*Serayu Valley Region*	
— At pasar kota	196	— From trader	32
— At toko	41	— From producer/farmer	16
— Own produce	23		
Kabupaten Banjarnegara		*Other part of Indonesia*	
— From trader	10	— From trader/producer	99
— From producer/farmer	66	— Own produce	6
— Own produce	3		

Source: Pasar Surveys

Such agents are a source of capital, as they are willing to allow some weeks delay payment; thus the part of the *pasar*, that is a chain in a national commodity circulation has this prerogative above those involved in regional circulation only. Strikingly not one *pasar* trader interviewed borrowed money from the *pasar* bank, a government bank, raised in particular to serve *pasar* traders. It was confessed that with its one-day-a-week opening scheme and the amount of paperwork involved market business people were hardly attracted. Trading enterprises need cash quickly, soon as they can make a bargain. Such is not delivered by the bureaucratic and careful *pasar* bank. No wonder money lenders are active at the *pasar*, snorted upon as rentiers by outsiders. According to informants 5 moneylenders operate at the *pasar kota*. They lend small amounts of money (Rp 5—10,000). Their regular clients are mostly small scale, capital-poor, *pasar* traders. Monthly interest rates are 20% and the loan has to be repaid with daily instalments. Compared to government bank rates (1.5—2.0% per month) such interest seems absurd, but it stands to the easy availability and possibility of prolonging in payment difficulties. Besides, in small scale trade at the *pasar*, a daily profit of 20% is common. With a daily turnover of Rp 5—10,000 (being very small scale trade) equal to the usual level of such loans, the revenue lost on interest to the moneylender is only 3% of total profit. Apart from informal 20% interest moneylending to solve short-term lack of capital, there is a habit of mutual money lending, particularly among larger scale traders. This does not entail huge sums either, not more than is necessary for daily purchases. Money borrowed this way is paid back quickly. Fellow traders do not reckon any interest, but it is customary to repay a little extra. On a monthly base such voluntary interest would come to about 2%.

For long term investment market traders relate to other sources. In this respect *arisan* are very important, credit cycles organized usually among traders of the same kind of merchandise. The *arisan* often serve as sources for trade ventures, but might be used for consumptive purposes as well. An *arisan* group can consist of any number of persons, though it will seldom surpass 10—30 members. Every day a certain amount of money is paid by all members, a realistic example would be Rp 1000, but contribution ranges from Rp 500 to Rp 2500. The head of the *arisan* collects the money and every 10 or 20 days the total sum is given to a member, appointed by a lottery. A winner is excluded from succeeding lotteries, but has to stay paying till everyone has had its turn. Often the head gets a little renumeration for administrative expenses. *Arisan* are an integral part of Javanese society, in all social circles there are *arisan*, among traders, civil servants, housewives and neigbourhood dwellers. It is the common man's way of saving.

Another paramount source of long term credit is money disposed of by relatives. Though such funding has not taken such flight as among the Chinese, 26% of market traders mention their families as a source of initial capital. If further investments are made, these are usually financed from a trader's own means or some other non family source is used. Some traders have even succeeded in applying for a low interest credit scheme at the *B.R.I.* or *B.P.D.* bank.

In chapter 4 we noted that competition within petty commodity sector is often conceived as different from, for instance, competition between corporate and petty commodity sector enterprises. Competition within the petty commodity sector is taken as an expression of, not as a limit to growth. It abstains from expelling fellow enterprises. The cooperation among rival traders at the *pasar* in *arisan* and by mutual money lending seems to support this assumption. Cooperation among *pasar* traders is common in selling and buying too, as well as in using scales. Fierce competition however is manifest in tying customers. Geertz (1963) has described how commerce at the market is dominated by a host of ad hoc arrangements and how consolidation of relations is unknown within the *pasar* walls. Such atomistic picture however, is not encountered at the Banjarnegara *pasar*. Half of the traders has, though to a varying extent, permanent customers, often tied by credit. Market traders frequently act as wholesalers, conform table 6.8, and such relations to other traders are marked by permanency.

Table 6.8 Market traders: groups of customers mentioned

Private persons	53%	Warong	10%
Intermediate traders	12%	Industries	5%
Hawkers	20%		

6.3 A CASE STUDY: CLOTHES TRADE AT PASAR BANJARNEGARA

Clothes trade is a major instance of *pasar* trade acting as a regional circuit in a national commodity circulation. Confection retailed at *pasar* Banjarnegara is produced in Central and West Javanese cities; only a rare local tailor supplies *pasar* traders. Pekalongan, Solo, Yogya, Klaten (for traditional cloth in particular), Bandung, Kudus and Jakarta are the main production sites. Travelling wholesalers intermediate between these national circuit textile mills and the *pasar* traders (see table 6.9). The exquisite hand-dyed *batik* cloth is distributed in a different network.

Table 6.9 Clothessellers at pasar kota: method of stock supply

Travelling wholesalers coming to Banjarnegara	79%
Trader buys at Banjarnegara toko	5%
Trader travels to wholesaler, industry or other pasar	11%
Trader sells own produce (Tasik and Klaten people)	5%

Source: Pasar Surveys

Periodically, every 5 or 10 days, these wholesalers or their agents frequent Banjarnegara town, and deliver to *pasar kota* and to *toko* in town. Every day 7—10 of these distributors visit the market. Some have their own pick-ups or minibusses, other wholesalers share and rent one together. Next to Banjarnegara, other *pasar* in the Serayu region are visited on such wholesale trips. Grossly the trajects are as follows: Kudus, Pekalongan and Magelang based merchants tour the eastern and northern part of the *kabupaten* and stop at *pasar* Kalibening, Karangkobar, Wonodadi, Mandiraja and Banjarnegara. Solo, Yogyakarta and Klaten businessmen plan their trip from Wonosobo, visit Banjarnegara, and travel back to Magelang. West Javanese wholesalers go to Purwokerto, Purbolinggo, Purworejo-Klampok, Mandiraja and as far upstream the

Serayu River as Banjarnegara. Minor *pasar* in the kabupaten like Kebutuh, Tunggoro and Madukara are occasionally visited by these extra-regional wholesalers, but usually retail traders at these periodic *pasar* have a route of weekly *pasar*, encompassing a large market, where they will supply their stock.

Trade credit integrates the circuits in clothes trade. Banjarnegara's clothes sellers in the survey all pay the wholesalers afterwards, often on the next visit. Interest is not assessed, but cash payment renders some discount. Apart from private persons, the clientele of *pasar* clothes traders is made up of petty traders, especially *tukang kredit*, delt with in the next paragraph. Delay payment regulations between travelling wholesalers and *pasar* traders are passed on to transactions between *pasar* traders and such hawkers. The prevalence of trade credit probably explains for the huge size of confection trade.

Clothes traders constitute an important section at the *pasar kota*. They occupy the central rows within the building, and at *lebaran* time additional stalls pop up. In the three monthly *pasar* surveys the number of traders varied between 76 and 117, depending on the time of the year. In the count on enterprises, enumerating enterprises in Banjarnegara town, 83 clothes traders were mentioned, including market and streetside traders and hawkers. To this figure one might add *tukang kredit*, to whom cloth and confection is one category in a wide assortment of manufactures.

Quantity and similarity of trade enterprises result in an intense competition for the same market segment. Therefore it is risky nowadays to start a clothes trading business and to keep it running. To upkeep a complete assortment of garment and cloth is expensive and average trading capital numbers up to Rp 286,000, needed to bridge the span between two successive visits of a wholesalers partly, though this sum might have been furnished by the wholesalers. The effort of retaining one's share in the face of numerous competitors is demanding and bankruptcy or near bankruptcy is not exceptional. A tragic example is Bu Kusnedi:

Bu Kusnedi has been trading on *pasar*, since she was a kid. Nowadays, she must be somewhere near her fifties. She covers four *pasar*: Banjarnegara, Wonodadi, Rakit and Madukara. She and her children share a permanent plot at a backrow of *pasar kota*. To do her job she has to travel a lot, and pay carrymen, *becak* and minibus drivers. As a result of harsh competition from *tukang kredit* and extraregional discount traders that penetrate both town and rural pasar and deal with customers directly, business is slack. Expenses are not covered by gains, that are only Rp 250 a day. Still she goes on, for she is used to it, trying to raise her turnover incessantly. It seems an impossible job to repay all her debts. She used her hushband's status as a civil servant to obtain a loan of Rp 400,000 at the *B.R.I.* An equal amount she owes to wholesalers, who now only sell to her when she pays cash. Besides she owes minor sums to fellow traders.

Though not a representative example because of the height of her debts, Bu Kusnedi is not the only one who complained about the present situation in the branch. The travelling salesmen penetrating the market with *lebaran* are an eyesore, they drain local trade of its peak demand. To many traders the overcrowded *pasar* is another problem, as well as customers reluctant to pay cash. Further, even though wholesaler's credit is common, many complain of capital shortage, for credit has to be passed on to the next chain in commodity circulation. To keep the amount of money invested in stock within margins, mutual lending of merchandise in case of shortage is common practice. Thus the laboursome procedure of borrowing *pasar* bank money is avoided, as well as the high interest taxed by money-lenders.

Entrepreneurial dynamism is not to be attached to this seemingly involuted section of the Banjarnegara *pasar*. After commencing business, investment to expand are rare. Neither did *pasar* traders interviewed specify any such plans. Profits indeed are modest, reaching from negative to a maximum of Rp 158,000 monthly. Averages, at Rp 67,000, are equal to what a bricklayer earns, whose occupation does not involve similar risk.

6.4 AMBULANT TRADERS

Traders with a fixed or a non fixed place are not the only exponents of commerce at the *pasar kota* complex, for peddlers pass the market and trade there as well as outside the market. Peddlers differ in assortment and route. Some peddlers, like cigarette vendors or foodvendors, are attracted to crowdedness and will operate near the *pasar*, the minibus terminal, schools or the cinema. Some of these foodvendors prepare the food themselves and are thus included as foodprocessors in the chapter on industry. A second type of peddlers trades its wares door to door and has a more or less fixed route, whereby some permanent customers are visited. Examples of this latter type are meat vendors, hawkers of traditional medicine and vegetables hawkers, who are discussed in paragraph 6.2. Despite all this diversity a tentative impression is that peddlers do not number as many in Banjarnegara town, as they number in big cities on Java. If peddlers are taken as the manifestations of the petty commodity part of the economy, one is tempted to assume that petty trading is not developed as intricately in Banjarnegara town as it is in other locations. Some types of peddlers, like newspaper vendors for instance, are absent in Banjarnegara.

It does not take too much private money to start as a peddler. Trading capital of peddlers interviewed averaged Rp 46,000. Loans to start trading are rare. Some peddlers rely on family money, but usually delay payment to the supplier serves as the source of capital. Both the petty commodity scale and the low number of capitalist characteristics stand out. On average a peddler's profit is Rp 29,400, slightly higher than that of a trader at one of the town's minor *pasar*. Such revenue is hardly sufficient for a family to sustain on and of all thirteen peddlers interviewed the family income was supplemented by the earnings of a second family member. On average the peddler's returns formed 50% of family income. Three peddlers even derived money from agriculture.

Peddlers are definitely local circuit. Their clientele is townsfolk or occasionally a rural dweller, who comes to Banjar-

Table 6.10 Supply of merchandise to peddlers (excluding tukang kredit): type and residence of supplier, origin of commodities supplied

Type of supplier (%)		*Residence of supplier (%)*	
Farming	9	Banjarnegara Town	69
Small scale industry	25	Kabupaten Banjarnegara	24
Pasar trader	57	Outside Kabupaten	7
Warong	3		
Toko	2	*Origin of goods (%)*	
Other enterprise	4		
		Banjarnegara Town	16
		Kabupaten Banjarnegara	56
		Outside Kabupaten	28

negara to visit the *pasar* or the cinema. Suppliers are town-based enterprises as well; as a rule *pasar* traders or home-industries. Products traded are regional products mostly (72%), as table 6.10 shows. All this contrasts the common peddler to the *tukang kredit*, often ambulant traders as well, who are reviewed in the next paragraph.

6.4.1 Tukang kredit

Clothes and garments, plastic kitchenware, and luxury items like television sets and refrigerators, are peddled by ambulant traders, called *tukang kredit*. They also go by the name of *cicilan*, *orang tasik* or *makelar barang-barang*. A *tukang kredit* will sell his wares on credit, whereby he splits the sum a customer has to pay him in a large number of small instalments. (The Indonesian term for an instalment is *cicil*; this explains the word *cicilan*.) This system enables lower income households to purchase consumer durables and those with more money to spend to afford luxury items, without having to take the effort of saving. Like money-lenders at the *pasar kota*, the *tukang kredit* will cash the terms periodically, everyday or every week during three to four months. *Cinamindring,* a Dutch word still applied to this practice, hints at the origin of the profession; it should be translated as Chinese reductions. It might have been the Chinese who introduced the selling on daily instalments system, but as a matter of fact Chinese nowadays refrain from this line of trade. At present a lot of people from Tasik Malaya (West Java) are engaged with the profession of *tukang kredit*, as is attested by its synonym: *orang tasik*.

Collecting the daily or weekly terms, it might be understood, is the most laboursome task to a *tukang kredit* and it comes as no surprise that sellers on instalments are less present in large conurbations, for population there is often mobile and anonymous, making it difficult to trace a defaulter. A customer has to pay a price that is raised 50—150% to a *tukang kredit*. At first this seems absurd, but is explained by the level of non-payment (5—20%) and the time and efforts a *tukang kredit* has to spend on getting paid. The labourintensive transactions, the multitude visits before an article is paid, lower total turnover to a *tukang kredit*, and make him classify as a petty entrepreneur, despite his selling commodities that are expensive per unit. Actually anyone who sells on instalments might be called a *tukang kredit;* the title is not reserved to peddlers, thought they number most, but might be allotted to *pasar* traders and shop owners as well. There is a difference in the manner the terms are cashed; the *pasar* traders or shop owners expect their customers to come and pay at regular intervals, while the peddler makes a daily or weekly tour to all debtors, which is a more effective way of getting paid. Some of these peddlers and *pasar* traders, especially but not solely the ones that sell luxury items, are allied to a *toko*. They note the wishes of a customer, and when it exceeds the usual portable assortment of clothing and plastic household items, the trader will go to the *toko* and bring the desired article on his next tour. If it is an expensive article, the *toko* will not demand the *tukang kredit* to pay cash. The *tukang kredit* will then take care of the final customer's payments. Such *tukang kredit* are called *makelar barang-barang*. Sometimes their profit margins are fixed by the *toko*. Quite remarkably, in this indirect manner, a *toko* will supply lower income people on credit. If not for the efforts of the *makelar barang-barang*, such customers would not be tolerated. Other *tukang kredit* do not have such fixed bonds with Banjarnegara retial shops, but operate independently and buy from a number of *toko*, or as applies to some of the traders from Tasik, are organized by non-*toko* wholesalers.

One such wholesaler interviewed, a man from Tasik Malaya himself, furnishes 10 Tasik *tukang kredit* with a merchandise of clothes, which they do not have to pay back immediately. He also appoints which villages the several *tukang kredit* have to frequent. This man cooperates extensively with fellow wholesalers from Tasik. They lend merchandise or money to one another and share a minibus to travel to Tasik Malaya to supplement stock. Sometimes even only one of them makes the journey to Tasik to buy for his fellow wholesalers.

Not all Banjarnegara *tukang kredit* are of Tasik origin, but many are. Neither do all *tukang kredit* that operate in the *kabupaten* reside in Banjarnegara town. Everywhere at the countryside one can meet these people at village *pasar* or peddling, travelling by foot, by bicycle or by pick-up. They often live in small regional centres or, when motorized, come from towns other than Banjarnegara. Those settled in the town constitute only a small fraction of the total population of *tukang kredit*. Their radius is limited, coinciding grossly with the town and adjacent *kecamatan*. Still even such limited trading area is more than the radius of the common peddler as discussed in paragraph 6.4. In many aspects a peddling *tukang kredit* differs from peddlers like food vendors or vegetables hawkers. While most peddlers sell daily household necessities, a *tukang kredit* will sell consumer durables or luxury items. This links a *tukang kredit* up with *toko* and, as was shown in pasar clothes trade, with the corporate sector in general. This alliance ensures some *tukang kredit* to have a large part of their working capital advanced by *toko* or wholesaler. Peddlers of daily necessities do not dispose of such source of capital, though they might be allowed by a *pasar* trader or a home industry to pay for their wares at the end of the day. As they almost sell out everyday, their total working capital might actually be funded by their supplier as well. A *tukang kredit*, for he is repaid only in 3—4 months time, has to have a larger capital stock. Mean present trading capital of *tukang kredit* interviewed was Rp 423.000, while initial investments averaged Rp 308,000. If the supplier does not provide this sum or if there is a time lag between payment deadline to a *toko* and the clients having their debts redeemed, family or private resources are returned upon. Bank loans to ambulant traders are unusual.

The contrasts between *tukang kredit* and peddlers of daily household necessities are matched in the higher turnover and profits to a *tukang kredit*; they average Rp 475.000 and Rp 65.300 respectively to a *tukang kredit*. a *tukang kredit* also distinguishes himself from other peddlers by his higher score of capitalist characteristics, as could already be made up from table 6.2. One peddling *tukang kredit* even employed a parttime labourer to carry his stock. Nonetheless selling on instalments is not a source of wealth to most of the people engaged with it. Many *tukang kredit* go bankrupt by non paying customers. The traders try to limit this danger by exchanging information on defaulters.

In a lot of households selling on instalments is taken up as an additional source of income and the activities might be of a temporary and ad hoc nature. Even established *tukang kredit* have their returns supplied by other sources of income within the family. On the other hand some signs of scaling up can be noticed in the *tukang kredit* business, for itinerant salesmen from other town, equiped with a pick-up truck, occasionally visit the affluent quarters of town, ringing door to door. These traders sell on periodic instalments too.

Chapter 7

RETAIL TRADE: SHOPS

The Indonesian language knows two words for retail shops: *toko* and *warong* (or *kedai*). This semantic division seems adequate in classifying retail stores. Confer to table 7.1. In form as wel as in structuring characteristics *warong* and *toko* diverge, whereby *warong* are without exception petty commodity sector and the median number of capitalist characteristics is 1. On the other hand 50% of the enterprises labeled as *toko*, are corporate sector enterprises. Degree of penetration of capitalist mode of production ranges, but most *toko* have 3—4 characteristics.

The difference between *warong* and *toko* goes further. The distinction is multi-facetted, as might be seen for instance in the way the stores get supplied. All *toko* interviewed get their stock from wholesalers from outside Banjarnegara, whether wholesaler's

Table 7.1 Structuring and form characteristics of toko and warong interviewed

Type of enterprise	*Sector*	*Number of capitalist characteristics*
Warong	Petty	1—3
Toko	Petty—Corporate	1—5

Table 7.2 Indicators of wealth in town and countryside in kabupaten Banjarnegara

	Banjarnegara town	Kabupaten excl. town
Monthly spendings per capita	Rp 10,674	Rp 5,639
	Kecamatan Banjarnegara	Other kecamatan
Brick and stone buildings	17.9%	5.4%
Number of motorized vehicles per 1000 inhabitants	11.2	2.9

N o t e : Kecamatan Banjarnegara includes more than Banjarnegara town, but below kecamatan level data were not available.

Source: Susenas 1980, Banjarnegara Dalam Angka 1980

agents or independent travelling salesmen. All *warong* on the other hand are tied to the local circuit; they are supplied by *toko*, *pasar* traders and—in case of sugar, frying oil and kerosene—by a local agency. Another distinction concerns the stock kept. Warong seldom specialize. If so, they specialize in dried fish, rice or sweeties. Most *warong* act as the grocer's shop around the corner, serving the common man with low priced groceries. Part of the *toko* is of the general store type too, but they deliver more exclusive and better quality goods, that cannot be afforded by lower income class people. Luxury items are only furnished by specialized *toko*. Demand for these items is concentrated in town. Table 7.2 demonstrates that purchasing power in town is twice as high as it is on the countryside of *kabupaten* Banjarnegara. Other indicators confirm this difference. Thus, not the expedience of settling in a central location, but the local pocket of high purchasing power seems decisive in the concentration of *toko* in Banjarnegara town. On the other hand *toko* do fulfil the needs of a population, that surpasses Banjarnegara town's

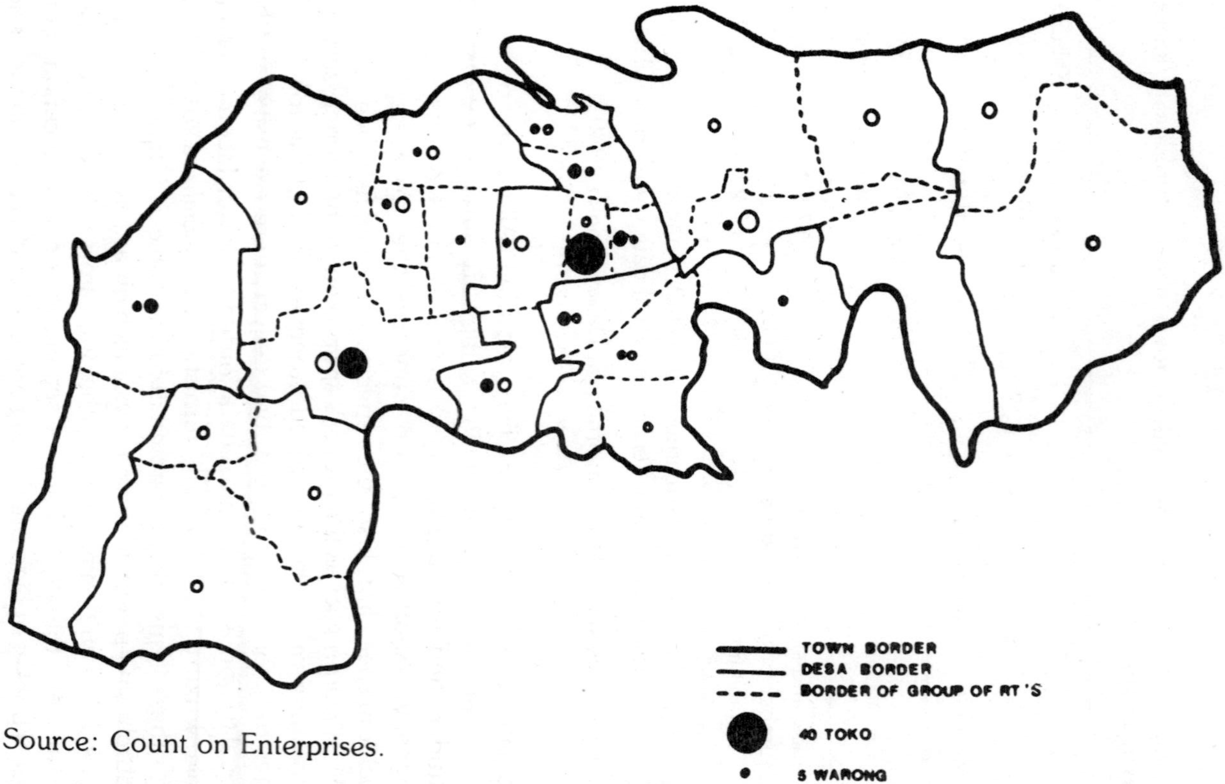

Source: Count on Enterprises.

Map 7.1 Dispersion of toko and warong in Banjarnegara town

borders: they definitely belong to the regional retail circuit, contrary to warong, that cater for neighbourhood demand only. From the nucleation of *toko* and dispersion of *warong* such difference in function might be conceived (see map 7.1).

In this chapter we will treat *toko* and *warong* seperately. In paragraph 10.3 a special case is added, where *toko* and hawker combine in gold trade.

7.1 TOKO

7.1.1 Toko: the Chinese resort

Banjarnegara *toko* are located in a few areas only; the streets bordering the town market are lined up with *toko*, especially the Jalan Veteran, to the west of the *pasar*. A secondary concentration is found along the provincial highway, with a node just west of Kali Tulis. *Toko* in this node are in state of decline however. In the past countryside dwellers used to walk to the town and stop to shop at these *toko*. The explosive growth of minibus traffic changed their fate though, for the minibusses drive past the *toko* in the node and stop at the minibus terminal, nextdoor to the town market and Jalan Veteran. The importance of non-town shoppers is indicated by this history.

Origins of the node west of Kali Tulis can be traced back to the Chinese quarter that used to have its site down there. During the anti-Chinese riots in 1965, many Chinese fled Banjarnegara. Only part of them returned and they dispersed all over the town's core. Nowadays most *toko* are still Chinese owned, especially the larger ones are. Out of 22 *toko* interviewed, 19 were Chinese owned, having an average monthly turnover of Rp 31,500,000. Monthly sales of the three Javanese *toko* interviewed, amounted to Rp 2,700,000 only; a very substantial difference. In the past all *toko* were Chinese enterprises; Javanese traders were by definition petty commodity sector. By that time the Chinese did not only dominate *toko* trade, but they dominated agricultural marketing, government wholesale and construction trade as well (SDS). Gradually they have been expelled from these branches. Usually at first it is decreed that one should have a license to operate in the metier and the next step is to refuse these licenses to Chinese. Discrimination does not stop: Chinese are extorted extra money by tax officials and some police and military personnel take it for granted that they do not have to pay in a Chinese *toko*. On an official plane, Chinese cannot apply for low interest credit schemes at government banks, like the *K.I.K.* or *K.M.K.P.*—a rule only very recently announced to be discarded.

The Chinese community counterbalances these adverse trends by being tightly organized. No young Chinese is in need of work. Young men willing to start their own enterprise are furnished with capital and merchandise, if the parents' budget allows. One hardware store owner for instance got his complete stock from his father-in-law, who runs a hardware store too. The *toko* building at the Jalan Veteran was bought by his father-in-law; rent to be paid is a symbolic Rp 100,000 annually. In this way the son-in-law is given the opportunity to build up his own clientele of artisans and contractors. Once established he might commence repaying debts to his father-in-law, but there is no hurry. A second hardware shop owner tells the same story. Both he and his father head a hardware shop. Though having seperate administrations, they cooperate extensively. Trips to wholesalers are made together; depot and personnel are shared. Part of the father's former clientele was transferred to his son. From jewelry and electronics shop owners we heard likewise tales. Borrowing from family members and using working space in family property are common practices.

Capital to start a toko, therefore, is seldom obtained from a bank; 95% of the *toko* owners use private funds: savings, inheritance money or a loan from a relative or a friend. Further investments might be paid for with a bank loan, a quarter of the *toko* keepers does, nothwithstanding the troublesome procedure. A special method of financing trade, peculiar to the Chinese community, is the *hwe* (Kelling 1928). It bears resemblance to the Javanese rotating credit scheme, the *arisan*, though chance does not play such a decisive role. How does an *hwe* work? A person—to be called the head of the *hwe*—who is in need of capital assembles a group of creditworthy people, usually some 10 to 15 persons. Beforehand the head of the *hwe* has fixed the amount of money and the periodicity of the *hwe*. Each member will bring the same amount of money. In Banjarnegara the contribution to a hwe ranges Rp 5,000—15,000 and a *hwe* usually congregates once or twice a month. At the first meeting the head will cash the money the members have brought. At the second meeting everybody, including the head, will again bring the same amount of money. Who gets the pool this time, is decided by the interest the members are willing to pay. Everybody except the head will write down an offer, the height of it depending on one's cash needs. Notes are folded up and on opening up it is disclosed who gets the money, which is the member that offered to pay most interest. Every next meeting he has to bring his share plus the interest he said he would pay. At the third meeting the procedure is repeated. It should be noted that the head of the *hwe* and the ones, who won the pool at a previous meeting are excluded from making an offer. The *hwe* will take as much meetings as there are participants. It is laboursome to estimate interest rates in a *hwe*, but it seems that they usually range 3—5% monthly. The head is free of duty in this respect, but he might be held responsible for default payments. Every *hwe* might have slightly different rules. For instance, in stead of paying a little extra every next meeting, the interest of the highest bidder might be subtracted from the shares the other members brought. In another version there might be no head and interest is offered already at the first meeting. In this version there is communal responsibility for defaulters.

Dispite its in-group cohesion, to which informal agreements on bottom prices should be added, it is our impression that *toko* trade does not flourish in Banjarnegara. Far larger amounts of money circulate in fruit trade (chapter 8) and construction (chapter 10). This is partly explained by discrimination towards the Chinese entrepreneur. Another reason might be, that

Table 7.3 Number and kind of toko in Banjarnegara town

Food store	21	Jewellery	5
Dispensary	6	Photo devices store	3
Clothes store	14	Electronics store	4
Household utensils store	8	Motorbike dealer	7
General store	61	Motorcar dealer	3
Furniture store	7	Other	7
Hardware store	9		

Source: Count on Enterprises

though Banjarnegara town is a concentration of wealth compared to its hinterland, a substantial and specialized *toko* apparatus cannot sustain on small town purchasing power. Table 7.3 gives an overview of number and sort of *toko* in Banjarnegara town. For luxury items, like latest fashion dresses and exquisite furniture, people have to go to other towns. Modern electric household equipment, like freezers or washing machines, cannot be obtained locally, nor can one buy a passenger motor car. Well-to-do inhabitants stated that for quality stores, whatever product, they went to Wonosobo or, more often, to Purwokerto or Semarang. The commodities might be available in Banjarnegara, but the bigger choice and lower prices of the city are preferred.

7.1.2 Toko: extraregional supply and regional retail

Toko are a major link in national commodity circulation. A minority of commodities, put up for sale at the *toko* in Banjarnegara, is produced within the *kabupaten*. It concerns essential foodstuffs, like rice, or building materials: the regional circulation of sand, stone and bricks is partly organized by some hardware stores; paragraph 10.3 will be dedicated to this line of trade. As is evident from table 7.4, these regional products are purchased from producers or intermediate traders usually, contrary to wares of *extra-*

Table 7.4 Origin of goods supplied by type of supplier to Banjarnegara toko interviewed (relative numbers)

	Origin of goods			
	Kabupaten Banjarnegara	*Elsewhere Indonesia*	*Outside Indonesia*	*Total*
Producer	*8*	*8*	—	*16*
Wholesaler	*6*	*54*	*7*	*67*
Intermediary	—	*2*	—	*2*
Retail store	*1*	*5*	—	*6*
Pasar	*8*	*1*	—	*9*
Total	*23*	*70*	*7*	

Table 7.5 Banjarnegara toko: origin of supplier mentioned

Kabupaten Banjarnegara	26 %	Purwokerto	21%
		Semarang	23%
Wonosobo	2.5%	Other C. Javanese cities	16%
Purbolinggo	6.5%	Elswhere on Java	4%

kabupaten origin that is. In such a case wholesalers will supply the merchandise. The interurban orientation of Banjarnegara *toko* now stands out. Most suppliers are wholesalers in higher level cities, notably Purwokerto and Semarang (cf. table 7.5). Semarang has a larger share in Banjarnegara supply than cities like Solo, Yogyakarta or Magelang. The latter offer specialized items only, like ready made garments, cloth and jewelry. Purwokerto, the biggest town in the Serayu Valley, has a large concentration of Chinese. Many people from Banjarnegara have relatives there and it is said that many refugees from the riots in 1965 settled in Purwokerto, instead of returning to Banjarnegara. Trade ties might have developed along kin lines.

Usually a *toko* keeper will pay his wholesaler afterwards, from a couple of weeks, up to two months after he has been delivered the goods. Thus, relations between the enterprises are strenghtened by trade credit. 90% of the *toko* is in permanent debt with his wholesaler. Dependent on the lag in payment prices might rise 5—10%, compared to paying cash. Debts will be discharged on some next delivery. The habitual pattern is that a wholesaler's agent periodically, every two or four weeks, will frequent a *toko* to do such delivery. Some Banjarnegara *toko*, take their own or rented car to go to a wholesaler. Occasionally, when a *toko* is short of stock, it might be supplemented by a fellow *toko* keeper.

Table 7.6 Type of deliverance to Banjarnegara toko interviewed

Visited by wholesaler or wholesaler's agent	55%
Transport taken care of by toko	5%
Both modes occur	40%

Despite the prevalence of trade credit, most Banjarnegara *toko* have not lost their independence. Branch stores are nearly absent in the town. Of 22 *toko* surveyed only one was entangled in a commission arrangement. This store sells furniture and motorbikes and is furnished by a factory and a motorbike wholesaler from Purwokerto. For every piece of furniture sold, the storekeeper can keep 5%; for every motorbike Rp 12.500. Wages, taxes and rent of the store are paid for by the storekeeper himself, but losses on stock are avoided; unsaleable furniture and motorbikes can be returned to the suppliers. The Purwokerto factory has similar contracts with *toko* in Purwokerto, Purbolinggo and Purworejo Klampok.

On the other hand, several Banjarnegara *toko* have such bonds with stores in *kecamatan* centres. A *toko* in electronic articles equips a store in Wonodadi, whose owner sells in commission at a fixed 2% profit margin. A Banjarnegara shop in cloth and garments even had a genuine store chain, reaching to Kalibening and Karangkobar. It should be noted that the distinction between dependent and independent shopkeeping often is an arbitrary one; in the cases mentioned however, the countryside stores were entirely dependent on one supplier, that delivered on credit. Some other stores in Banjarnegara have ambulant commission salesmen, *tukang kredit,* already commented upon in paragraph 6.4.1. Some of these *tukang kredit* look for customers at the countryside, note their wishes and pass them on to a connected *toko*. Such *tukang kredit* might have his profit margin fixed by the *toko*. Most *tukang kredit* however, operate independent from *toko*. Traders, it might be clear, whether ambulant or established, are an important category of customers to *toko*. Some *toko* even seem to specialize in wholesale. The survey included a question into the major group of customers. Though the answer to this question cannot be interpreted as a reflection of the actual number of customers, it stands out from table 7.7 that traders, including *warong* keepers, take care of a large part of the *toko*'s turnover. In table 7.8 the degree to which town and countryside are served is shown. Town dwellers score high too, considered Banjarnegara's limited population, in comparison to the countryside. Generally it seems that though Banjarnegara *toko* serve the countryside as well, this hinterland is confined to *kecamatan* near Banjarnegara.

Moreover as a wholesaler the Banjarnegara *toko* are increasingly by-passed by extra-*kabupaten* wholesalers' agents supplying rural stores directly. Banjarnegara's wholesaling position cannot match Purwokerto or, in the northern districts, Pekalongan and

Table 7.7 Major categories of customers stated by Banjarnegara toko

Private persons	50%
Hawkers and intermediate traders	30%
Warong	7%
Institutions and industries	12%

Table 7.8 Origin of customers stated by Banjarnegara toko

Town	39%
Kabupaten Banjarnegara	56%
Outside kabupaten	5%

Tegal. The small town *toko* are circumvented in another respect too. Market traders at *pasar kota*, selling manufactured goods, less and less purchase the wares from Banjarnegara *toko*. Especially in the textile branch, as was detailed in paragraph 6.3, itinerant wholesalers called *pendatang*, take up the supplying of market traders. In the *pasar* survey, encompassing all *pasar* traders, the number of traders, that mentioned a *toko* as its supplier was a mere 5%. Commodity exchange between *toko* and *pasar* traders in town has almost dropped to nihil, as table 7.7 shows.

7.1.3 Aggregating the branch

Serving the needs of town and countryside is what the service centre concept is up to. Do Banjarnegara *toko* fit in such a concept? The previous paragraphs give the impression that they do, but to a limited extent. Distributing manufactured products is the main function of most Banjarnegara *toko*. In this respect they cover part of *kabupaten* Banjarnegara, but not the whole of it. Consider wholesaling by stores in Banjarnegara: shops in the *kecamatan* periphere to the town are oriented not to Banjarnegara, but to other towns, like Purbolinggo, Pekalongan and Wonosobo. Even some traders and small stores in the vicinity of Banjarnegara are supplied by big city wholesaler's agents directly. Though the *toko* cater for customers and traders in the *kecamatan* nearby as well, the conclusion seems justified that the main service role of Banjarnegara *toko* is geared to the needs and desires of the local upper and middle class: the bureaucrats and their clientelist appendix.

Supporting rural production is another concept noted,

wherein the *toko* branch might have a role to play. One aspect of this concept, the marketing of primary and secondary produce, hardly has a place in Banjarnegara *toko*. The Chinese toko-owners are hardly allowed to. An occasional exception entails the repaying of debts at a *toko*, with copra or clove. A second aspect of the rural motor concept, is selling tools and other inputs to rural enterprises. This is done by some urban *toko*, but if there is sufficient demand, the inputs might be sold in rural shops, as well as on rural *pasar* too. The service area of the town in this respect is hardly larger than *kecamatan* Banjarnegara. Densely populated Java can sustain such points of supply outside the regional centre.

The management of *toko* is comparatively capital extensive, for most use a wholesaler's trading capital. Only 7 *toko* interviewed have a value of capital goods per employee, that is higher than Rp 250,000. Still the branch cannot be called labour-intensitive. In the 22 shops questioned 104 people find employment. Extrapolating it might be assumed that some 700 jobs are created. Though a substantial figure, it is not too much for the largest urban centre in a *kabupaten* of 670,000 inhabitants. Besides shop assistants are reputed for the low payments they receive.

7.2 WARONG

Petty commodity retail stores are very uniform in appearance. Nearly all offer a standard assortment of household necessities: packed and non packed foodstuffs, batteries, spices and packed *jamu*—factory produced traditional medicine—. They cater neighbourhood demand. Only one *warong* keeper interviewed, had regular rural customers; a few hawkers operating in hamlets nearby. Of all *warong* surveyed one third stated that they were patronized by ambulant traders, who, though townsfolk, not always sell there. Like a minority of *toko*, the *warong* have a fixed clientele, mostly persons tied by debts or at least the absence of the obligation to pay cash. The latter are also the prime problem of managing a *warong*: debtors. Trading capital is swallowed by badly paying customers.

This drawback is only partly offset by trade credit from wholesaling *toko*. Profit opportunities of *warong* keepers depend to a great extent on wholesale discounts from the supplier, which they only receive when they pay cash. A *warong* keeper thus, has narrow margins to work in. Lasono, Suwandi & Lawen (1981) describe the difficulties of starting and running a small store. Their example emphasizes the necessity of tying customers by an attractive sales organization and personal appliance to keep going under harsh circumstances.

Both in forward and backward linkages *warong* are locally oriented: 87% of all suppliers origin from Banjarnegara town. Symbiosis seems to pattern the linkages between pre-dominantly corporate sector *toko* and petty commodity *warong*, as is demonstrated by trade discounts given to the *warong*. Interestingly most products

Table 7.9 A Banjarnegara warong's assortment: articles put up for sale, type of supplier and origin of articles

Kind of article:		*Article produced in:*	
Foodstuffs	25	Kabupaten Banjarnegara	14
Cigarettes	7	Purbolinggo	8
Sweets	5	Purwokerto	9
Drugs and medicine	47	Gombong	2
Spices	7	Semarang	20
Sandals	1	Magelang	2
Stationary	2	Solo	8
Other household necess.	5	Elsewhere Central Java	2
		Jakarta	20
		Bandung	2
Type of supplier:		Elsewhere West Java	3
Own produce	1	Surabaya	5
Pasar Banjarnegara	7	Kediri	3
Toko in Banjarnegara	92	Elsewhere Indonesia	2

Source: Stocktaking of Warong Krandegan, June 17th 1983.

sold in *warong* are factory-produced. In the national circulation of these commodities, *warong* are the local retail circuit. In table 7.9 all articles sold at one *warong* are enumerated according to sort, origin of supplier and origin of producer. Only 14% is produced locally: foodstuffs and one brand of cigarettes. It strikes that such a large part of drugstore wares are included. It witnesses the diversity in traditional and modern medicine in Indonesia. A host of powders is consumed for all sorts of diseases.

Many *warong* in Banjarnegara are managed by women. This is in line with an observation of Nibbering & Schrevel (1981) on rural *warong* in East Java that these shops are usually managed by widows or divorced women, while rural *toko* are financed by rich farmers to supplement their income. In the small town the preponderance of civil servants should be noted. Some of the small shops are owned by low and medium rank bureaucrats and run by their families. At least half of the *warong* interviewed served as a secondary or second source of income to their owners. Many a *lurah* (desa-headman) in town seeks an income out of shopkeeping. Bereft of their rights to sawah land and restricted to official salaries as these urban *lurah* are, they search ways of adding income. Their regular salaries entitle them to bank loans, often necessary to finance the start of a *warong*.

Warong keepers do not cooperate like *toko* owners do. Collective purchasing or mutual advancing of money or merchandise is unusual, nor do informal price levels exist. The average *warong* owner operates independently, resembling Geertz' (1963) picture of the *bazaar* economy entrepreneur.

Employment created in the branch is modest. A dense network of neighbourhood shops serves the urban population. Despite low turnovers and profits, it provides work to a significant part of female labour force; extrapolating survey data we estimate 440 persons. It is an easy entry section of the economy, capital intensity and common skills do not impede access. Initial investments can be very low indeed, but on average number Rp 100,000, which is only a fraction of what is needed to set up at the *pasar kota*.

Confronted with small town development concepts, *warong* do not play any significant role. Geared towards neighbourhood demand, sevice centre or rural motor concepts thus cannot be applied to this branch. As employment creators, these shops have some function. It is limited though, for it is only derived from the size and wealth of the town's population.

7.3 GOLD TRADE: A SPECIAL CASE

In the last paragraph it was stated that *toko* and *warong* or ambulant traders interlink in a way, that might be called symbiosis, whereby a *warong* survives on trade discounts granted by a *toko* and a *toko* enlargens its turnover through these patronizing *warong* keepers. Symbiosis is not the opposite or the absence of competition, it is interlinking to mutual benefit of parties involved. This case study on gold trade is another prove of such symbiosis. In a way gold trade is a special case, for it entails an upward as well as a downard flow, in contrast to the common *toko* and *warong*, that are wholesale and retail stores only. High inflation rates, unstable economic prospects and the psychological gap between the common man and the banking system are some of the causes of the prevalence of gold trade. Besides Javanese are traditionally fond of jewelry; it is the first luxury one will afford. Gold has a solid value, tied to world market prices. As artisanal wages are low in Indonesia, the price difference between bare and fashioned gold is low. The amount possessed is a clear indicator of a person's wealth. Farmers after the harvest, civil servants with money to spare, traders after a lucrative transaction, all invest in gold. Some Chinese *toko* keepers have the habit to save by purchasing 10—20 grammes of gold each week. Gold can be turned into capital at any moment. To buy agricultural inputs, to buy capital goods, to finance a trade transaction, to purchase a house or a plot of land, to pay for a wedding, gold is easily resold, resulting in a fast circulation of bare gold and fashioned gold. Another way of turning gold into money is to bring it to the government pawnshop.

7.3.1 Makelar, trader, toko

Three types of enterprises are involved in Banjarnegara gold trade: brokers, traders and *toko*. A transaction may involve all three levels, but occasionally a level is skipped, not to mention private transactions. Usually however, a townsman or a rural dweller that intends to buy a piece of gold or have a piece of gold sold, will go to a *makelar* (broker). A broker is someone who has sufficient understanding of jewelry and is familiar with the trade. One will find such persons in every village and at every pasar. A person desiring to buy or sell gold will ask a *makelar* to bargain on his or her behalf, because he or she is afraid to be deceived by a gold trader or at a jeweller's shop. These *makelar* will then mediate between private persons or between private persons and traders or toko. The *makelar* might have a permanent relationship with a *toko* or a trader; they will use its scales and are paid a fixed price per gramme, Rp 200—300 below market quotation, which ranged Rp 10,000—13,000 at the time of the survey. Private persons dealing directly wtih a *toko* are said to be paid at least Rp 400 below official price level, so the fright of being cheated seems justified. Malpractices positively exist. Intentional misinterpretation of carat content and adapting world market prices to a customer's ignorance are examples.

While being a broker often is a casual profession—the occasion makes the *makelar*—, traders in gold and jewelry are occupied fulltime. They differ from brokers as they have their own trading capital and can operate independently They usually have more experience. Risks of miscalculation are for their own account, but profits can be high for they have the possibility to wait and speculate on price fluctuations.

Banjarnegara gold traders are tightly organized. Without consent of fellow traders access to the trade is impossible. It is not too difficult to bankrupt an intruder by collective action, considered the extensive cooperation that exist in this branch. Some agreements: in the first place everybody keeps to his or her own clients. Most traders have consolidated contacts with rural *makelar*, that might even come from *kecamatan* as distant as Punggelan and Karangkobar. Besides the rich of town and countryside, that do not hesitate to deal with these traders directly, are divided among gold traders. Cooperation even goes as far as, in case of absence, replacing a companion and taking over calling customers, while profits still accrue to the absentee. Secondly, a maximum buying price is agreed upon, so that nobody will go bankrupt, because of rapid price fluctuations within one day. Thirdly, at a large and attractive transaction, money is pooled, so the cooperating traders can compete with the *toko*. *Pasar makelar* do the same sometimes, collectively carrying out a trader's job. Finally, traders consult each other on carat content of gold and gems, to circumvent misinterpretation. Estimation of carat content of gems especially is an intricate job; there is hardly any trader that dares to bid independently.

So there is no competition among traders. This is not to say it is a smooth trade. Now and then interests of traders and brokers clash, when the former, if asked to do so by a customer, take up brokerage for it is often quarrelsome for a trader to sustain trade on his own means. A daily turnover of Rp 200—500,000 is usual. If a trader desires to await price fluctuations, he sometimes has to keep his merchandise in stock for several days. Trading capital will then be drained; one reason to take up broking.

A special version of gold trade is buying pawned jewelry. Persons in need of money often bring their valuables to the government pawnshop. When they are unable to repay debts within proper time, the pawned goods will fall to the pawnshop. The only way out is to sell the receipt to a trader, who of course offers a very low price and obtains the goods at a bargain this way.

In contrast to the majority of traders in town, it is quite usual for traders in gold and jewelry to apply for a loan at a government banking institution. Landed property or the regular wage of a member of the family might serve as a guarantee. It gives an impression of capital needs and of profitability and stability of this trade. Gold traders indeed are enterprising men and women. Traders as well as jewellers often started as *makelar*, saving and investing through the years. All *makelar* and traders interviewed delineated investment plans within the branch. *Makelar* want to become traders and traders aspire to set up a jewelry shop.

Jewelry shops are the links to the outside world in gold trade. At the moment of survey there were 5 jewelry shops in Banjarnegara town, all except one Chinese owned. Cooperation between the shops is faulty compared to the traders; there is only mutual information exchange by telephone on price levels every morning. Distrust among the *toko* is flagrant, especially between the three long established shops and the two newcomers in the trade. The problem is that these new shops are doing very well, while two of the three established jewellers have slumbered in. Besides buying and selling from and to Banjarnegara traders, that might pace up and down in front of the *toko*, and—through brokers—from and to common people, jewellers sell old jewelry top Magelang and buy bare and newly fashioned gold for use in *kabupaten* Banjarnegara. The jewellers interviewed stated that especially after the harvest of rice or clove demand for gold and jewelry in *kabupaten* Banjarnegara staggers. As supply from the *kabupaten* at this time is accordingly low, and as it is very expensive to keep a large amount of gold in stock, in such periods bare and fashioned gold is imported from Magelang, a centre of gold smithing. Only one Banjarnegara *toko* employed a few artisans, that shape the precious metal and melt old ornaments to 24-carat bare gold for sale to Magelang or to be used for shaping again.

Supply to the *toko* is not as peaked as demand is. Farmers may turn gold into money to pay for seeds or other inputs at the start of the planting season, but others save gold to pay for a house, to invest in a non-agricultural enterprise or to finance the pilgrimage to Mecca. Urban supply is still more evenly spread for it is less tied to farming than it is to business cycles.

Next to the urban jewelry shops, jewellers have established in the *kecamatan* centres Karangkobar, Kalibening, Wonodadi, Purwonegoro and Klampok. Those shops belong to the occasional clientele of the Banjarnegara *toko*. They mainly pertain to a local intra-*kecamatan* circulation, but at times of high demand or supply, they are backed up by town establishments. Rarely the rural jeweller will contact Magelang enterprises.

So it can be concluded that in a network of *makelar*, traders, rural jewellers, the Banjarnegara *toko* represent the national circuit, though local and regional circulation are customary too. As illustrated by incidents, soon as traders take up broking, position of everyone in business is strictly defined: symbiosis by consent.

One thing to be noted comments on the analytic model as outlined in chapter 4. In this model we operationalized petty commodity sector versus corporate sector by among others turnover. Consequently, because of high gold prices, all jewelry shops and traders in our survey belong to the corporate sector. Brokers, as they have no turnover are classified as petty commodity sector. Often corporate scale correlates with a high score of capitalist characteristics. In gold trade however, but for one exception, stores, traders and brokers have 2 or 3 capitalist characteristics at most. Gold trade is, notwithstanding the big volumes of capital involved, structured on pre-capitalist lines.

Chapter 8

MARKETING OF CASHCROPS: FRUIT, VEGETABLES AND RICE

8.1 CASH CROPS IN BANJARNEGARA

This chapter treats the marketing of some of the cashcrops in *kabupaten* Banjarnegara, notably fruit, vegetables and rice. Marketing of cashcrops is a foremost element in the rural motor concept, reviewed in paragraph 2.1.3. A question central to this concept and central to this chapter is the extent to which town traders are able to organize the marketing of hinterland produce. In paragraph 2.3 attention has been directed at the phenomenon of by-pass. Studies by Grant Anderson (1980) and Mai (1984) indicate that cashcrops, increasingly, instead of moving upward to national commodity markets through a chain of local and regional circuits, are bought directly at the farmgate or at the village *pasar* by merchants from out of the region. Hence the position of the regional centre is undercut. This chapter has the marketing of fruit, vegetables and rice as its subject and contemplates whether by-pass undercuts Banjarnegara's position too. An impression of cashcrop production and marketing channels in the past is included to assess what factors probably determine trade flows and whether or not by-pass is a new trend in *kabupaten* Banjarnegara.

In paragraph 2.3 too a comment was made on how national commodity circulation combines with large scale of production. It seems correlated with large scale commerce as well; table 8.1

Table 8.1 Structuring and form characteristics of fruit, vegetable and rice traders

Type of enterprise	*Sector*	*Number of capitalist characteristics*
Fruit exporter	Corporate	4—5
Village trader in fruit	Petty-Corporate	3—4
Pasar fruit vendor	Petty	2
Pasar vegetable wholesaler	Petty	2
Pasar rice wholesaler	Petty	1—3
Rice mill	Corporate	5

classifies enterprises trading primary commodities. Exporters seem structured on capitalist lines. In the mix of capitalist and precapitalist characteristics typical for village traders and pasar retail traders, precapitalist elements prevale.

Fruit, vegetables, partly exported from the region, and rice, circulating regionally, are respectively outlined in paragraph 8.1, 8.2 and 8.3. These are not the only commercialized products from the hinterland of Banjarnegara. Chapter 9 treats livestock fattening in *kabupaten* Banjarnegara. Some minor cashcrops, lumber and coconuts, are dealt with in paragraph 10.3 and 11.3. Other products cultivated for monetary income, however are not reviewed within this thesis. Cassave is the major omission. Part of it is used for autoconsumption and part of it is retailed locally, but cassave from *kabupaten* Banjarnegara is partly exported to Cilacap's tapioca mills as well. As the tapioca is sent abroad periodically, this links Banjarnegara cassave prices to world market prices (Unnevehr 1984).

8.1.1 Growing fruit

Growing fruit trees in ubiquitous in Banjarnegara town.

Whoever has some room left at his compound, will grow banana, papaya, mango, clove or some other tree crop. The harvest is for home consumption, but might occasionally be sold as well. The important fruit surplusses however, come from the countryside, notably the agroforestry areas at medium high altitudes: *kecamatan* Sigaluh, Madukara and Punggelan. A multitude of tree crops is cultivated there, in a seemingly disordered, but actually well-patterned interculture of annuals, biannuals, shrubcrops and perennial tree crops. Fruit crops are seldom grown in monoculture.

At the turn of the century, so the Mindere Welvaartsverslagen (MWV 1907) mention, the major fruit crops in the *kabupaten* were *durian*, mangosteen and *duku*, cultivated at compound gardens. Agroforestry was absent then in the surroundings of Banjarnegara. The main farming systems were wet rice cultivation and dry land cultivation (*tegal*) of cassave and corn, and tobacco in the long since commercialized Northern Serayu Mountains. On the 'empty' slopes north and east of Banjarnegara, coffee cultivation had been forced by the colonial government in the second part of the nineteenth century. At the turn of the century, however, a disease virtually ended the culture. It has been hypothesized by Palte et al (1981), that the way these plantations were abandoned was decisive for further land use. Where the land was completely cleared after the leave disease had killed the coffee shrubs, there dry land *tegalan* farming was the prime alternative. But on plots where coffee trees interspersed with original plant coverage, agroforestry became feasible.

In the twenties a considerable mangosteen production seems to have developed: yields were so abundant, that a third of it was left rotting, for it could not be sold (SDS Morpey 1917). *Petai*-beans were exported from Banjarnegara and Bawang subdistricts in the twenties. An informant told us that at that time the crops were gathered at a big merchant's warehouse, who sent them to West Java by rail.

Nowadays fruits have stabilized as a cash crop in Banjarnegara *kabupaten*, especially on the slopes east of town, alongside the road to Wonosobo. Many peasants use their cultivation as an extra income. Production per crop is dispersed over a wide area, contrary to vegetable growing, neither are surplusses large and concentrated. Probably this explains why so many local and regional traders are involved: small surplusses do not attract large scale merchants. Regional export is mainly handled by Banjarnegara town traders, operating at the *pasar kota*.

Bananas, *cengkol, petai* and *duku* are the important cash crops. Cloves, a spice more than a fruit, are the coming crop: for this reason a seperate paragraph pays attention to it. Some specialization has taken place in fruit trade, in sofar that most merchants trade clove or trade bananas or trade a combination of *cengkol, petai*-beans, *salak* or *duku*. At the time of survey banana trade was very low in Banjarnegara, for the peak season is the second half of the year. Besides, the major flow of bananas is handled at *pasar* Wonodadi. Therefore banana trade is not treated in this paragraph.

8.1.2 Fruit export from Banjarnegara: hierarchy

Fruit, as it hangs on the tree, often does not belong to the peasant anymore. He might have sold his fruit crop to a village trader (*bakul*), just before it is mature. Quite regularly, however, peasants sell their crop up to three months before maturing, forced by cash-needs. The harvesting is arranged by the *bakul*, employing part-time or piecework pickers. Depending on the time interval between selling and picking, the price the farmer is offered is 50 to 70% of the market value expected. The longer the time-lag, the harder it is to estimate what a tree will yield. An instance: when a tree is estimated to yield a Rp 15,000 crop in due time, a peasant might recieve Rp 10,000, when he sells the crop six weeks before it can be picked. Part of the sum he might receive at the moment of transaction (Rp 3,000), part of it afterwards (Rp 7,000). When the yield does not come up to expectations, the peasant is nonetheless sure of being paid the full price. This is not too big an advantage, as estimates are often very conservative and a high yield means a high profit for the *bakul*. The interest on cash receipts in such a *tebasan*-deal, resembles interest in *ijon* deals, where a peasant has to repay debts to a trader with crops harvested himself and sold at a low per kilogram price. *Tebasan* seems to be widespread in the agroforestry areas between Banjarnegara and Wonosobo-town, though peasants also bring a substantial part of their fruit crop to village markets (Nijkamp &Peeters 1984, Hunink & Stoffers 1984). *Tebasan* is customary too in the impoverished southern part of *kecamatan* Banjarnegara, where *petai* and *cengkol* is grown. Another arrangement, called '*rampasan*', is found there too: a peasant sells five to ten harvests beforehand. It will be highlighted in the next paragraph. Such practice is not reported in the agroforestry area at the upstream of the Serayu River.

Once the fruit is picked, the *bakul* will transport it to the town market, where they are awaited by corporate scale traders (*tengkulak*). Small *bakul* use bicycles to go to Banjarnegara or walk, others use public transport or rent a minibus. There are 8 Banjarnegara *tengkulak*, wholesaling and exporting *petai*-beans, *cengkol, duku* or *salak*. On March 17th, at the peak of the *petai*-season, we asked all fruit traders at *pasar* Banjarnegara, where their supplier came from. The heavy weight of the *petai*-producing *kecamatan* Banjarnegara is significant from table 8.2, though intra-*pasar* trade distorts the picture. The absence of suppliers from the agroforestry *kecamatan* at *pasar* Banjarnegara is no sign of regional traders being by-passed. Market officials at *pasar* in these *kecamatan* acknowledged *pasar* Banjarnegara's central function for fruit trade. The *salak, petai, duku* and *cengkol* thus handled is destined for big cities in West Java.

A *tengkulak* might buy from his *bakul 'timbangan'* or *'borongan'*. In the first system goods are being weighed and a price is settled per kilogram, in the latter the price is settled per basket or per load. Small amounts are traded *borongan*. Relations with *bakul* have a fixed character, prompted by consensus among *tengkulak* in town, that prohibits a *bakul* to change *tengkulak* suddenly. However to the regret of the Banjarnegara fruit merchants, their position has

Table 8.2 Origin of suppliers to fruit traders at pasar Banjarnegara per kecamatan, March 17th 1983.

Banjarnegara	44	Banjarmangu	5	Sigaluh	1
Rakit	3	Wonodadi	8		
Purwonegoro	3	Bawang	4	**Kabupaten**	
Punggelan	2	Madukara	2	Wonosobo	3
		Total	75		

Source: Pasar Surveys

been undercut recently. Some money-rich West Javanese merchants have gotten a foothold at the *pasar*. They sent free-lance representatives to Banjarnegara, who are called *'makelar'* (broker) by the Banjarnegara *tengkulak*. *Bakul* have an alternative now and prices are raised. For some however, it is hard to switch to these *makelar*, as they were advanced money by the *tengkulak*, to pay farmers long before harvesting is due. Those *bakul* with some working capital of their own to sustain on, on the other hand, have a free choice and help to erode Banjarnegara traders' oligopoly.

Fruits are sent by truck. Two Banjarnegara fruit traders own a truck, but most rent one. As for many things in present day Banjarnegara's economy, there are brokers for truck rental. Groups of 3—5 transport brokers operate at the fruit section of the *pasar*. One of them will go to the provincial highway and try to halt a truck, that returns empty from Central Java and is heading for West Java. The other brokers try to assemble enough traders for one direction, so a truck can be loaded. It might take a couple of traders to fill the 3—4 tons a truck can convey. The driver will pay the transport brokers 10% of what he gets from the traders that board his lorry. A fare to Jakarta might cost Rp 120.000. Truckers are quite keen on such extra transport, they know about transport needs along their routes. The fast growth in truck transport versus fruit export stands out: some years ago a driver was taxed only 5% by the petty brokers.

When fruit supply is at high tide, times are best for the transport brokers. The pasar gets flooded with petty scale fruit traders, both from West Java and Banjarnegara. These try their luck in exporting fruit, infringing marginally on the big merchants oligopoly. Such small scale traders sell a couple of quintals, and 5—10 of them have to share a truck, arranged for by the transport brokers.

Before the fruit harvesting season has started, most Banjarnegara *tengkulak* have already contacted merchants in West Javanese cities. The big city merchants are consulted on quantities needed and these are agreed upon roughly. When the bulk of fruit from the region starts to come off, the *tengkulak* gathers the fruits and sends them to—predominantly—Jakarta. A *tengkulak*, his assistant or a driver employed, will receive cash or cheques on the next trip. The price level at the big city market by then, determines the prices in transactions between Banjarnegara *tengkulak* and Jakarta fruit wholesalers. Risks are beared by the *tengkulak*. One fruit trader interviewed, remembered large losses one time, when his *petai* shipment to Jakarta coincided wioth an excellent harvest in South Sumatra. Jakarta prices dropped below what he had agreed to pay his *bakul* and he lost some million *rupiah*. A different method is practized by some other Banjarnegara merchants, who settle their price themselves, based on West Javanese price level and adapted to Banjarnegara market prices.

Occasionally a Banjarnegara *tengkulak* avoids all risks by bargaining with the *bakul*, that the price they receive accord to what the *tengkulak* is paid for on the West Javanese market. In such a deal the *bakul* pays for price fluctuations. Such bargains occur mainly between *tengkulak* and *bakul*, that have no consolidated relation.

In the peak season of fruit harvesting, 5 to 7 trucks daily depart from *pasar* Banjarnegara, conveying a total of 20—25 ton. January to April are the busy months, though sometimes the season extends to July. Before the season starts cash needs are most urgent among town *tengkulak*, because they have to pay the *bakul* a sum in advance, for these often lack trading capital. When a *tengkulak* has agreed with a West Javanese merchant, he might be forwarded some cash by him. Those that have no such contacts might try the bank, some *bakul* do too—a time-consuming prodecure and therefore often abandoned—or invest some private money. Trading capital ranges accordingly among traders surveyed: Rp 50,000 to 10,000,000.

The big part of Banjarnegara's fruit crop enters national circulation. The merchandise moves upward in a hierarchy of local, regional and national circuit, conform model A in diagram 2.1. These circuits are chained to one another, not only by supply, but by payments in advance as well. By-pass is unusual. Banjarnegara traders however are now rivaled in what has long been their stronghold: exporting fruit from the *kabupaten*. In this part of the national circuit they are met by both large scale and petty scale traders from West Java.

Part of the Banjarnegara fruit crop does not leave regional circulation. On the Banjarnegara *pasar* some 30 fruit traders operate, selling to local customers. This might be peasant-wives selling small surplusses or retailers that are supplied by Banjarnegara wholesalers. Besides, numerous general store type of market traders sell some fruit. Other retailers are encountered at Banjarnegera town's three small markets: *pasar* Parakancanggah, *pasar* Wage and *pasar* Garam. They usually purchase at the main market, but purchase from *desa* people too. Volumes in this kind of trade are small. Finally, some fruit import might be noted: this is put up for sale at *pasar* Banjarnegara by people from Solo and Yogyakarta.

8.1.3 Clove

Clove is the coming crop in the Serayu Uplands. In *kabupaten* Banjarnegara clove trees acreage increased at least 10% annually in 1977—1980, as diagram 8.1 depicts, and in 1983 its expansion was going on unabatedly. Clove trees are grown at compound gardens and in mixed agroforestry. Pockets of monoculture clove cultivation are found too—in contrast to most other fruit

Diagram 8.1 Area under clove cultivation in kabupaten Banjarnegara, 1977—1980

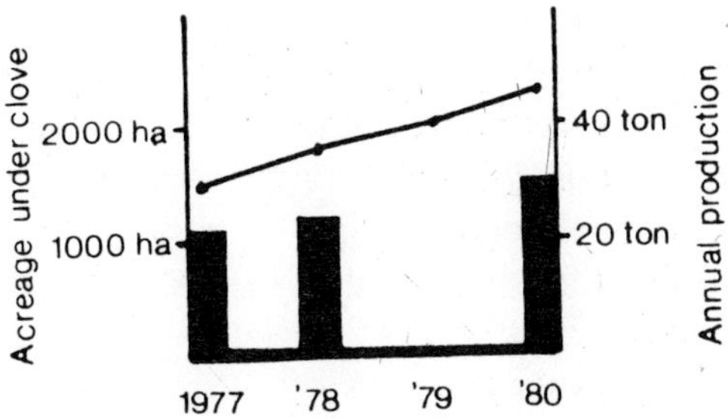

Source: Banjarnegara Dalam Angka 1980

crops. A few years ago clove prices were very high, but since then they have slided back. It is however still very rewarding to grow the spice; demand at Indonesia's clove cigarette (*kretek*) industry is not satisfied yet by national production. A fully blossoming 15-year old tree might yield 6 kilogram dried clove, which equals a sum of Rp 50,000. The only adverse factor is the changeability of clove yields. In some years the clove does not blossom at all.

While clove cultivation is rewarding to the peasants, it is even more rewarding to the traders. In Banjarnegara five big traders and several small ones export clove. At the time of survey, when clove harvests were extremely high, they made gigantic profits. The town-based traders collect wet or dried cloves from village traders or from farmers that travel to Banjarnegara to sell their crop. Some town-based traders will dry the clove bought wet, odouring the streets of Banjarnegara with clove's spicy scent. Others will keep to collecting only and send a daily freight of wet and dry clove to agents of *kretek* factories in Banyumas or Purwokerto. Though Banjarnegara's importance as a clove centre should be noticed and ***bakul*** as far as Wonosobo go to Banjarnegara town to sell clove, the town's traders do not control clove flows. Well-to-do rural traders might go and deal with the factory agents themselves, by-passing the regional circuit. Countryside *pasar*, like *pasar* Wonodadi, are important for clove export as well.

To illustrate the profitability of clove trade, Banjarnegara's biggest *tengkulak* is portrayed. Bu Hermana owns a stall near the *pasar*. In the clove season she trades clove and coffee. On a standard day she might buy 1.5—2.5 ton wet and 1—2 ton dried clove Per kilo she will pay respectively Rp 100 and Rp 150 below what the factory agents will offer her and this is her prifit. On transport and on porters' wages she spends Rp 25.000 a day. The final destinations of her cloves are the *kretek* factories of Gudang Garam and Djarum. She traders six days a week. On Sunday the factory agent is closed and Bu Hermana's storage facilities are too small to keep and stock overnight. On busy days her net gains are up to Rp 520.000, which is a peak income indeed. Other Banjarnegara *tengkulak* handle less than one ton daily, but often take up drying, unlike Bu Hermana.

Wealth also accrues to *bakul*, that visit peasants and see if they can be persuaded to sell their crop. Some of such *bakul* are town-dwellers. The clove *bakul* interviewed estimated that half of all cultivators arrange the picking of cloves themselves, before selling per kilo to a *bakul*. The other half of the peasants opt for a *tebasan* arrangement, whereby the *bakul* pays per tree and organizes the harvesting. This *tebasan* deal is similar to the one frequent in fruit marketing. Some time before ripening, would-be buyers roam the countryside, estimating a peasant's clove crop and making bids. Two of the traders surveyed even employed a professional for such intricate job, who is paid Rp 10—15,000 daily, thus reducing the risk of miscalculations.

Next to selling per kilo or per tree, a third system was encountered, called '*rampasan*'. In a *rampasan* contract, a peasant sells claims to 5—10 successive crops of a tree. The picking and providing of dung in these years is the trader's duty. Prices are very low to a farmer then, but the risk of crop failure in this period is to the claimant. Cash needs compel a peasant to such arrangements; he is paid 5—10 crops beforehand, but will be devoid of income on the

Diagram 8.2 Calculations of returns to peasant and traders in three methods of selling clove

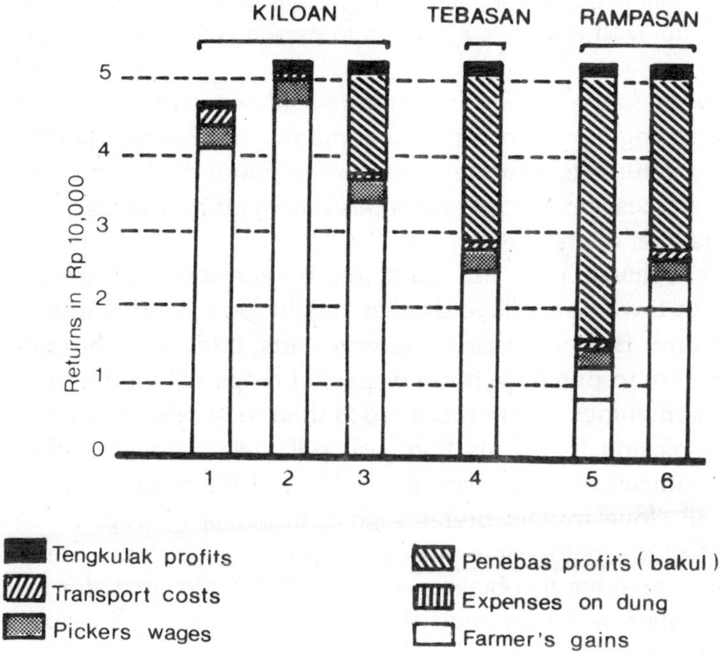

Notes:

* In this example we assume a tree's crop is sold, yielding 20 kg wet clove and 14 kg wet tanke. Tanke is the twig, which is picked too. It has a slight clove flavour and is used for cheap kretek and clove oil. When dried, a volume of 6 kg clove and 4 kg tanke is left. A tree crop as large as this example takes three menday to pick.

1 = KILOAN. Peasant selling wet clove and tanke to a town based tengkulak.

2 = KILOAN: Peasant selling dried clove and tanke to a town based tengkulak.

3 = KILOAN: Peasant selling dried clove and tanke to village bakul.

4 = TEBASAN: Peasant selling a tree's crop to a bakul, who dries it before selling to tengkulak.

5 = RAMPASAN: Peasant selling a tree's crop to a bakul five years in

advance, who dries at before selling to a tengkulak.

6 = RAMPASAN: Like 5, but with a correction for interest losses. An interest of five percent monthly was taken, which is above bank rate, but not the least excessive in person to person credit transactions.

tree for a very long period. In diagram 8.2 we compare three mothods of selling clove, in order to compare the shares a farmer gets. The low returns to a farmer under a *rampasan* deal stand out, though if one takes into account the interest benefits to a farmer, this picture somewhat alters.

Clove cultivation is not confined to agroforestry farming systems. Both town and village dwellers might grow a clove tree in their compound. Before the clove harvest starts, traders go through the town and try to purchase these dispersed crops still on the tree. These men sometimes obtain more crops than they reasonably can arrange the picking for. Thus they will sell their claims to other traders. An indication of the high profitability of the trade.

Not all clove traders prefer such a dispersal of trees to be harvested. Clove's high value makes it appealing to theft. Some traders therefore strive to obtain crops in a nucleated area, for instance a plantation with hundreds of trees, where guarding the clove trees can be done efficiently.

8.2 VEGETABLES

8.2.1 Marketing of vegetables: a non Banjarnegara trade flow

The Banjarnegara mountain districts have a long history of commercialization. Tobacco cash-cropping is reported from the Batur drylands as early as 1800 (Titus 1982). At the turn of the century, the cultivation had spread to the Karangkobar district too and covered 65% of the area tilled in the Batur district (SDS Oltmans 1905). Tobacco trade was controlled by Chinese merchants, who exported most of the upland tobacco to Pekalongan and Batang. From these ports the tobacco was shipped to Bantam (West Java), where the smoked Batur species was in high demand (SDS Hillen 1898, Oltmans 1905). This northcoast route was the least expensive and therefore Banjarnegara town networks had no share in the trade. Carlier (1980) is surprised to find commercialized cultivation preceeding the opening up of this isolated enclave. She concludes that road accessibility is not such a thriving force in commercialization as is often supposed. Tobacco is a special case of low transport requirements however, for, as it is smoked, it is not a perishable product. Though Banjarnegara town trade networks had no share in the marketing of the Batur tobacco, it should be mentioned that Banjarnegara served as a transit town for tobacco from the Wonosobo regency prior to 1917. In 1917 the Serayu Valley narrow gauge railway was extended to Wonosobo and Wonosobo traders sent their merchandise to the Preanger residency directly.

Since 1910 tobacco cultivation was on its way back. Acreage did not expand and yields fell (Carlier 1980). In the thirties export from the Serayu upland districts declined; quality had deteriorated and competition from cigarette industry loomed up, for which production the Wonosobo and Batur tobacco were unfit (SDS). It seems that ever since, and very gradually, vegetable cultivation has been taking over. In the first quarter of this century some vegetable cultivation seems to have developed already (MWV), geared to Europeans' demand and sent by rail to Preanger (West Java). Most vegetables however were intercropped with tobacco to attract insects and keep them away from tobacco plants (SDS).

It was not until the sixties that vegetable production could take a high flight, probably due to improved road transport. At presence, the major vegetables growing *kecamatan* are Wanayasa and Batur (see map 8.1). Cabbage, potatoes and onions are grown in monoculture. Equiped with lorries, big city merchants penetrate the *desa*, where production is concentrated. Entire harvests are bought up at once, up to three months before maturing. Under such *tebasan* deal the merchant will bring his own labourers to cut the crop (Palte et al 1981). Destinations are Pekalongan and other northcoast cities and Serayu Valley cities and towns. Occasionally the perishable vegetables are even sent as far as West Java.

Thus local and regional circuit are by-passed, in contrast to

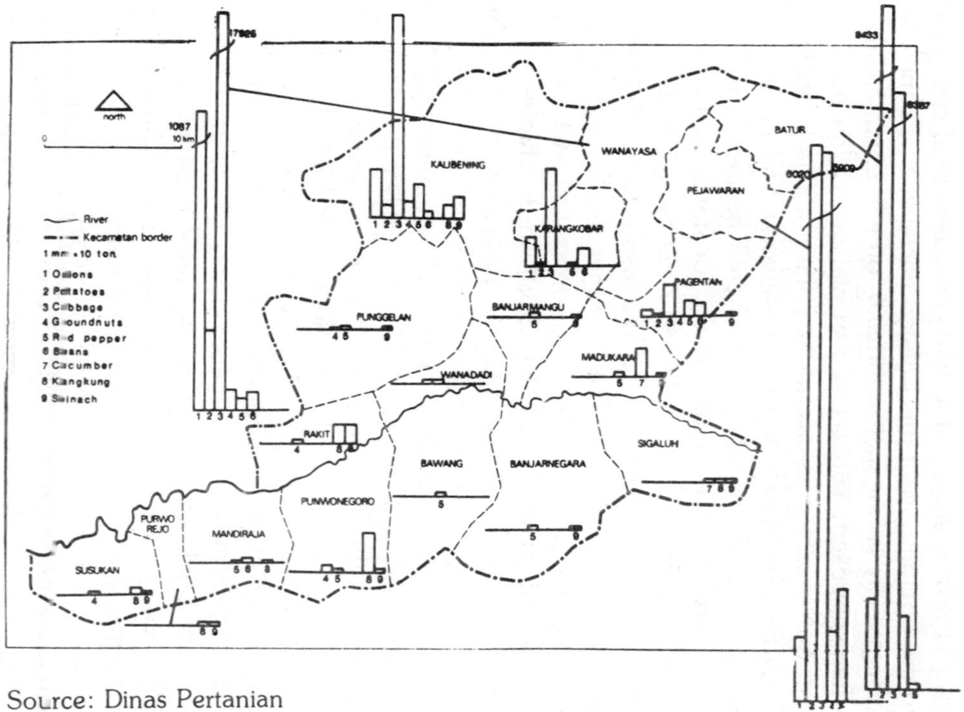

Source: Dinas Pertanian

Map 8.1 Vegetable production in kabupaten Banjarnegara 1982

fruit trade. This difference might be linked to the concentrated character of vegetable cultivation vis-a-vis dispersed fruit cultivation. This by-pass is not the only model relevant for vegetable trade in the upland districts. Part of the crop is bought and harvested by rural traders, rich farmers oftenly, that will sell to extraregional markets. The upland markets have a bulking function too; some peasants take their crop to the market or prefer to sell to petty village traders, who will bring the vegetables to *pasar* Karangkobar or some other upland *pasar*, where big city merchants await them (Wolters 1984).

Ostensibly Banjarnegara town traders have no share in the bulking of cashcrops from the Northern Serayu Mountains. They never had one either. Vegetable trade in town is confined to the regional retail circuit. Collecting traders from Karangkobar and Batur descend to Banjarnegara and sell the vegetables to local retailers or to intermediaries, who bring the wares to other markets in the vicinity. Only occasionally, when supply and price differences allow, big city merchants trade with these upland traders at *pasar* Banjarnegara, instead of going to one of the *pasar* in the Northern Serayu Mountains.

8.2.2 Vegetables retail: the Pasar Sayur

The vegetable section of *pasar* Banjarnegara is situated next door to the general trade section. At the time of the survey it was unroofed and unstructured, but a market hall was under construction, that should be ready by now. Activity changes from day to day on the Banjarnegara vegetable market. At the main market day in Kalibening, business is low at *pasar* Banjarnegara; for the bulk of the vegetables from *pasar* Kalibening is siphoned off to northcoast cities. At the main market day in Karangkobar however, vegetable trade in Banjarnegara bustles. Small scale vegetable merchants, renting trucks with 5—10 fellows, transport the merchandise to Banjarnegara.

Almost all vegetables are weighed before trade starts. It is a lively scene to see the freights of vegetables enter the market.

Porters, always at hand, unload the lorries, carrying bags up to 180 kg on their bent backs, waddling like mother ducks. With amazing speed the weigh-man (a private enterprise) weighs the stock, he notes the results and the haggling begins. The vegetable merchant is surrounded by some 10 wholesaler traders, mostly women, who try to settle a fair price. They offer a price per kilo for the whole bag, when the weight is not know yet. Only afterwards the neutral weigh-man calculates the amount each vegetable merchant brought to him and accordingly these are paid by the wholesalers. The costs of weighing are only Rp 50 per bag, and when a trader has had a bad day selling, he only has to pay Rp 25 or in case of losses even nothing at all. Probably to show off goodwill, which helps the weigh-man to keep his monopoly.

According to the weigh-man the amounts of vegetables, that pass the scales on a normal day are: cabbage 10 ton; potatoes 4 ton; *sawi/pecai* 2 ton; onions and garlic 2 ton; red pepper 0.3 ton. These volumes might double on busy days, while 70% is measured on low days. If these figures are correct and they most likely are, it seems that some 15% of the upland vegetables produce is destined to be retailed through *pasar* Banjarnegara. Diagram 8.3 makes such comparison.

Apart from the merchants, some peasants also come and bring their crop to the Banjarnegara vegetables market. Hoping to get a better price by selling to wholesalers directly or by retailing the vegetables themselves. The amounts are small. The weigh-man is their major customer and he has a daily turnover of 700—2000 kg, most of it potatoes and cabbage. Interestingly he does not use his scales in buying. He said he trusted his capability to estimate the weight of the bags with vegetables and tried to make some extra profit this way.

The survey included three *pasar* counts. Table 8.2 presents some results as to origins of traders at *pasar* Banjarnegara. It is striking how a substantial number of non town-dwellers make a living at the vegetable market (50—70%). In the first *pasar* survey a question was posed into the origin of commodities traded. The pre-

Diagram 8.3 Major vegetable crops in Kabupaten Banjarnegara (1982): Production figures and volume retailed at Pasar Banjarnegara

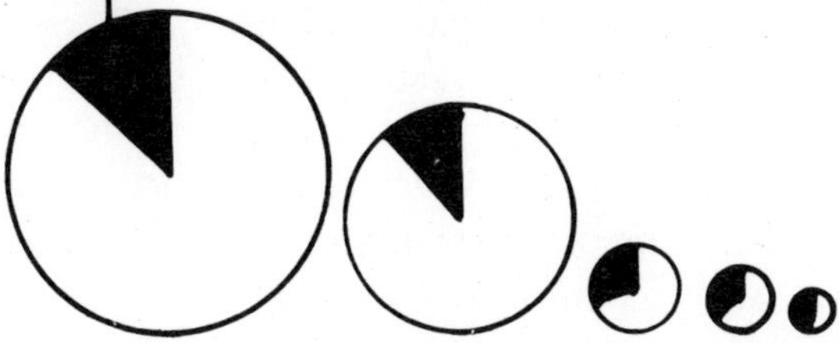

Source: Dinas Pertanian, Tukang Timbangan

Table 8.2 Number of traders to origin on the vegetable section of pasar Banjarnegara

	Banjarnegara Town	Kabupaten Banjarnegara	Other Kabupaten
March 17th, 1983	20	26	4
May 9th, 1983	33	23	7
June 14th, 1983	27	36	14

Source: Pasar Survey

valence of intra *pasar* trade stands out. It occured that traders (39 out of 50) purchased the vegetables at the Banjarnegara market, even though many of them are non-urbanites. Those that did not purchase at the *pasar* were peasant traders, selling their own crops and a few outsiders, traders who bought at markets in Wonosobo and Purwokerto or from producers in these *kabupaten*.

Overall only 16 out of 50 traders sold some products originating from other *kabupaten*: Purwokerto (6), Wonosobo (6),

Tegal (2) and Magelang (2). It underscores that vegetable trade at *pasar* Banjarnegara confines to a regional retail circuit. Extraregional trade is from *kabupaten* nearby and is not very substantial.

An example of profit margins and turnovers on the *pasar sayur*, table 8.2 gives the daily result of one of the wholesalers surveyed. This woman might be taken as representative. Spices and lowland vegetables (not treated specifically in this paragraph) are sold too. It looks like some products are put up for sale, not so much for their profits, but to complete assortment, in order to attract customers. Profit margins amount to 15% of total turnover, which is in line with usual trade profits of 10—20%.

In a way the term 'wholesaler' used for traders at the *pasar sayur* is deceptive, for most sell to consumers. Still, all wholesalers at the vegetable section of *pasar* Banjarnegara have other traders among their clientele: intermediate *desa* traders, hawkers and petty retailers at *pasar* Banjarnegara and on other *pasar* inside as well as outside town. These receive trade discounts of approximately 10%. Amazingly and signalling the labour absorptive character of the

Table 8.3 Average daily turnover and prifits (in Rp) as stated by a representative vegetables retailer on Banjarnegara vegetable market, May 1983

	Price bought for/kg	*Total amount*	*Price sold for/kg*	*Turnover*	*Profit*
100 kg cabbage	80	8000	100	10000	2000
50 kg beans	80	4000	90	4500	500
35 kg walu	50	1750	60	2100	350
1 pack muncang	4000	4000	4500	4500	500
8 kg red pepper	187	1525	225	1850	325
7 kg potatoes	150	1050	160	1120	70
6 kg kencur	150	900	200	1200	300
3 kg ginger	450	1350	500	1500	150
3.5 kg garlic	1300	3250	1500	3750	500
1 kg onions	450	450	500	500	50
		26275		31020	4745

branch, the last chain has not been reached yet, for intermediates sell to *warong* keepers and very small scale hawkers.

Cooperation is often posed as a way-out for problems met by small scale enterprises. Among traders at the *pasar sayur*, there is cooperation both to solve practical problems and to improve bargaining position. Wholesalers join together to buy bags of vegetables from the merchants, especially the ones of which only small lots are sold, like red pepper and spices. A few years ago balances used to be shared, but as everyone has bought his own balance now (on credit usually), this type of cooperation is out of custom. Besides, there is consensus on minimum retail prices, to keep losses at a margin.

Like fruit traders at these markets, the vegetable traders at Banjarnegara town's three small *pasar* go to *pasar* Banjarnegara to replenish their stock every two or three days. These traders are of a scale different from the wholesalers at the vegetable maarket, a fact they are aware of. While the wholesalers at *pasar* Banjarnegara might near corporate sector scale, the traders at *pasar* Parakancanggah. *Pasar* Wage and *pasar* Garam are definitely petty commodity enterprises. Table 8.4 provides such a comparison. Assortment of the traders at these *pasar* is less specialized and volumes of each product are small. Often salted fish and soybean cakes, even some pre-packaged food, are sold next to vegetables. Only few traders possess balances, and these are used by others as well. Small scale hawkers are one type of clients, discussed below. These hawkers get 5—10% trade discount when they pay cash or receive credit without interest. Another type of clients are final consumers. As traders at the small *pasar* have to ask a slightly higher price, consumers are apt to walk a little longer to the *pasar* Banjarnegara. The traders cope with this danger by not demanding the customers to pay cash. Clients are more fixed than they are at the vegetable market. Most come from *desa* surrounding town, which is not surprising since these small *pasar* are located near rural feeder roads (see map 5.1).

Table 8.4 Monthly turnover and profits (in Rp) of traders sampled at the vegetable market and small pasar in Banjarnegara town.

	Mean turnover	Mean profits
Pasar Sayur	5,220,500	88,000
Other Pasar	1,810,000	17,000

Hawkers of vegetables and other perishable foodstuffs constitute the final link between producer and consumer. In the morning and the early afternoon they roam the streets and alleys of Banjarnegara town, selling their wares door to door. Usually they have a fixed route and some fixed customers. Stock is diverse and covers, next to vegetables, all essential fresh household necessities; rice, corn and cassave; fruits; *tahu* and *tempe* (soybean cakes); sometimes meat or salted fish. When one can afford it, the ease of being served at your roomgate, instead of going to the *pasar* stands to the fractionally higher prices. As the hawkers try to be the first ones in the morning at the *pasar*, they have the best pick. Their profits partly stem from the trade discount, they get at buying. Most of these vegetable hawkers are women originating from rural *desa* surrounding the town or living in a quarter at the town's outskirts. Like table 8.2 already illustrated, it is plain that many rural dwellers make a living by trading in town. Sometimes, part of the merchandise is own produce, but the lot of their suppliers are met in Banjarnegara; wholesalers at the vegetable or general store section of *pasar* Banjarnegara; fish sellers in stalls bordering the main market; *tahu* and *tempe* vendors and producers from Karangtengah or Wangon.

Only one of the traders interviewed travels to other regions to get his wares. He (the single man among vegetables hawkers interviewed) goes three times weekly to Magelang using public transport to buy vegetables at the vegetable market there. His clientele also differs from the usual clientele: shops, restaurants and foodstalls. Though he is a national circuit trader, he hawks the merchandise himself. However monthly turnover distinguishes him from other hawkers: Rp 7,450,000, against an average of Rp 1,109,000. Six men from Banjarnegara are involved in this kind of interurban trade, according to the informant, exploiting the lower prices and extensive assortment at the Magelang *pasar*.

8.2.3 Comparing fruit trade and vegetables trade

This last subparagraph on vegetables retail trade attests that vegetables may change many hands before they reach their final consumer. Descending in the retail trade chain a trader's assortment becomes less specialized; ultimately a woman hawking vegetables door to door will offer all foodstuff, needed daily. The fine-mazed interlinking between traders in this branch seems a reflection of high labour absorption. By-passing of regional or local circuit is unusual in vegetable retail (in contrast to vegetables marketing). An exception to the rule is the man hawking Magelang vegetables to *toko*, restaurants and foodstalls. In general symbiosis, maintained by trade discounts, patterns vegetables retailing, whether among petty enterprises or between petty and corporate enterprises.

Banjarnegara is the central node of a regional vegetable retail circuit, that encompasses the southeastern part of the *kabupaten*. It is not the centre in the bulking of vegetables. Local and regional circuit in this line of trade are made up of people from the northern *kecamatan*. These circuits however are often by-passed by merchants from outside the *kabupatèn*. Significantly such export has never been organized by merchants from Banjarnegara town.

Banjarnegara on the other hand serves as a staple town for fruit export. Village traders gather the crop, that they have often bought long before and bring them to the town, where Banjarnegara *tengkulak* await them. Recently the position of the Banjarnegara traders is eroded somewhat by exporters from other regions penetrating *pasar* Banjarnegara. A first instance of by-pass is mentioned too: rural merchants—in case of clove—selling to factory's agents directly. As the town's marketing function is essential in the rural motor concept, it might be concluded that Banjarnegara has a modest role only in facilitating commercialized agriculture in this respect. Only the dispersed fruit crop is bulked in town. It seems that in present day Java the expedience for a staple town is limited. It does not take too much effort to export cashcrops from the countryside directly.

This point is proven in the next paragraph as well. It reviews rice trade. Rice mills, some of them set up by the government, decentralized to the countryside, are the nodes in rice marketing. Regional circulation is more extensive than national circulation, but in neither respect Banjarnegara town has a significant role to play.

8.3 RICE TRADE: A SECOND NON BANJARNEGARA TRADE FLOW

The rice belt in *kabupaten* Banjarnegara stretches out along the Serayu River in the western districts: Klampok, Rakit, Susukan- and Purwonegoro (see Chapter 5). Reports from the past mention that *kabupaten* Banjarnegara never was a prime rice export region, nor a rice import region. Nowadays the extent of national circulation is still limited, at least not as large as it is in fruit and vegetables marketing. A huge portion does not even enter marketing at all, as it is used for autoconsumption. We will first proceed from where we started in the paragraph 8.2.2: *pasar kota*.

On the *pasar* rice trade is represented by a few wholesalers in the first place. Other salesmen, that have a permanent place trade in rice as one of the main articles within an assortment of basic foodstuffs, next to corn, beans, *mie* and *sohoen*. Two further groups of enterprises can be distinguished: those that supply the market, *bakul* and rice mill owners channelling surplusses to the *pasar*; and those that buy at the Banjarnegara *pasar*, intermediaries, that transport the rice to other *pasar*. Both last categories have no permanent place at the *pasar*.

In the *pasar* survey we asked all rice traders at the Banjarnegara market, whom they were supplied by. Table 8.5 gives an overview. Three groups of suppliers stand out: *bakul* and rice mill owners and *pasar* traders. This latter intra*pasar* trade concerns the wholesalers, that supply general foodstuff enterprises. 93% of all transactions takes place at the *pasar*; *bakul* and rice mill owners visiting the market. Only 7% of the *pasar* traders travels to Purworejo-Klampok *kawedanan* to buy rice. The 18% part of traders that stated that their merchandise originated from this region comes low, for it is the major rice producing district in the *kabupaten*. By far the most rice at *pasar* Banjarnegara originates from the *kecamatan*, surrounding the town. Which indicates the low importance of Banjarnegara as a rice collecting centre to the whole of the *kabupaten*. A majority of the regional surplusses is probably

Table 8.5 Supply channels of rice to rice wholesalers and basic foodstuff traders at pasar kota, March 17th 1983, (in relative number of traders)

	Origin of rice	*Residence of supplier*	*Location of transactions*
Banjarnegara town	—	21	93
Kecamatan Banjarnegara	11	4	—
Kawedanan Banjarnegara	57	40	—
Kawedanan Wonodadi	4	—	—
Kawedanan Purworejo Klampok	18	14	7
Serayu Valley Region	11	11	—
	Kind of supplier		
Toko	7		
Pasar wholesaler	21		
Bakul or rice mill owner	61		
Farmer	11		

Source: Pasar Surveys

handled by Purworejo-Klampok traders, while the bulking is organized by countryside rice mill owners.

Bakul and rice mill owners, making up 61% of the suppliers to the town market, are not by chance mentioned under one heading. Frequently *desa-bakul* are connected to rice-millers, tied by financial agreement. An instance: one Banjarnegara rice-mill owner has two mills. One in Pucang (*kecamatan* Bawang) and one in Semampir (*kecamatan* Banjarnegara). Twenty *bakul* trade in the countryside, mainly buying threshed rice or paddy as it stands on the *sawah (tebasan)*. Each one of them is advanced capital by him (Rp 500,000). He does not expect them to pay back, though officially it is a loan, but he considers it as an insurance to their loyalty. All their merchandise is polished and dehusked at his mills and he buys the milled rice and forwards it to *pasar* wholesalers. His profit margins in this respect are not exhuburant (Rp 10—15 per kilo), but milling costs and selling the waste of dehusking and polishing, at Rp 5 per kilo, raise his gains.

Kabupaten Banjarnegara counts approximately 100 rice-mills and a mere 7 are owned by town-dwellers, not at all an astonishing figure; it proves weak town-hinterland connections in this area. Rice-mill technology is a unique example of decentralized technology. Formerly, less rice was polished at the mills, hand pounding prevaled. Some rice-mills existed by then, owned by Chinese. Nowadays rice-mills can be found spread over the countryside in a dense network. Each year some 210,000 ton of rice is produced in the *kabupaten* (Banjarnegara Dalam Angka 1980) and by far the most passes a rice mill.

Besides places of processing agricultural produce, rice mills are centres of marketing. Farmers and *bakul* bring the rice to the mill to be dried, dehusked and polished. Trade transactions take place before and after these processings and prices differ accordingly. Wet and dry threshed rice yield Rp 10,000 and Rp 12,000 per quintal respectively (March 1983 prices). The costs of polishing are Rp 800—100 per quintal. A farmer's returns differs according to the way he sells his crop. Depending on his cash needs, a peasant might sell *ijon* or *tebasan* to a *bakul*; when resources allow the farmer might sell the rice wet or dried at the mill or sometimes even bear the costs of milling himself and sell to *pasar* wholesalers directly (see table 8.5). At the mills intermediary traders (named *bakul* as well) and occasionally *pasar* wholesalers gather to collect polished rice or buy from farmers, before milling, Rice mill owners intervene as well and frequently sell to *toko* or *pasar*. The fast growth of rice-mills thus changed trade patterns. A number of these rice-mills are not private property, but are owned by state-induced *Koperasi Unit Desa* (*K.U.D*).

A story on rice marketing cannot be complete without a short discussion of *K.U.D.* functioning. These village cooperations—part of the *Bimas* programme—do not deliver directly to *pasar* traders, but still play an important background role in rice trade. Some 25—30% of total *kabupaten* rice produce is marketed through *K.U.D.* units, that operate rice-mills and storehouses in almost every *kecamatan* centre. Banjarnegara town, consequential upon this decentralized marketing institution, does not play a significant role in rice trade. Only as a *kecamatan* centre it gives home to one of the *kabupaten's* rice-mill units.

One of the most important functions of these *K.U.D.* is rice price stabilization throughout the year. Formerly, rice price was very low during the harvesting season and shortly after, and in the *musim paceclik*—the 'last weeks before the rice harvest sets off—prices soared at a high level. Nowadays, due to a growing acreage of technically irrigated rice fields and the use of modern inputs, several crops a year are harvested and price fluctuations are less extreme. Still they are significant and stabilization by the *K.U.D.* is required. Rice is bought at guaranteed bottom price and stockpiled in government storehouses. When demand exceeds supply, and prices rise above a fixed maximum, the stock is sold at this maximum price. The stockpiled rice also serves to supply government officials with their monthly rate of rice.

Another purpose of *K.U.D.* is the battling of *ijon*. Transactions, whereby traders lend money to peasants, that can be repaid by selling rice for a price below standard, however are not extinct yet in the Banjarnegara region. Presently insiders (village traders) estimate the extent of *ijon* to be 15% of all paddy purchases in some villages. 6 to 8 weeks before maturing, peasant borrow money from *bakul*—usually fellow villagers—to finance their *paceclik* purchasings. After the harvest they are obliged to sell their crops to the mentioned *bakul* at 50% of the usual price. *K.U.D.* do not pay in advance, but at worst several weeks later, and peasants in financial trouble run to a *bakul*.

Like in fruit marketing and vegetables marketing, *tebasan* is another popular method of selling paddy. Again *desa bakul* purchase the forthcoming crop some two weeks before harvest time. Money shortage is one reason for a peasant to prefer *tebasan*, but circumventing traditional harvest sharing customs is another. The trader organizes harvesting and the peasant gets a sum of Rp 7,500 per quintal threshed rice.

Unless the *K.U.D.* price is higher (Rp 11,000 per quintal threshed rice), the number of farmers selling to the cooperative is low. Bureaucracy is one of its handicaps. To sell to the *K.U.D.*, at the guaranteed price-level, one has to be a member of the cooperative, with concomitant administrative commitments. Members are favoured, they can obtain cheap rice in the *paceklik* season and productive loans at 2% interest a month. *K.U.D.* could be a wonderful institution, if not for its inadequate functioning.

It was noticed that Banjarnegara is not a staple town for rice production in the *kabupaten*. At *pasar* Banjarnegara 15—20 wholesalers operate, handling on average 2—3 ton a day. As a very rough estimate 15,000 ton rice a year is handled at the *pasar*, which is a tiny fraction of 210,000 ton annual rice production in the *kabupaten*. To this fraction the—unknown—amount of *toko* sales should be added. Some *toko* buy from *bakul* too.

Where is *pasar* commerce destined for? First, as was noted, intra*pasar* deliverances are frequent in rice trade. Next to those traders keeping a stall with basic foodstuffs, all kind of other enterprises sell small quantities of rice, bought on the market. Secondly, some *toko, warong kedai, warong makan* and hawkers are other, non-*pasar* purchasers of rice.

Clientele from outside the town is limited, though Banjarnegara is a transit town to some extent. The upland *kecamatan* are net importers of rice, notwithstanding their own low quality rice species and corn and cassave being staple foods. A lot of rice is channeled to these districts by the *K.U.D.* or private rice mill owners. At *pasar kota* several intermediary traders operate as well, that send at regular intervals bags of rice to the northern districts too. Some wholesalers take up such jobs next to the usual local distribution. To Karangkobar, Kalibening and Wonosobo 5 traders each operate and to Wonosobo 2 wholesalers send weekly shipments. Quantity numbers 2—3 ton every five days.

So rice trade at *pasar* Banjarnegara is a local and regional circuit affair. No external merchants are involved. The *K.U.D.* marketing board and large scale traders (rice mill owners), handling large surpluses might follow national circulation channels, but these by-pass Banjarnegara town. As the western lowlands are the main rice-producing territories of the *kabupaten*, Purworejo-Klampok traders are renowned in this respect. In vegetable marketing Banjarnegara neither had a say in bulking of the cashcrop, as was shown in paragraph 8.2. Still the town trade networks have a central role in the distribution of vegetables in the southeastern part of the *kabupaten*. For rice retail, Banjarnegara is not so crucial a node though; paddy is cropped near Banjarnegara and autoconsumption and local *desa* circulation diminish Banjarnegara's place in this respect. What is left is some transit trade to the upland districts.

Chapter 9

LIVESTOCK TRADE

9.1 ANIMAL HUSBANDRY IN KABUPATEN BANJARNEGARA

Initially the expansion of livestock fattening in the upland districts of *kabupaten* Banjarnegara was linked with the growth of commercial tobacco cultivation. Cows, kept in sheds, provided manure to the tobacco fields. Apart from widespread peasant animal husbandry, a few specialized farms were founded in the area. Total population of cattle (cows, some buffaloes and some horses) in the regency amounted 11,000 head in 1916 (SDS). Because of Banjarnegara's and Wonosobo's cattle stock, cattle waggons were introduced on the narrow gauge railroad, that connected these regional centres with West Java. This introduction benefited Banjarnegara in particular, for its cows, since they were kept in sheds, were unable to walk long distances. Wonosobo livestock was fattened on pastures and could, before the new railroad connection, already be transported all the way to Purorejo (South Kedu), to be railed to West Java. Though the traders themselves made no bones about walking long distances, the cows however lost much weight on such trips. One informant, a cattle trader since 1947, told us about his weekly 24-hour trip to Kebumen, where he bought young cattle. Originating from the southcoast region, these steers were taken through the South Serayu Hills to sell them on the nest market day in Banjarnegara.

Prompted by a combination of improved transport facilities and price differences between Banjarnegara and West Java, the amount of cows fattened and exported racketed in the 20's and 30's. According to *Dinas Peternakan* officials, the number of fattened cattle shipped to other regions amounted to 40—50,000 head annually just before 1940. Cattle population must have grown fantastically then, considering the figure of 11,000 in 1916. Wolters (1984) estimates a still enormous number of 30,000 head exported every year in the thirties. As it was impossible to breed enough new stock, the staggering volume of exported cattle had to be counterbalanced by a huge influx of steers. In the course of time however, it led to drainage problems and a law was promulgated prohibiting the slaughtering of female cows below the age of six. This restricted export trade somehow, although in the fifties fattened bulls put on transport to West Java still numbered 20,000 head yearly (Wolters 1984).

At the end of that decade and in the sixties animal husbandry in Banjarnegara must have declined severely. Notwithstanding counteractive government policy, the region was gradually depleted of cattle and other areas in Indonesia increased their share on the West Javanese market. Lampung (South Sumatra) and Nusatenggara developed into cattle export zones. It diminished opportunities for fattening in the Serayu Valley and caused an ongoing fall in population numbers. In 1978 the amount of cattle exported was 8271 animals (Wolters 1984). The most recent statistics indicate that the decline has not stopped yet; 2382 bulls were exported in 1982 (*Dinas Peternakan*). This sharp statistical decline might be partly due to a new regulation. In order to protect Central Javanese traders, the Provincial Government forbade West Javanese traders to operate on Central Javanese cattle markets. One reason of this new rule is the recurrent neglect of some West Javanese traders to pay accumulated trading debts. It is common practice in cattle trade to pay afterwards for a piece of cattle. Meant to favour local traders,

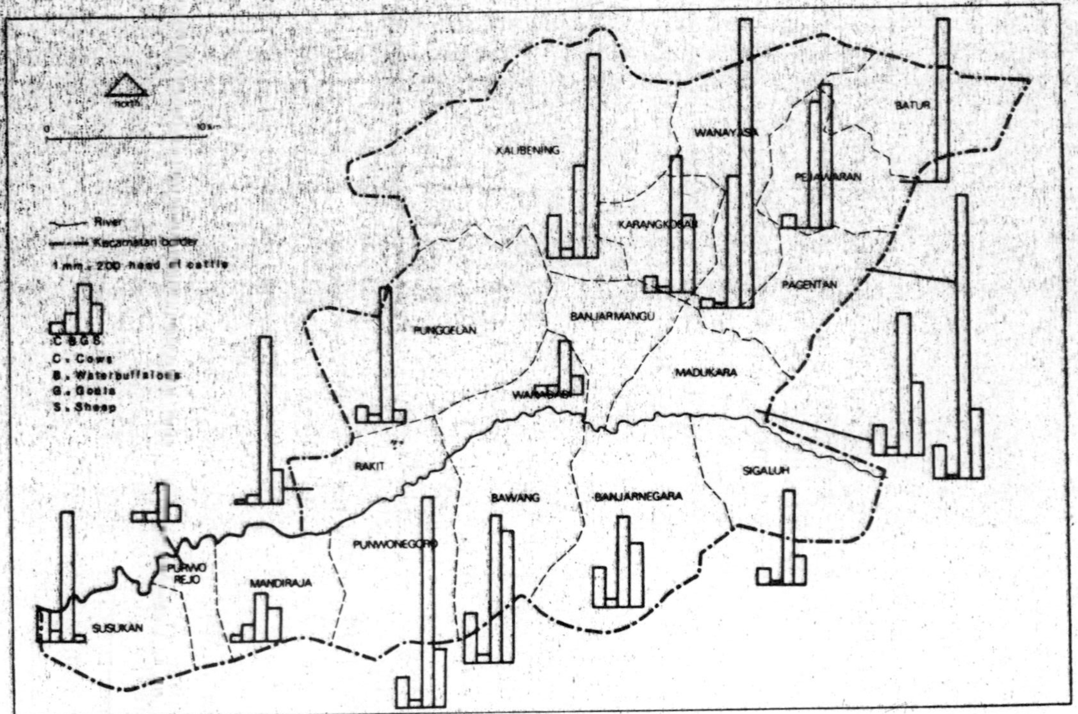

Source: Banjarnegara Dalam Angka 1980.

Map 9.1 Distribution of cattle in kabupaten Banjarnegara

the decree by the Provincial Government had drastic repercussions for cattle export however. Banjarnegara traders usually have great pains to gather sufficient working capital; they could not immediately take over from their larger scale Sundanese colleagues. Most likely the decree will not have enhanced fattening activities in the area.

Map 9.1 depicts how bovine cattle is spread over the *kabupaten;* the northern districts are still endowed with most fattening activities, though cattle population has fallen in these districts. Next to diminished marketing opportunities, ecological factors might have had a say too; as landuse in the northern districts has intensified, it has become harder to gather leaves and grass used for fodder. Besides, the increased use of chemical fertilizers has probably made dung supply less necessary. Diagram 9.1 states that cattle population in *kabupaten* Banjarnegara has stabilized at low level. Diagram 9.2 gives an overview of cattle import and export. For cows the figures range near 2500 head.

The fattening pattern has hardly altered since 1920.

Diagram 9.1 Cattle population in kabupaten Banjarnegara, 1972—1982

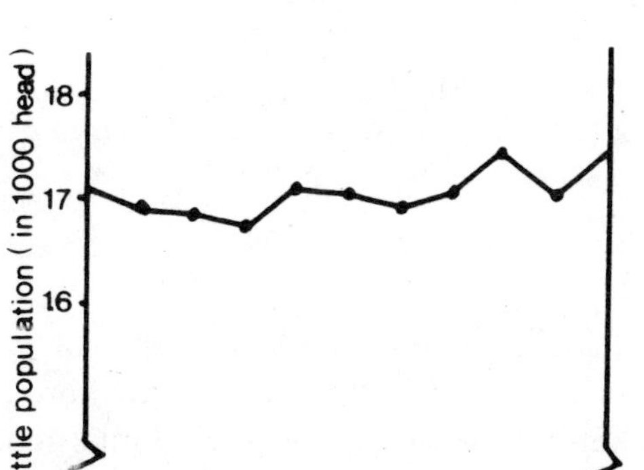

Source: Statistik Kabupaten '73/'74, Banjarnegara Dalam Angka 1980
Dinas Peternakan 1982.

Diagram 9.2 Import and export of cattle in kabupaten Banjarnegara in 1982

a) Number of cattle to kind, import and export

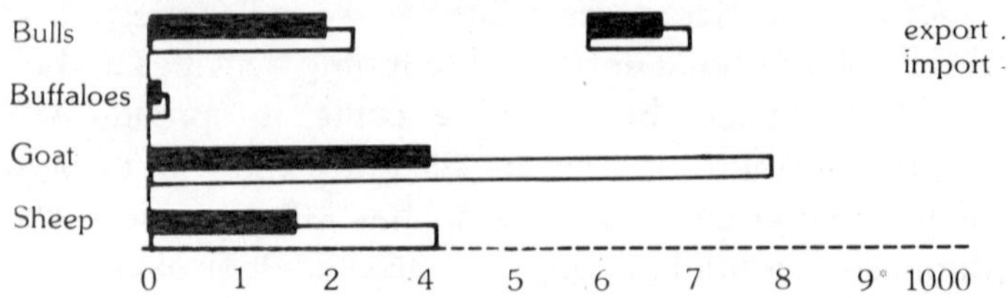

b) Number of imported and exported cattle to kind and origin or destination.

Origin	*Cows*	*Buf-faloes*	*Goats & sheep*	*Destination*	*Cows*	*Buf-faloes*	*Goats & sheep*
Bumiayu	227	—	—	Bumiayu	38	—	—
Sokaraja	836	—	—	Sokaraja	625	29	—
Purbolinggo	149	6	—	Pekalongan	—	—	1580
Wonosobo	120	245	5700	Wonosobo	137	43	440
Kebumen	535	—	55	Kebumen	54	—	48
Purwokerto	70	4	—	Purwokerto	479	2	—
Ajibarang	480	15	—	Pati	46	—	—
Blora	237	—	—	Jakarta	65	—	9370
Sokayasa	76	—	—	Tanggerang	880	37	950
Pati	111	—	—	Other cities in West Java	59	15	—
Total	2481	271	5755	Total	2383	126	12388

Source: Laporan Bulanan Perdagangan Ternak 1982.

Nowadays young bulls, some 4—5 months of age, bred in Kebumen or Gunung Kudul (South-Central Java) are brought to be Petambakan market, some miles north of Banjarnegara town. A peasant might buy a steer at the *pasar*, but more frequently the young animal is bought by a prosperous farmer, who will put the steer '*in de kos*' by a fellow villager. This is a board and lodging arrangement, whereby the fellow villager, a peasant, tends the cow in his shed and provides it with fodder, usually leaves and grass cut from the roadsides and forests. At intervals the dung is collected and used to fertilize the peasant's plot or otherwise it is sold. The peasant is compensated for his care in fattening, by monthly payment or by sharing in the trade profit (*maro bahti*). Within one and a half year of fattening, the weight, and hence the value, of the bull has doubled. Frequently *bakul* will visit the *desa* and offer to change the fattened bull for two young ones. Otherwise the bull is brought to the market by his owner and sold with the help of a broker (*tukang panteng*).

In former days many town inhabitants used to invest in fattening too, having hundreds of cattle lodged at numerous farmsteads (Wolters 1984). Today such venture is restricted to a few people, that are expert on animal husbandry. The wife of an employee of the Veterinary Service, pre-eminently, owned 250 head of cattle in various upland *desa*. Monthly payments to the tending peasant are Rp 3,000—4,000, which means a profit to the owner of 35% annually, for a young bull bought at Rp 125,000 is resold within 18 months for Rp 250,000. Such revenue is not excessive and in line with bank interest, but untouched by inflation.

Thus far we have delt with cattle export. Fattened cattle bound to be slaughtered is sold on *pasar* Petambakan to intermediaries of Purwokerto butchers or to big traders sending the animals to West Java. Diagram 9.2 gave an incomplete picture of livestock trade, since there is a substantial regional circulation of cattle as well. *Pasar* Petambakan is a central node in this respect too. Part of the bulls is destined for regional consumption and is sold to intermediaries of Banjarnegara butchers. Other regional commerce concerns draught animals and goats. Before we will pause at these lines of trade and return to cattle export, we will pay attention to *pasar* Petambakan in the subsequent paragraph.

Pigs trade and poultry trade are not treated in this chapter. The volume of pigs trade is small and is centred at Purworejo Klampok. In the past—until the 50's—pigs used to be reared in Banjarnegara town, south of the former Chinese quarter. Such animal husbandry has disappeared by now. Poultry is circulated in larger quantities, especially at the Purwonegoro and Mandiraja markets. At the town poultry market (*pasar* Ampera) small amounts of chicken are sold to Purwokerto everyday.

9.2 PASAR PETAMBAKAN

The major cattle market in the *kabupaten*, *pasar* Petambakan, has its locus eccentric to the cattle fattening zone of upland *kabupaten* Banjarnegara. *Pasar* Petambakan lies on the road from Banjarnegara to Karangkobar, a few miles north of the town, notwithstanding the fact that a huge part of commerce at the market is destined for or originates from the northern districts. Until 1977 the *pasar* was even situated near the town's centre, opposite the hospital. This site was reached by foot easily by Banjarnegara town traders, who could keep bought cattle overnight in stables, near their homes. In 1977 the *pasar* was removed for sanitary and congestion reasons. This move imposed extra costs of transportation at the expense of profit, according to informants, causing some small scale traders to abandon business. Most animals are moved by truck nowadays. Merchants from the town however, still have a major stake in cattle trade, both at *pasar* Petambakan and in the *kabupaten* as a whole, as will be shown in paragraph 9.3 to 9.5.

Locating the cattle market outside the cattle fattening zone is not so astonishing as it might seem at first sight; its ratio is that next to trade in fattened bulls, trade in waterbuffaloes and, to a minor degree, trade in goats and sheep are focused on *pasar* Petambakan. Diagram 9.3a shows the major channels to and from *pasar* Petambakan, with respect to livestock. Diagram 9.3b is taken from Wolters (1984) and maps goat trade in the northern and eastern part of the *kabupaten*. Each of the three market days at Petambakan seems dedicated to one line of cattle trade; monday afternoon is spent by big merchants selecting export quality fattened bulls, brought in from the northern districts. These merchants have the best price to offer. The remainder passes the night at the market, to be sold the next morning to medium scale traders. At this day other lower quality

Diagram 9.3a Cattle trade to and from pasar Petambakan

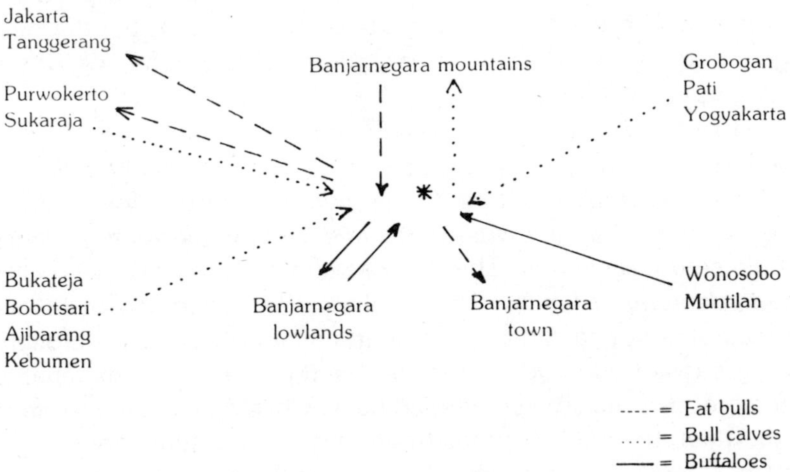

Source: Dinas Peternakan; Survey Cattle Market

Diagram 9.3b Goat and sheeps trade in the Serayu Uplands

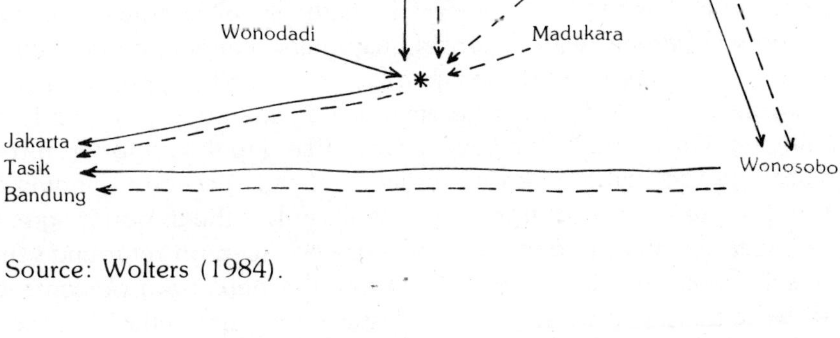

Source: Wolters (1984).

fattened bulls as well as steers and waterbufalloes are transported to the market. There is some goat trade on tuesday too, but the peak of goat trade is on fridays, whereas bulls and waterbuffaloes for sale are a minority on friday.

Counting activities at *pasar* Petambakan one would be surprised to find that cattle brought to *pasar* Petambakan is outnumbered by human visitors. On an average tuesday for instance, 100 cows may change owner, but some 150 people seem engaged with these transanctions. The hub of them are brokers, men called *tukang panteng*. At *pasar* Petambakan 20—25 groups of *tukang panteng* operate, each group consisting of approximately 4 brokers. Such groups of *panteng* mediate between peasants and merchants. Some groups specialize in fattened bulls, while others keep to steers or to waterbuffaloes. In goat trade singular *panteng* operate, as Wolters (1984) has described. To illustrate the *tukang panteng* profession we depict *Pak Sutawar*.

Pak Sutawar has joined a *panteng* group, that mediates in transactions of steers. He spends every tuesday and every friday at *pasar* Petambakan. On other days *Pak Sutawar* works at the Wonosobo or Sukaraja cattle market. Early in the morning his group awaits the merchants, who bring the bulls they import to the region to the market, and the *panteng* will settle a (realistic) bottom selling price for the steer, for instance Rp 90,000. When the trader has agreed upon this price, the *panteng* will try to find people interested to buy the particular animal at a price, that surmounts the price agreed with the importer. Individually all members of the group will bargain with potential customers, keeping contact constantly, until one of them has managed to settle a proper price, for instance Rp 97,500. The difference will be shared among the four *panteng*. Occasionally the initial price, offered to the importer, turns out to be too high. When the brokers do not succeed in finding a client, there will be not transaction at all, unless the importer agrees to lower his price. In general traders are not keen on returning with unsold cattle and the importer will pay the *panteng* a percentage (2%) of the final, lowered, price. Usually the price settled between *panteng* and importer is unknown to would-be buyers. Sometimes unexperienced peasants, only rarely attending the cattle market, do not know that they are dealing with a broker. Such ignorance is exploited by the *tukang panteng*; they will cheat the peasant by suggesting competition, as two or more *panteng* from the same group bid different, but exaggerated prices.

The example of *Pak Sutawar* depicts a *panteng*, that negotiates on behalf of a merchant importing young bulls. Other groups act on behalf of peasants, willing to sell a fattened bull; for a peasant, though he might be deceived by the *panteng*, might be too shy to haggle with a merchant. A merchant on the other hand, cannot afford the time-consuming process of bargaining with the peasants. Still some traders at *pasar* Petambakan will refuse the services of a *panteng*; motivated by profit-seeking or status. Village *bakul* are experienced enough to sell. Big merchants are often annoyed by the presence of the brokers and state that they skim revenues. *Pasar* Sukaraja and *pasar* Wonosobo have a worse reputation in this respect. For *panteng* groups consist of 8—10 persons at these cattle markets, hence bargaining becomes an exacting process. At *pasar* Petambakan entry to the profession is restricted; when somebody new wants to try his luck as a broker, he first has to opt for a permit, i.e. getting registrated informally at an established *tukang panteng*. In broking goats there is no such seclusion mechanism, as every broker works on his own account.

Notwithstanding the low opinion held of the *panteng* by some traders, as a third party, the brokers mitigate the gap between peasant and merchant. For to survive at the cattle market is a laboursome thing; one has to know the tricks of the trade. The major skills are to bargain and to estimate an animal's net weight. A goat or a bull might be put on a balance, but there is not linear correlation between live weight and dead weight. The correlation is among others distorted by the salt water trick. Before going to the *pasar* the bulls and goats are refreshed with salt water. Becoming thirsty they drink more and because of the salt, the water is not secreted. Hence the animals gain weight and, besides, their appearance is more fleshy.

Experienced traders all assured to see through this swindle, but nevertheless the trick must pay off, considering its frequency. Waterbuffaloes cannot be quenched with salt water, for they drink while bathing.

In paragraph 6.1 we described how institutionalization at the general market in Banjarnegara town impeded access to new traders. Such institutionalization is unknown to the cattle market, though it is dotted with rules and regulations. One has been mentioned: West Javanese traders are prohibited to trade on Central Javanese cattle markets. The effect of such regulations should not be exaggerated; the number of West Javanese traders has decreased on *pasar* Petambakan, but one will still find West Javanese at the market, whose presence is condoned, for these particular traders are known to be creditworthy. Other regulations apply to market tax, which has to be paid when livestock enters the *pasar* and when it is exported out of the *kabupaten*. These obligations are sometimes simply ignored by cattle traders.

Though regulations are dodged and institutionalization does not narrow the opportunities of making a living in cattle trade, other phenomena do. To establish as a cattle merchant demands skill and capital. Skill in assessing net weight and in bargaining, capital to finance transactions, for one fattened bull might cost Rp 250,000 and there are additional costs on transport and care. Importing and exporting cattle merchants still have a higher treshold; the minimum turn-over is one truck-cargo of animals, because a partly empty truck would be loss. The one activity at *pasar* Petambakan that can be executed without trading capital, neither is open to everyone; to become a *tukang panteng* one has to be allowed to by other brokers.

Livestock traders can be discerned by two criteria; traject and number of animals traded. The usefulness of this latter criterion reflects the importance of trading capital. Traject and turnover are correlated. Village *bakul*, the regional circuit, will hardly ever handle more than 2 or 3 bulls per market day, incurring low turnover, making them petty commodity sector. The national circuit, cattle importers or exporters, will handle 10 animals at least per week and

TABLE 9.1. Structuring and form characteristics in livestock and meat trade

Type of enterprise	Sector	Number of capitalist characteristics
Exporter of bulls	Corporate	3–4
Importer of steers and young waterbuffaloes	Corporate	3–4
Village bull trader	Petty	3
Exporter of goats	Corporate	3
Village goat trader	Petty	3
Tukang panteng	Petty	3
Butcher	Corporate	3
Meat trader	Petty	2

multiplying this figure with cattle price, the sum makes them enter corporate sector, like table 9.1 depicts. There hardly seems to be dif ference between corporate sector and petty commodity sector cattle traders regarding the mode in which the enterprises are managed, however. A cattle trader might be large scale or small scale, and this scale might influence how he is running his business, like how many assistants he will employ or what type of transport he will use. But structuring elements, like ownership of enterprise or type of labour employed, are constants within the branch.

Below the three sections of livestock trade, present in the town, are highlighted: trade in fattened bulls, in draught animals and in small ruminants. In the succeeding paragraphs we will often portray a trader, justified not only by his representativeness, but because, since cattle trade is controlled by so little people, every trader is responsible for a considerable portion of livestock trade.

9.3 TRADE IN STEERS AND FATTENED BULLS

In the previous paragraph we reviewed *pasar* Petambakan,

just north of Banjarnegara town. Banjarnegara traders no longer control trade at the cattle market. According to Wolters (1984) they did in the thirties, but their position is captured by capital rich West Javanese traders. Table 9.2 reveals that Banjarnegara merchants only have a say in the import trade of steers and young water-buffaloes. There are six Banjarnegara importers, five of them brothers. Theirs is a family of cattle traders, for another brother concentrates on cattle export. One might suspect some cooperation to exist between the brothers, but they operate as atomistic as any other cattle trader. Even solidarity is absent; one brother, a cattle trader since 1957, had gone bankrupt a year before. He used to send cattle to West Java and had been deluded by someone, who

Table 9.2. Merchants operating at pasar Petambakan

Type of cattle	Number of traders	Residence	Sellers Stock bought in:
Bullcalves	6	Town	Purwokerto, Ajibarang, Sukaraja
	1	*Kabupaten*	Bobotsari, Bukateja, Grobongan
	3	Kebumen	Kebumen, Pati, Wirasari (Yogya)
	2	Sokaraja	
Fat bulls	11	*Kabupaten*	Northern districts *kabupaten*
Buffaloes	4	Town	Wonosobo, Muntilan
			Buyers Destinations of stock:
Fat bulls	5	Town	Town
	1	Town	Jakarta
	4	*Kabupaten*	*Kabupaten*
	5	Purwokerto	Purwokerto
	4	Sokaraja	Sokaraja
	1	Tanggerang	Tanggerang
			Buyer and seller Origin and destination:
Bufalloes and oxes	9	*Kabupaten*	*Kabupaten*

Source: Market Warden at *Pasar* Petambakan

failed to repay accumulated trading debts of Rp 8,000,000, worth 30 head of fattened bulls. At the time of the survey he tried to get some of his money back by court. In the meantime however, he was not helped financially by his brothers and fellow traders. Trading capital is crucial in the branch, for one can get 10% trade discount on paying cash, which is a fair reflection of risk thus avoided in these long distance transactions. Banjarnegara traders will send as far as Jakarta and fetch their merchandise on distant markets, like Blora, Pati and Ajibarang. One of the importing brothers exemplifies this need of capital:

Next to importing steers from the Muntilan market, *Pak Muliyono* is engaged in trading draught animals within the Serayu Region and occasionally he will purchase fattened bulls to sell them to Banjarnegara butchers or aged waterbuffaloes to sell to Wonosobo butchers. He regularly rents a lorry to travel to Muntilan, where he will purchase 12 steers at the cattle market, equal to the cargo of the lorry rented. Selling these young bulls on markets in the Serayu Region, he will use *tukang panteng*, who manage to extract higher prices from the future owners. *Pak Muliyono* tries to improve his profit by purchasing at slack days and selling at hey-days. Often he has to visit several *pasar* (Petambakan, Wonosobo, Sukaraja, Bobotsari), before he gets rid off his stock at an appropriate price. His target is a profit of Rp 15,000 per bull. Because of the short-term speculation and the time-lag between buying and selling an because of him allowing delay payment, he has to have a buffer of working capital. Therefore he obtained a loan from *B.R.I.*, amounting to Rp 2,500,000.

In contrast to import trade, export of bulls is not so much a Banjarnegara town matter. Only one Banjarnegara merchant, from the cattle trading family, sustained on this type of trade. He send 75 head to Jakarta every month, bought at *pasar* Petambakan and *pasar* Wonosobo. For transport he uses a truck from a befriended contractor, whose billnotes are used by him as well, for he thinks the legal *C.V.* (limited liability) status suggested might impress clients in Jakarta. He has got three customers in Jakarta and this is a crucial step in setting up export linkages; finding reliable trading partners, for delay payment is common and a partner not meeting obligations can shipwreck a trader. This hints at an alternative explanation for the occurrence of extraregional traders at the *kabupaten* cattle market, for such West Javanese are familiar with local retail situation in their area. A second activity of this trader is purchasing steers, young buffaloes and goats at *pasar* Blora, Pati and Wonosari. Every 5 days, at the rhythm of the Javanese week, he will go to these rice cultivation zones, paying his suppliers on the next trip. To avoid miscalculations the merchant employes experienced helpers at each *pasar*. These part-time employees are expert on prices and fluctuations in demand and supply. They can assess an animals weight without balances and know the ropes of the trade. Such precious assistants are paid accordingly: Rp 10—15,000 a day.

Though only one Banjarnegara trader actually exports fattened bulls, some other tradesmen in town are engaged with it. They are Purwokerto butchers' intermediaries, furnished with initial capital, worth Rp 2,000,000 by their client. These intermediaries were excluded from the market warden's overview, as presented in table 9.2. Two of them were interviewed. They will gather fattened cattle at Petambakan, Wonosobo and occasionally Sukaraja, Bobotsari and Bukateja. At *pasar* Petambakan they will meet the butchers and transfer the animals. Sometimes the traders will even transport their stock to Purwokerto themselves, renting a truck at Rp 2,000 per animal. Usually 5 or 6 six bulls are handled per market day, totalling 30—40 monthly. The usual price for a fattened bull is Rp250—300,000 and is paid afterwards by the butcher. Net profit ranges Rp 8—10,000 per animal. Despite their fixed outlet, which labels them as intermediaries, the traders have not lost independence. Now and then, one of them trades with other customers at the *pasar*. So merchants in town have a minor stake in the marketing of fattened bulls. They neither have a hold on trade to and from the *desa*, which is controlled by rural dwellers. The merchants stated that circumventing the *pasar* would not pay off in this respect, for peasants are aware of real market value, informed as they are by *bakul* and *panteng*.

Banjarnegara intermediaries however have a stake at the regional circulation of fattened cattle, as table 9.2 informs. A portion of the bulls at *pasar* Petambakan are slaughtered by Banjarnegara butchers. Diagram 9.4 gives a rough estimate of regional circulation vis-a-vis national circulation and might be compared to diagram 8.3 on vegetable retail. There are five butchers in Banjarnegara town and all but one use local intermediaries to select bulls at the market. Risk of misestimation is entirely borne by the intermediary, for he is paid a price per kilogram net weight (flesh and bones), i.c. after the bull has been slaughtered and blood and dirt has been drained. Such slaughtering is done by the butchers' personnel at the town's abatoir. Within a radius of 6 kilometer around the town's slaughterhouse, private slaughtering is prohibited. Next to the government abatoir, there are private slaughterhouses in Punggelan, Bawang, Batur and Klampok. Costs of using Banjarnegara's slaughterhouse totals Rp 6250—part tax, part inspection fee and part cost of hide preparation and cleansing of the slaughterhouse.

Diagram 9.4 Cattle fattening in Kabupaten Banjarnegara: Total export from pasar Petambakan and volume sold to Banjarnegara butchers, 1982.

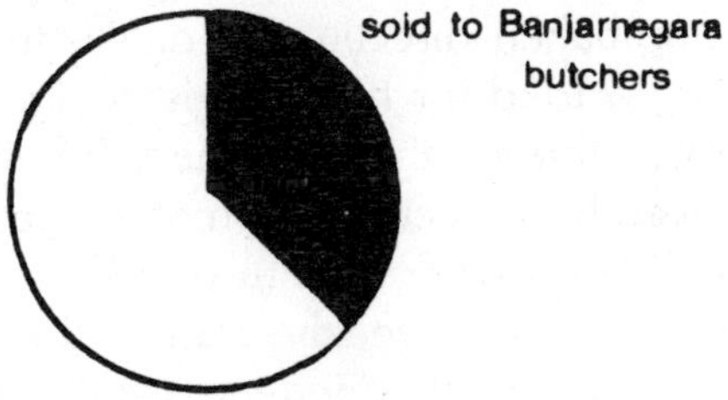

Number of bulls: **3903**

Source: Dinas Peternakan; Survey Cattle Market.

Table 9.3. A bull's output as stated by a Banjarnegara butcher

	Weight	Price/Kg	Returns
Live weight	250		250,000
Net weight	125		
— fresh meat, incl. fat	100	2100—2700	240,000
— meat processed into *abon* (4.5 kg)	2	6000	12.000
— lyngs turned into *paro kripik*	1.5	2000	3.000
— horns and bones (for comb industry)	10	35	350
Remainder			
— hide dried and conserved with salt (alternately it might be sold fresh)	8 (25)	2600 (500)	20,800 (12,500)
— waste (blood, dirt, remnant)		—	—
Dung sold once a year after 300 head			700
Total			Rp 276,850 (268,550)

Only one butcher in Banjarnegara felt expert enough to buy at *pasar* Petambakan directly. He differs from the other four butchers in havig a *toko* for his commerce, in stead of selling on the general market, though the Veterinary Service plans to have all five butchers moved to a special section of the general market. Turnover of the *toko* is 50% higher than turnover of *pasar* traders: 10 versus 7 cows are slaughtered weekly. Part of the meat is processed into *paro kripik* (fried lungs), *dendeng* (strips of dried meat) or *abon* (dried and shredded meat). Besides he prepares the skin to be sold to a Wonosobo trader, who sends the leather to Semarang. Table 9.3 lists the butcher's statement of a bull's output. 50% of the meat is sold to private customers in the butcher's shop. The other half is wholesaled to meat traders and small scale hawkers. The latter receive Rp 100—200 discount per kilo and are allowed to return meat unsold; this butcher is fortunate to own a freezer.

The *pasar* based butchers have a partly fixed clientele too, consisting of *tukang bakso*—foodprocessors hawking soup— and meat traders. Those petty scale meat traders might operate at the *pasar* as well, retailing the meat obtained from fellow *pasar* traders. Their turnover is small. Consider for instance one woman, that shares her spot at the general market with four other meat traders. Her daily sales are 3 kilogram meat, 3 kilogram fat and 3 kilogram bones. Her major worry is to sell out everyday. Unsold meat she will boil and hope to sell the next day, albeit at a dropped price, because of the high perishability of meat. Sometimes she is even forced to consume the meat herself or have it consumed by relatives. The perishability of meat explains why it will not change hands below the level of such petty traders, in contrast to vegetable retail illustrated in paragraph 8.2, for the meat will not last too many transactions.

9.4 TRADE IN DRAUGHT ANIMALS

Map 9.1 showed, beside fattening activities being concentrated in the upland districts of *kawedanan* Karangkobar and Batur, that the lowlands are not devoid of cattle either. It concerns cows and waterbuffaloes (*kerbau*), that are kept to work, not to become fat. Using animal traction in agriculture requires level terrain and monocropped plots, that are not too small in size. These conditions are met in the lowland *sawah* areas, in contrast to the hilly drylands up north. Waterbuffaloe, the major draught animal, needs daily bathing; this makes them less suited for the mountain districts too. Cows might be an alternative; it ought to be remembered however, that it is not possible to combine traction and fattening.

A minor part of the farming households has the privilege of owning draught animals. Most till their *sawah* with *pacol*, or occasionally hire animal traction, whether or not with labourers included.

Draught animals are sometimes bought for a short period only, used extensively for the preparation of the owner's and the lessees' land and sold afterwards. These farmers might take the animals as an object to invest cash earned at a previous harvest, the rent of traction power constituting interest to capital. Such short term ownership causes regional demand and supply to have an uneven character, with consequential low prices at the end of the preparation season. To some this loss (5%) stands to the expenses of tending the waterbuffaloes outside the preparation season. Obviously an intensive regional circulation of draught animals is the result. From diagram 9.3a it could be inferred that short and medium distance transactions prevale in this line of cattle trade. There is an entrance and an exit to the system however. Young buffaloes are transported to the Petambakan market by Banjarnegara traders, who went to *pasar* in the Solo—Magelang area to purchase the buffaloes. Exit to the system is the butcher. At the end of their productive lives the draught animals are sold to Jakarta or Wonosobo to be slaughtered. Buffaloe meat is not consumed in Banjarnegara town. Sometimes the animals are even slaughtered after the end of their lives. Prices will drop 50% then. Other dead animals are slaughtered in the village itself.

Waterbuffaloe export has such a casual character, that there is no merchant specializing in it. Import of waterbuffaloes, on the other hand, might be combined with steer import as the example in the previous paragraph shows, but it is a full-time profession to 4 Banjarnegara merchants (confer table 9.1). Two of them are pictured:

Pak Abdul Mardiana has been engaged in waterbuffaloes import for 33 years now and is beyond ambitions to maximize and invest. He runs his business on routine. He will go to the Wonosobo and Muntilan market once every five days, using a rented truck, and purchases 10 head every trip. The young waterbuffaloes will be sold at markets in the Serayu Lowlands; Petambakan, Bobotsari, Sukaraja and Bukateja. At these markets he will not use *tukang panteng*, for, as he states, *panteng* drain a merchant's profits. Usually he will deal with peasants and village traders directly. A colleague, *Pak Sudirdjo*, from the cattle trading family, set up six years ago as a buffaloe importer. He used the Rp 750,000, saved from his former profession, bicycle trading. Unlike *Pak Abdul Mardiana*, *Pak Sudirdjo* wants to expand business. Though his scale and method of working at present is similar to *Pak Abdul Mardiana*, except for his importing from the Solo Region, *Pak Sudirdjo* aims at importing 50 head per week. He acknowledges that to expand is a discontinuous process, every step being equal to 10 head: the cargo of a truck. One cannot afford to rent a truck and return half empty. The major bottleneck to enlarge trade is the lack of funds; capital is dissipated on delay payments. At the moment he obtained a loan at the *B.P.D.*, worth Rp 2,000,000, to finance operations.

In the regional circulation of waterbuffaloes, the reciprocal arrows in diagram 9.3a from the village to the market and back, Banjarnegara town traders hardly interfere. *Bakuls* and brokers walk with the animals or have them driven to one of the markets in the rice belt; Petambakan, but occasionally Bobotsari, Purbolinggo or Sokaraja. One part-time broker interviewed gets orders from fellow villagers to sell or buy their waterbuffaloe, whereby the villager has settled his price beforehand. Usually the owner or owner-to-be does not accompany the broker on these missions, but trusts him to do what he was asked. His profit is the difference between the price settled in advantage by the villager and the price settled at the market.

In cattle trade the range a trader covers is not limited to *kabupaten* Banjarnegara. Merchants, but *bakul* and *panteng* as well, the less so for fattened bulls, will operate on several markets in the Serayu Valley Region. Banjarnegara traders might not control trade at *pasar* Petambakan, but it should be remarked that they have a foothold at cattle markets in adjacent *kabupaten*.

9.4 GOAT TRADE

A third type of livestock trade, that we will pause at, is goat trade. Goats and sheeps are the small man's bank account. Expenses to buy a young goat will not surpass Rp 8—10,000, and this is within the common man's budget. The animals might be tended by the owner or there might be a putting out relationship, similar to what is decribed in cattle fattening. Goats presence is ubiquitous. They are fed leaves and grass and their dung is an additional resource, next to their meat. In the upland region by eminence, keeping goats is integrated in the rural economy.

In contrast to cattle trade, there is a goat market in virtually every *kecamatan* centre and in many villages too. Purwonegoro is the major market; 1500—2000 head are sold monthly. Petambakan, the *kabupaten* cattle market, accounts for a mere 1000 head per month (see diagram 9.5). Goat trade to a major extent is regional circulation. It seems that every month some 12,000—13,000 goats are sold; 4,000 of these are exported to other regions. Next to registred transactions, numerous goats change owner unreportedly, in spite of the obligation to report transactions to the *desa* officials. Such trade is mainly local circulation. It

Diagram 9.5 Volume of goat trade at pasar in kabupaten Banjarnegara, 1982

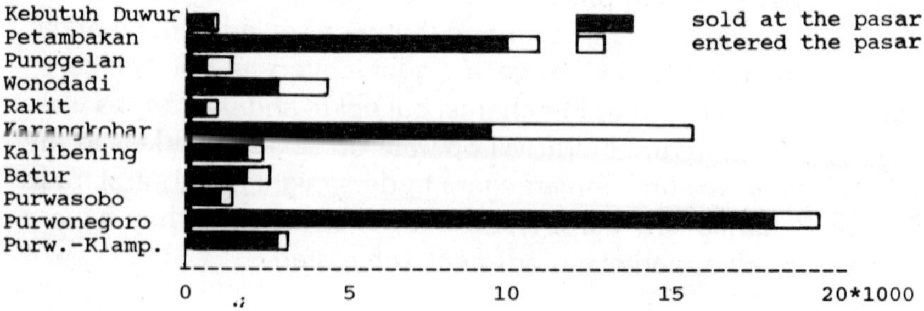

Source: Laporan Bulanan Perdagangan Pasar Ternak, 1982.

often does not take place at a livestock market; part-time peasant-traders might buy and sell on the rural spot. One such *bakul* interviewed was ordered by peasants to buy or sell them one or two goats. Sometimes a bottom price or a ceiling price is agreed, and this man—trusted by his fellow villagers—bargains freely and receives a commission, no matter what price has been reached. He uses his own capital in this venture. One time he borrowed bank money, but he felt twisted at that time between peasants' delay payments and the burden of monthly instalments. This man exemplifies the scale of transactions in regional circulation, which amounts one or two goats usually, and ten goats at the most. In trading, a *bakul* might be assisted by a *panteng*. They will settle a bottom price and the two of them will try to find customers willing to pay more. The surplus is shared by *bakul* and *panteng*.

Banjarnegara town traders do not concern themselves with this local or regional circulation of goats and sheep. The more so do they master the export of small ruminants. In fact, one trader from the town, acquainted with the family of cattle traders, is trying to monopolize goat export: *Pak Darsono* is a well-known person on livestock markets in *kabupaten* Banjarnegara: Petambakan, Purwonegoro and Karangkobar; in *kabupaten* Wonosobo: Wonosobo, Kaliwiro, Kretek and Sapuran; and at *pasar* Purbolinggo. On these *pasar* he has got intermediaries trading for him, for *Pak Darsono* neither has the time, nor the skill to do the bargaining. A total of 10 intermediaries supply *Pak Darsono*. Tying these intermediaries is his system of consolidating business. Payments to those, that work completely on his behalf, are faster, than to those that have not given up independence. One of the first type of intermediaries was interviewed:

Two days a week *Pak Bendi* boards *Pak Darsono's* minibus to go to the livestock market of Kaliwiro or Petambakan. He will buy goats, but is not allowed by *Pak Darsono* to sell to any other trader. The price he is paid is the price he paid for the goat plus a fixed allowance of Rp 500 per goat. Thus he might as well be labelled a piecework labourer. Actually on two other days in the week, he is on *Pak Darsono's* wagelist, tending the goats to be sent to Jakarta. Contacts to the Darsono family go back 40 years, when *Pak Bendi* started trading for Darsono senior. Other intermediaries will offer fattened goats to both *Pak Darsono* and his rivals. *Pak Darsono* is no guaranteed outlet to them. Their profit margins are the result of bargaining. A third kind of intermediaries might be called brokers, though different from the *panteng* they are ordered by the buying party. *Pak Darsono* states a price to them and the brokers try to fix him with goats, they have bought for a lower price. Gains to the last two types of intermediaries range Rp 500—1000 per goat.

Pak Darsono sends four shipping of 125 goats each to Jakarta monthly, using his own lorry. Profits per goat are Rp 1000—1500, which is the difference between Jakarta and Banjarnegara prices (Rp 2500) and expenses on fuel, forage and labour (Rp 1500). Next to goat trade the Darsono family runs a conglomerate of enterprises: a stationary shop, a construction company annex building material wholesale trade. Besides they are the only ones in the town that butcher goats at the abatoir, to sell the meat at the *pasar*. They slaughter 300 goats monthly. Other people butchering goats in Banjarnegara town are restaurant owners, using one goat daily.

As a goat exporter *Pak Darsono* is equaled by few other traders. One other large scale exporter has his base in Banjarnegara town. This *imam* sends 400—600 goats to Cirebon every month. However he prefers other livestock markets to Petambakan. Another channel to goat export from *kabupaten* Banjarnegara is *pasar* Kaliboning. Goats are sold to Pekalongan. Neither *Pak Darsono*, nor the *imam* visit this distant market.

9.6 RESUMING LIVESTOCK TRADE

All livestock trade is hierarchy trade. It differs from the bulking of vegetables and clove, where model B and C of diagram 2.1 have introduced themselves. Circumventing the livestock markets and penetrating the *desa* would not pay off to livestock exporters or importers, as one respondent explained, for it would be hard to find, for example, a fattened bull in the first place. In the second place the owner would expect an inflated price, knowing it is bitter for a trader to return empty-handedly, because of transport costs already made by then. Similarly a cattle importer would be wellcomed with expectations of a low price. Frequently village dwellers are visited by fellow villagers, *bakul* or *panteng*, so they can assess what a head of livestock is worth. *Bakul* and *panteng* control trade in and out of the village; in this respect they are the link between peasant and corporate sector merchant and the interface between village trader and merchant is the livestock market. The first argument mentioned, the hardship in finding merchandise, suggests a parallel with fruit marketing, which is hierarchical as well and surpluses are of a spatially dispersed character too.

A trend that—to a lesser degree—was signalled in fruit trade at *pasar* Banjarnegara, applies to the cattle market too: merchants from out of the region have penetrated *pasar* Petambakan. Purwokerto butchers and West Javanese cattle merchants outnumber exporters from *kabupaten* Banjarnegara; at *pasar* Petambakan there is only one trader from Banjarnegara town, who exports to West Java. In the past the proportions used to be different. Some explanations suggested for this change are the general lack of trading capital of Banjarnegara town traders and the trouble of finding a reliable partner on the remote West Javanese markets; and an assured outlet seems a pre-requisite for such expedition to Banjarnegara traders. It seems that fetching prevales in national cattle circulation, for traders from Banjarnegara town do master the import of steers and young waterbuffaloes from East Central Java. Supplying a hinterland, that even surpasses *kabupaten* Banjarnegara, this activity fits perfectly in the rural motor concept. Goat export does too, for in contrast to cattle export, a few merchants from Banjarnegara town dominate the forwarding of small ruminants to Cirebon and Jakarta. Regional circulation of goats however is much more substantial than export trade, like intervillage circulation of draught animals is more substantial than their import or export. In such regional circulation, though partly focused on the Petambakan market, Banjarnegara town traders have no hold.

The place held by traders from town in the national circulation of regional livestock should not deflect attention from the plain statistics, that show how such national circulation has shrunk to less than 10% of what it used to be in the thirties. In its trail commercialized cattle fattening has declined, like—and maybe because—tobacco cultivation declined, to which it was closely linked. Ecological factors might account for the fall, but deteriorated marketing opportunities offer a prime "because". We like to suggest that these marketing opportunities might improve, if cattle fattening becomes interlaced with local agro-industries. At present local processing is geared to local meat demand. Part of the fattened bulls enter the *kabupaten's* slaughterhouse, to be turned into a host of products, as table 9.3 shows. A neglible quantity of meat, the leftovers actually, is processed into *dendeng* and *abon*. We think processing meat into dried products merits more attention. It is highly valued, non perishable and easy to transport; and hence could ameliorate marketing opportunities for livestock in *kabupaten* Banjarnegara and keep a substantial part of the added value within the region. The other products of a slaughtered animal, bones and hide, could be an input to other industries.

Thus far in this paragraph, we reviewed livestock trade with a hindsight to the rural motor concept. Reviewing the service centre concept one should also point to government services benificial to rural animal husbandry that do exist in the town. The new cattle market, the extension activities by the veterinary service, the veterinarian clinic to be built and the slaughterhouse facilities attract and benefit activities in the cattle branch. New types of animal husbandry adapted to the local situation are propagated and introduced. Compared to other branches, services in this branch are well-developed.

Finally, livestock trade cannot be called a labour absorber, at least not in Banjarnegara town. Capital per unit is large in the first place. A young bull already costs Rp 90,000. But trading units of cattle merchants usually are even larger, namely one truck load of livestock, for an exporter or an importer cannot afford to convey one animal only. Therefore, albeit Banjarnegara traders have a stake at such trade, the number of people employed is little and covers one family mostly. The people that are numerous at the livestock markets are livestock brokers, that are rural dwellers mostly. At *pasar* Petambakan, as was noted, entrance to this profession, is restricted.

Chapter 10

CONSTRUCTION: AT THE BOOM

In Banjarnegara the construction branch has acquired the proportions of a boom sector. Those few, that have some money to invest, are attracted to it as well as those many seeking well-paid work. Taking into account both construction workers and those engaged in activities closely related to it, in Banjarnegara construction has become one of the big employment generating branches, outside agriculture and trade. Its peak is impelled by the increase in infrastructural works from 1970 on and the increased overall wealth that accelatered private housing construction. In Banjarnegara construction activities mainly take two forms; the '*proyek*'; being the infrastructural improvement works coordinated by *kabupaten* government or provincial departments; and private house-building, usually managed by the future resident himself. Organization differs in these components of the construction market as will be shown in paragraph 10.1. Van der Erve's (1983) actor-diagrams represents the two different forms (diagram 10.1).

The major exception to these methods of organization is the construction of the Mrica hydro-power dam, carried out some 15 kilometers west of Banjarnegara. The multi-milliard *rupiah* project is handled by a Swedish-British joint-venture. When work is in full progress, it will employ 2300 construction workers, most from outside the *kabupaten*, as Banjarnegara construction workers lack the

proyek	private housing
owner	owner
•	• •
builder	supplier workers
• •	
supplier workers	

Diagram 10.1 Organization in the construction market

skill to handle the advanced machinery, that was imported from Sweden and Britain for the purpose. A hundred foreign engineers will supervise the construction. Such capital-intensive way of working is in stark contrast to the low-technology, labour-intensive construction of *proyek* or private housing in Banjarnegara and quite significantly only the *kabupaten's* biggest contractors were subcontracted minor parts of the Mrica-project. The hydro-power dam was outside the scope of our research and we will stick to private housing and *proyek* only. Nonetheless we want to comment on some consequences of the Mrica project for the construction branch in Banjarnegara.

One can imagine that after the hydro-power dam is completed some of the machinery will be sold to local entrepreneurs, which would hasten mechanization of construction industry. Another consequence might be the local raw materials being used up. The Tampomas lime quarry will be exhausted and some rivers will virtually be depleted of sand and stones, suitable for building materials, for these are used for filling the dam. It will leave sand and stone diggers down there without work.

10.1 CONSTRUCTION WORKERS

As construction has turned into such a big industry, it

provides work to a large number of people. According to our count on enterprises in Banjarnegara there are some 378 carpenters and bricklayers, self-employed or employed on a temporary base. In addition there are another fifty specialized construction workers like welders, electricians and painters. Add those being paid for carrying stones and sand at the building site or assisting the *tukang* (skilled craftsmen) and those with a permanent contract from a construction company: the total number of construction workers is easily doubled.

The next part will concentrate upon the craftsmen most important absolutely, the carpenters and the bricklayers. In case they are not engaged in a permanent labour contract, they should be considered petty commodity sector enterprises, usually low in capitalist characteristics (see table 10.1). Construction workers have two markets to operate upon; the private house building market and the government ordered, contractor-organized project market. From their point of view, in Banjarnegara at least, there is no segregation between these two markets, they tend to work intermittently in both sorts of building work, though every construction worker prefers one of the two markets to the other.

Organization differs between the two markets as was stated. First private housing construction; when a *tukang* gets work at constructing someone's home, he is visited by the owner and asked to do so. Someone who intends to have a house built or reconstructed usually goes to a *tukang* living near and they will haggle over the work and the payments. If the *tukang* is already engaged or in case

Table 10.1 Structuring and form characteristics of construction enterprises

Type of enterprise	Scale	Number of capitalist characteristics
Construction worker	Petty	0—2
Contractor	Corporate	4—5

the private builder needs extra craftsmen, the *tukang* will recommend someone else. The *tukang* is allowed to bring his own helpers, who are his trainees usually. Sometimes they make up a more or less permanent team, as Geertz (1963) has described a '*stel*'. Yet above this level lasting bounds are scanty among construction workers.

There are two types of labour arrangements. Either *tukang* and assistants are paid on a daily base (*harian*) or on a contract base: a certain amount of work is decided upon and a fixed price is settled for the *tukang* to complete it. In this latter *borongan*-arrangement the *tukang* himself is paid partly during the job, partly afterwards. *Borongan*-arrangements in general permit a higher profit to the carpenter or the bricklayer. In both sort of arrangements however materials are supplied by the owner of the house. Tools are always brought by the *tukang*. It is hard to say whether the *harian* or *borongan*-arrangement is more common in private building, but it seems that for some sort of jobs, making a well for instance, there is always a *borongan*-deal.

In working for a contractor-company, *harian* and *borongan* arrangements occur too and have a similar content, but here daily payments prevale. There is a ditto system, with the contracting company providing building materials and the craftsmen bringing their own tools. When one opts for temporary employment at a project, the job finding procedure is different however. A *tukang* has to be known by a *mandor* or else go and subscribe at the *mandor's* place. A *mandor* in this respect is an overseer, who is on the contractor's pay-roll. Only very few construction workers are on a permanent wage list of a contractor, apparently the most skilled ones only, moving from project to project. This system tends to employ workers from a wider area than when a private home is built. The majority of the construction workers however will come from near the site where the project is undertaken.

In Banjarnegara wages hardly seem to differ between the markets of private dwelling market and project market. Probably building private homes earns slightly better, as the workers are always provided free meals. More important in determining a *tukang's* remuneration seems to be his skillfulness. If a *tukang's* skill is proven to his employer he can bargain for a better payment per day. People, who have been working for a contractor before, start out at a higher level. When someone begins working for a contractor, his wage might be raised if he turns to be a hard worker. In general carpenters seem to earn more than bricklayers. Table 10.2 illustrates this. A similar conclusion was reached by Nibbering & Schrevel (1981) for rural construction workers.

Table 10.2 Daily returns for a number of male professions in Banjarnegara (estimated)

Chief bricklayer	Rp 2100	Krupuk-vendor	Rp 1500
Bricklayer	1500	Tukang kredit	2000
Bricklayer's assistant	800	Krupuk factory worker	400
Chief carpenter	2250	Tahu factory worker	750
Carpenter	1750	Coconutoil factory worker	750
Carpenter's assistant	1000	Ice factory worker	400
Carpenter furniture factory	1500	Shop assitant	750
Sanddigger	1000	Land labourer	650
Sawyer	800	Porter	1200
Tile factory worker	1000	Becak-driver	1500
Brick factory worker	750	Bamboo-plaider	1250
		Copra-dryer	1250

Though some start as a carpenter's assistant or, graduated from *STM*, set up as a *tukang* outright, a frequent pattern for an aspirant construction worker is to commence working as a bricklayer's assistant. Bricklayers generally need most assistants. Having acquired the skills which on average takes 6 to 12 months, the trainee buys his own equipment and starts as a bricklayer himself. Some widen their opportunities by learning carpentry-work too. This involves an extra invenstment on tools. Table 10.3 shows a carpenter's outfit being more extended than a bricklayer's. On

Table 10.3 A carpenter's and a bricklayer's standard equipment

Bricklayer		Carpenter	
Trowels	Small hammer	Saws	Hammer
Spade	Rule	Chisel	Rule
Pencil	Levelling instrument (10 mtr hose)	Planes	Levelling instrument
Thread		Handdrill	Screw-driver
		Carpenter's square	Pair of pincers
		File	

average a carpenter's tool-kit comes to Rp 45,000, while a bricklayer only has to spend Rp 10,000.

Nearly all tools are bought at a Banjarnegara hardware shop; very few *tukang* seem to use tools that are for sale at the *pasar*. The extra costs for buying carpenter's tools deters some people from entering this profession, despite the better returns and despite the advantages of less strenuous work and having furniture making as an alternative for the slack season. In buying their tools all *tukang* use private sources. There is no credit scheme whatsoever for them. *Tukang* might use their own savings or ask friends or family to lend them the money.

Table 10.2 might also be used to see how a construction worker's earnings stand out among other professions. They seem to be some 50 percent higher, compared to other types of own account work that indulge physical labour and that are taken up by *tukang*, when they are out of work: sanddiggers, land-labourers, sawyers or *becak*-drivers. A construction worker's income is also on a par with professions where commercial skills prevail, though within each line of work returns fluctuate. Even a *tukang's* assistant earns Rp 750—1000 a day, more rewarding than working in Banjarnegara's coconut oil factory for instance. On the other hand it should be noted that being engaged as a construction worker leaves little scope for secondary income opportunities, as one is occupied from 7—12 h and 1—4 h

Though a lot of people have changed their job for working in the building branch, the end of the influx is not yet met, so it seems. Contractors keep complaining about the lack of skilled craftsmen.

10.2 THE PROYEK; AN EXAMPLE OF CLIENTELIST ENTREPRENEURSHIP

If ever a measure to enhance indigeneous entrepreneurship has met success, it has been presidential decree *Kepres 14a* of 1980. This decree identified building trade as a context for the *pribumi* businessmen to sharpen their talents. In fact in Banjarnegara no type of enterprise expanded recently like the building trade did. In August 1982 only 23 contractors were registred at the *Kantor Bupati*. To these 23 contractors one should add 11 branch-quarters of contractor companies, that originate from outside the *kabupaten*. Quite often such contractors are from Semarang. They have a branch-office established in the *kabupaten* to capture orders budgeted below 100 million rupiah, for which being established locally is one of the requirements. In June 1983 the number of contractors had racketed and passed the number of 60 limited liability companies, the majority of them having their office in Banjarnegara town. The town-based contractors include all but one of the *kabupaten's* big contractors; those who are licensed to execute projects with a budget, that surpasses 20 million rupiah. The legal status of at least a *CV*—limited liability company—is obliged to be eligible for a government order and government orders are the corporate sector contractor's sole specialization. So one can assume the registration to be exhaustive.

Why has *Kepres 14a* preceded the rush toward building trade? *Kepres 14a* eased the procedures for indigeneous entrepreneurs to get a working permit. Having such a permit a contractor with landed property to serve as a guarantee can go to the bank and get a 35% advance loan on the cost for completing an order.

This so-called *Kredit Kelayakan* thus solves liquidity problems. Contractors can also apply for other low-interest credit schemes, designated for what is labeled the '*golongan ekonomi lemah*', i.e. the economicly weak. Most contractors use such credit schemes. A considerable part of the *K.I.K.* and *K.M.K.P.* loans issued by the *B.R.I.* bank in Banjarnegara are usurped by contractors. As a guarantee is demanded for both the working permit and the low interest loans, this serves as a restriction to entering building trade. The haves are the ones to start a contractor-*CV*. Congenial ties can serve as a reference too. Many Banjarnegara contractors are acquainted to one another. Some *CV's* appear to be set up to catch a maximum of orders for one's relatives.

But the major reason for the peak in the building trade is it being so lucrative. Contractors interviewed mentioned their monthly profits to be in the Rp 1—10,000,000 range, but it could even be higher. The number of infrastructural projects has staggered in the past decade and as since 1980 Chinese contractors are discriminated to the favour of Javanese entrepreneurs, the chances to make a handsome profit are abundant.

The job of contracting is actually quite simple. Special skills are not involved. A flexible system has developed which enables the *C.V.* that gets hold of a government order to execute the project with a minimum of commitments, if the *CV* desires so. Labourers are employed for the duration of the project only on a daily base and large parts of the work can be subcontracted. In getting building materials consolidating your enterprise is unnecessary too. Transport is the key issue here. It would be an illogical thing to do, to stockpile building materials, especially the most bulky ones like sand, stones and bricks. It reduces transport costs to bring these from production site directly to building site and they are always in ready supply. A contractor can order a building material wholesaler to do so or hire a truck and have the materials fetched. Neither does a contractor have to own a single engine: all equipment necessary for finishing a project can be hired.

Of course most contractors do not take such avoidance of commitments to the extreme. Though leasing machinery is common practice, a number of Banjarnegara contractors own trucks, diesel engines and pumps, confer table 10.4. Of the contractors surveyed all had personnel employed on a permanent base. Usually it concerns staff jobs, but sometimes a select group of overseers and skilled craftsmen has a labour contract as well. With regard to building materials: in this instance some contractors control their inputs too. There is a thin and permeable line between being a contractor and being a building material wholesaler. Some of the medium-sized contractors even have their own exclusive sources of supply from which they sell to other contractors and occasionaly to private persons.

Table 10.4 Commitments of contractors

Contractor	Minimum labourers	Maximum labourers	Value of machinery owned	Own inputs
A	22	97	Rp 15,950,000	yes
B	20	200	Rp 4,500,000	no
C	50	500	Rp 21,000,000	yes
D	30	51	—	no
E	20	250	Rp 14,300,000	yes
F	50	300	Rp 631,300,000	no

Thus one can see the contours of agglomeration benefits in Banjarnegara-town's building trade. Its spatial nucleation in the *kabupaten* capital reflects the importance of keeping close contact to the *kabupaten* government. In fact this is the most crucial point to becoming a successful contractor; getting the attractive projects. The *proyek* taken up by Banjarnegara contractors spring from two sources, the *kabupaten* government and the provincial departments. First we will describe the official procedure for the *kabupaten* government to decide which contractor is allotted the order.

The *kabupaten* government—the *bupati* and his staff—is

entitled to hand out orders from the *Inpres* funds, entailing primary schools, *interkabupaten* roads, *pasar* buildings and policlinics. For this purpose the provincial department puts a lumpsum at the disposal of the *kabupaten* government. This sum is based on the number of primary schools or policlinics or *pasar* buildings to be built. It is more or less fixed as there is blueprint for constructing such buildings. For roads budgets differ. A contractor can apply for an order, if he has the right permit. For all types of construction—bridges, roads, buildings, waterworks—permits have to be obtained that allow a contractor to handle projects of a certain category. These categories are shown in table 10.5. In Banjarnegara only one contractor had a license to operate in the B2-class, for roads and buildings. Projects that surmount Rp 100,000,000 can be

Table 10.5 Contractor permits, for project categories at the kabupaten level

Category	Project's budget
C 2	< Rp 20,000,000
C 1	Rp 20— 50,000,000
B 2	Rp 50—100,000,000

Source: Kantor Pembangunan

applied for by *non-kabupaten* contractors. Below this amount of money projects should be offered to *kabupaten* enterprises. Once a project is announced, contractors are invited to subscribe to it with a detailed plan stating the costs to be made and the material and labour used. This plan is called the *bouwsoom*. In a *bouwsoom* labour costs usually take up a quarter of all expenditures. Table 10.6 gives an example. To this sum a contractor is allowed to add 10% as a reward for this services. For all projects in the C 1 and B 2 categories, the tender is open to every contractor with the right qualifications. A committee decides which contractor will execute

Table 10.6. An example of a bouwsoom for constructing an office building (relative numbers)

	Percentage of total costs	Material costs (%)	Labour costs (%)
Preparation works	3	30	70
Masonry and plastering	36	72	28
Carpentry	35	74	26
Roofing	7	87	13
Finishing (painting, plumbing, electricity)	14	77	23
Other costs	5	73	27

Source: C.V. Angkatan Kaya

the order. The committee consists of the *Bupati* and his staff and people from the local department under which authority the finished building will resort (f.i. Education Department when a primary school is built). The contractor with the lowest price gets the order usually, unless he has a bad reputation. Projects below Rp 20,000,000 are administered by the Department of Public Works of the *Kabupaten (D.P.U.K.)*, that approaches three to five contractors to make an offer. It is said that for these low budget projects contractors without a *CV*-status also qualify, as a subcontractor to the *D.P.U.K.* There are some projects no one is eager to undertake. If there is no candidate, the *D.P.U.K.* will take up the job.

For building projects under charge of departments outside the *kabupaten* the official procedure is quite similar. They include e.g. orders to build local offices and highschools, provincial roads and irrigation infrastructure. The departments most important in this respect: *Dinas P dan K* (Educational Department) in Purwokerto, *Cipta Karya* (Physical Planning) in Cilacap and the provincial *D.P.U.* that has a branch office in Banjarnegara town. A specialized consultant determines the budget and by means of a tender contractors have to do a bid below this sum.

The actual procedure for both *Inpres* and outer *kabupaten* projects delimits these guidelines to mere formalities. Concerning the *Inpres*-projects the contractors themselves distinguish between projects that render a huge profit (*proyek manis*) and projects, that allow a meagre profit only. Roads belong to the first category, while primary schools represent the second category.

As has been outlined, the provincial government puts a budget at the disposal of the *kabupaten* government, that has to be spent on a fixed number of projects. From this sum the *kabupaten* government is allowed to subtract the costs made to appoint and inspect the building site and to organize the tender. Normally these costs should average no more than 8% of the lumpsum, but the building committee—the *bupati* and his secondants—will take 13—15%. This malpractice leaves 85—87% of the budget to the contractor to finish the order. The *bupati's* staff major worry is that all building projects will be executed. To this end they will visit contractors and ask them to take up the projects. Frequently the contractors, that have been approached congregate and settle who gets which project. To compensate for taking up low profit projects, a contractor after having completed some primary schools for instance, is rewarded an order to construct or upgrade a road. Such a project incurs a 25—35% profit margin. This high profit stems from saving on material expenditures. Using less materials than stated in the building plan—a thinner layer of asphalt—is the major fraude. So it comes as no surprise that most roads deteriorate rapidly after completion. Other clauses to make extra profit; purchasing building materials of a minor quality, for a price below that stated in the *bouwsoom* and the fact that construction plans issued by the *kabupaten* government take no account of material that is already available at the building site; constructing a road is often asphalting a gravel-road an one can use this for foundation. In erecting a building, like an *Inpres* primary school for instance, chances for such abuse are less. Making profit is limited to buying cheap building materials and does not outreach 5—10%. Because, as one contractor put it, one cannot leave out building materials unseenly. After some primary schools in the *kabupaten* collapsed while being completed, people are more watchful.

Two pecularities of this informal process of project allotment should be noted. First, within the whole process money-transfer between contractors and civil servants is limited. Secondly, as a contractor is demanded to take up the construction of some less profitable school buildings, before he is eligible for a profitable road project, surplus (preparation costs) tends to level out between the *kabupaten*-level departments concerned. It seems that for those projects, that are allocated by departments at province level, no such leveling effect is in force.

Within the construction branche, the image of the clientelist entrepreneur comes to the fore: absence of free competition, the dependency on government orders, the weight of connections. The success of the presidential decree *Kepres 14a* seems to be very superficial only. It does not seem to be the best avenue to enhance indigeneous entrepreneurship. The need to organize one's enterprise efficiently and keen is absent: building trade grows with speed of speculation. As a contractor is dependent on his bureaucratic patrons and as the number of projects can fluctuate widely, a contractor will tend to short term investments only. It refrains him from consolidating relations with labourers and suppliers.

The present system of handing out government building orders has some serious consequences. The squandering of building funds is obvious. Only 60—70% of the money designated for *Inpres*-roads is actualy spent on the roads to name the worst example. Another consequence is that the way, the budgets for each project are settled, renders some of them very attractive, while others are not attractive at all. As the project budgets are hardly adapted to their locations, pre-eminently primary schools at isolated villages or in the northern part of the *kabupaten* are not popular among contractors. Remembering the weight of transport costs, this is easily explained. The elevated northern part of the *kabupaten* being unattractive also is correlated to its shortage of sources of building materials. Bricks do not dry as quick in this in this area and the ma-

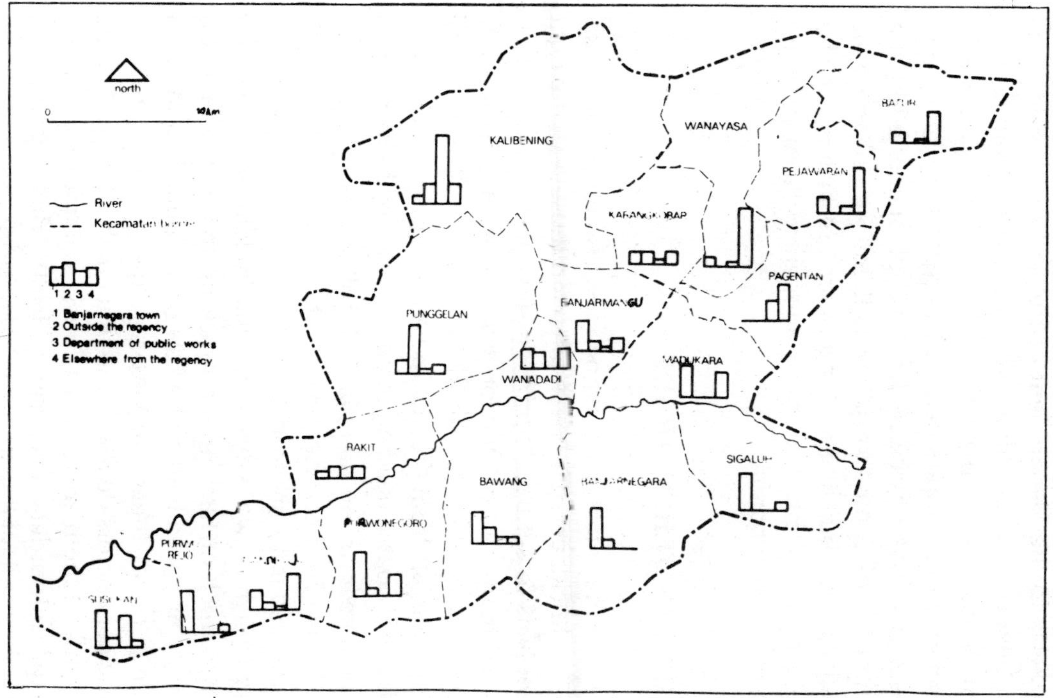

Map 10.1. Projects in kabupaten Banjarnegara: origin of executing contractors

Source: Kantor Pembangunan

jor rivers flow too brisk to take sand and stones out. Usually if a Banjarnegara contractor takes up a project up north, he is eager to subcontract large parts of it to local people. Quite often contractors leave such projects to the Department of Public Works or to non-Banjarnegara town contractors, that have been able to spring up in these northern subdistricts. Map 10.1 shows this. For in general for a contractor having your address near to the seat of the *kabupaten* government is a pro. The service centre concept, suggested by the spatial concentration of contractor-*CV*'s, is therefore only partially true. The Banjarnegara building entrepreneurs are inclined to the most rewarding projects only and these happen to lie outside the northern part of the *kabupaten*.

10.3 BUILDING MATERIAL TRADE

The peak in the construction branch has inspired many to skill as a carpenter or bricklayer. The peak attracted those with the right capital and contacts to set up a contractor-*CV*. It had a spin-off in building material trade and production (subject of paragraph 11.1) as well. Because of the high transport expenses, a contractor will prefer building materials from the *kabupaten*. Diagram 10.2 depicts that most bulky and coarse building materials used by Banjarnegara contractors originate from the *kabupaten*. Roofing tiles are the major exception and they are from Kebumen. Those inputs with a high value added per kilogram are from elsewhere.

A contractor has two ways of getting building materials; he can use his own truck or hire one and pick up the materials at the place where they are produced or he can order a building material wholesaler and have them delivered. The building material wholesalers the contractors deal with, are habitually of the corporate sector type. Some of them are former Chinese contractors, who are denied government orders ever since 1980. Building material wholesale is often combined with a hardware store. Such an enterprise, might gender equally high profits: Banjarnegara's richest man

Diagram 10.2 Building material supply to Banjarnegara town contractor-companies

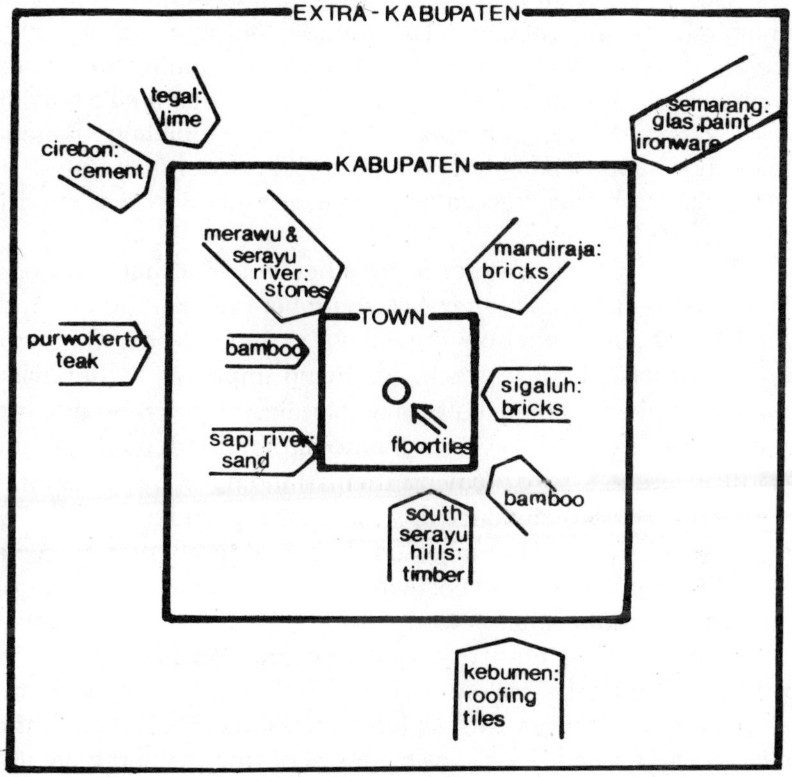

is a contractor, but number two is a building material wholesaler. A wholesaler's stock is diverse. The expensive extra *kabupaten* inputs (except roofing tiles) they will have in ready supply; a contractor will always recur to a wholesaler to get these (unless he is wholesaler himself). Other inputs they will order from producers of building materials. These small producers are working on request. For most the step towards working piecework for a wholesaler is a small one however. Some wholesalers in Banjarnegara have now taken up organizing production themselves. For instance: they might have obtained a concession to exploit part of one of the *kabupaten's* rivers, like pre-eminently the Sapi River or the Merawu River for winning stones and shingles. The sanddiggers working at such a place are paid per cubic metre. For wholesalers putting your name to a certain patch sometimes is a gamble; but if in due time a building site is planned near, it pays off. Some building material wholesalers—apparently not the Chinese—extend business in another direction too, becoming contractors, as is commented in paragraph 10.2.

Timber trade is distinct from other building material trade. Timber merchants usually specialize in timber only and do not trade anything else. It is the only building material from within the *kabupaten* that is kept in stock, as drying improves its durability. Contrasting other building material wholesale, considerable advance payments are involved—even to the point of a trader buying young trees at a farmer's yard, leaving them standing there for another 2—5 years to be maintained by the farmer. Under such an arrangement—it resembles *rampasan* described in chapter 8—a tree costs 40% of what it would cost when fully grown, so we were told by timber merchants interviewed. One of them even had agents to buy the trees. Most timber in Banjarnegara comes from the impoverished Southern Hills and concerns albizzia, a species that matures within 10 years. Not all farmers sell their trees, before they are big enough to cut. Some call in a *stel* of sawyers and have their trees sawn into shelves and next sell the shelves. All sawyers questioned were paid on a piecework base, making Rp 500—1000 a day. Other farmers sell their fully grown trees to traders, who arrange the sawing and marketing part. Earnings are shared usually, under such a deal. At present timber is the only building material from the *kabupaten* put up for sale in other districts. Some timber, especially timber from the State Forest, is exported to the Cilacap region. But most of it is used by Banjarnegara's builders and industries. There is import of timber too; teak and mahogony are brought in from elsewhere.

Thus far we have dealt with building materials for the *proyek*. Private builders might also order at corporate sector wholesalers mentioned above, but it is not customary. The polarization within the construction branch comes to the front again. Private builders have another type of suppliers, who are of a petty commodity scale. It includes a trader in secondhand roofing tiles that was interviewed. Farmers selling fresh-cut shelves at the tiny *pasar kayu* (timber market) are included too or timber merchants having trees cut on customer's request. Sand and stone diggers belong to it, who work at parts of the river, that are not accessible to motorized traffic, and therefore unattractive as a concession. These sanddiggers supply fellow villagers, whose building site might be out of reach of truck transport too. Some petty scale brickmakers operate in the same margins. In a small town like Banjarnegara such a pattern is still possible, since walking distance from sites of production to private building sites are not too long. When such petty commodity sources are not quite near or road accessibility facilitates otherwise, however, a private builder might turn to a '*leveransir*' (supplier), someone that on request hires a truck and will deliver sand and stones. When bricks are required, a deal is made before production, as quality and price differ.

In the next chapter we will pay attention to building material industries. Suffice it here to say that the segmentation within construction trade is mirrored within building material production.

10.4 AFTER THE BOOM

Will the boom in the construction branch last? Some prognosises were bleak in 1983; Indonesia's oil revenues dwindled; a balance of payments deficit was a fait accompli and savings on national expenditures were necessary. One indication: In July 1983 the Mrica hydro-power project, financed by export credit from Sweden and Britain, was temporarily stopped to negotiate for a new contract in line with Indonesia's payment perils. *Inpres* is ultimately paid for by the central government. Though allocation of its funds went on, and is hard to stop since it serves as an additional payment to an important part of the civil servants corps, a change in tempo is not unlikely.

Will the construction boom trigger off something lasting or will everything collapse as soon as government orders collapse? We have argued that the clientelist entrepreneur, thriving on government orders since 1980, is not an innovator liable to set up an alternative enterprise outside the scope of institutional protection. A decline in government contracts might mean their farewell to business.

At a fast rate people have become absorbed in construction labour. Banjarnegara town is not a specific labour absorptive growth centre in this respect; both urbanites and rural dwellers have taken up bricklaying or carpentry. The skills these people have acquired are not very unique, neither very sophisticated, as stands out from the hydro-power dam attracting highly skilled construction labour from outside the *kabupaten*. Should work opportunities at contractor-*CV*'s diminish, a number of construction workers will have to change professin probably, or try for constructing someone's home; but the labour market might be flooded.

Resuming we think that though license policy enabled the construction sector to become the core of propulsive growth, we expect that this complex looses its reasons of existence soon as government orders decline.

Chapter 11

THE REAL EKONOMI LEMAH; INDUSTRY

Small-scale industry is frequently supposed to remedy all sorts of problems; high unemployment rates, shortage of managerial skills, basic needs not being met. Its growth is probably considered a panacea, because problems seem so present and small scale industry seems so absent.

In their study on home and small scale industry in Central Java Thoma & Lempelius (1977) however take another stand, stressing the low prospects for labour absorption in the petty manufacturing sector, because (sic) it still is so small. They estimate a meagre 1.3% of the growth of the labour force is going to be engaged in the branch. As their figures are based on enterprises enlisted at the *Dinas Perindustrian*, they underestimate the branch's size. In table 11.1 we compare this registration—in Banjarnegara the most complete—with our count on industrial enterprises.

Taking into account the unregistered enterprises and petty trade, that is sustained by petty industry, the branch is a bigger employer than held for by Thoma & Lempelius. But could small scale industry relieve unemployment in Banjarnegara town? A substantial part of the people looking for a job are highschool graduates. Small scale industry seldom provides jobs, that match their aspirations. Table 11.2 presents unemployment figures for the male population. It is based on the voluntary ascription for a job

Table 11.1 Small scale industries in Banjarnegara twn according to registration at Dinas Perindustrian (June 1982) and according to the count on enterprises (February 1983)

	Dinas	Count		Dinas	Count
BUILD MAT INDUSTRY			*OTHER INDUSTRY*		
floortile production	9	9	tailor	58	123
brickmaking	14	20	shoe-maker	2	13
bamboo-plaiting	5	35	woodcraft	4	7
sanddiging	—	15	iron furniture	3	6
			printshop	6	6
FOOD INDUSTRY			cock shuttle	1	3
coconut sugar	4	4	ceramic	—	8
tahu processing	11	15	tool production	—	6
tempe processing	76	71	stamp-making	—	6
ice production	23	40			
krupuk production	40	13	*REPAIR*		
kecap production	—	2	car-motorbike repair	3	23
other foodprocessing	11	123	bike-becak repair	12	21
			wielding & smithing	—	36
AGRO INDUSTRY			tv-radio repair	8	13
rice mill	7	4	watch repair	2	24
copra-drying	10	12	tyre repair	—	7
			miscelleneous	3	13
			(Total	310	729)

Source: Dinas Perindustrian, Count on Enterprises.

at the Mrica hydropower project. A wide range of unskilled, semi-skilled and skilled jobs were offered. Wage prospects were good, so the registration reflects the need for (better) work. Unemployment runs at 7.7% of the male population of 15 years of age and older in Banjarnegara town.

Does Banjarnegara's industry differ from those in the *kabupaten*? As map 11.1 depicts for the southern part of the *kabupaten*, and map 5.5 based on different statistical data for the whole of the kabupaten: main strongholds of rural industry are coconut sugar production, bamboo processing and building material industry. These rural industries are geared to what is in abundant supply locally. In contrast, the composition of the town's secondary

Table 11.2. Male persons looding for a job at the Mrica-project by level of education (February 1983)

No education	54
Elementary School	117
Junior Highschool	146
Junior Technical School	12
Senior Highschool	169
Senior Economic School	148
Senior Technical School	129
Academic	35
Other	35
Total	845

Source: FBSI Banjarnegara

sector seems oriented to small town urban demand: food-processing industries make up the hub of activities. Still urban industry has a diversified character compared to rural production activities, where often whole villages specialize in one type of industry.

It is instructive to compare home industry in the *kabupaten* at the turn of the century with the situation today (see table 11.3). Some changes stand out. Assuming the Mindere Welvaarts-verslagen give an accurate overview, the branch seems to have grown substantially, which comes as no surprise, regarding the tripling of population figures and marginalization within agriculture. The Mindere Welvaartsverslagen mention that the needs of the population were sufficiently covered at that time by agricultural production. Simple agro-industries existed in 1907, and continue to exist until today, even to an enlarged extent. On the other hand, artisanal

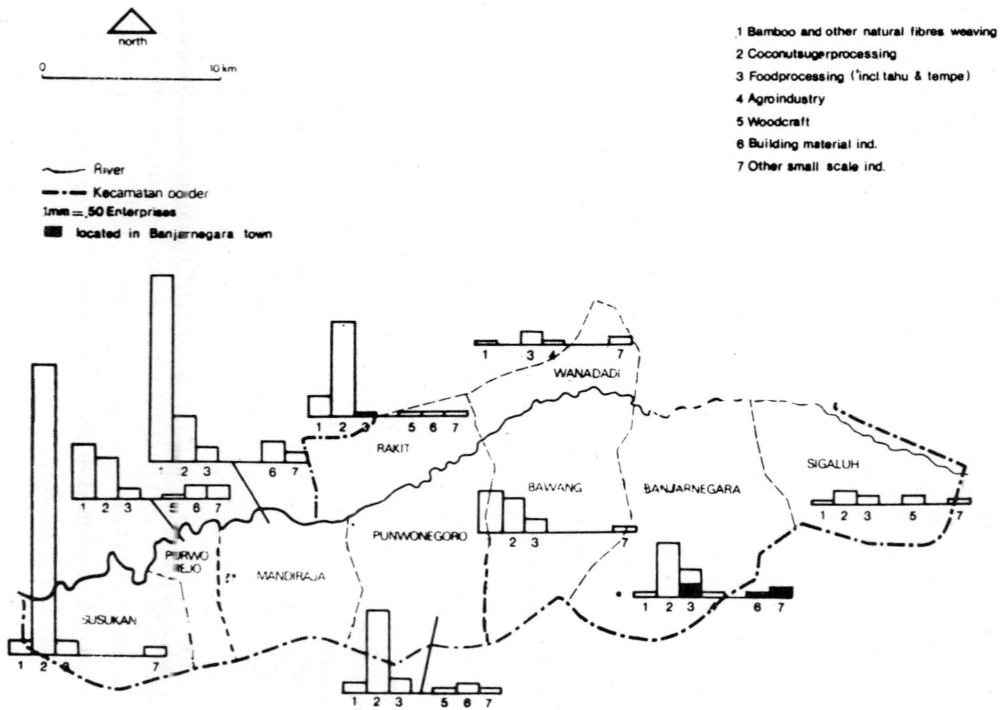

Map 11.1. Small scale industry in southern part of kabupaten Banjarnegara per kecamatan (November 1982).

Source: Dinas Perindustrian.

Table 11.3 Small scale industry in kabupaten Banjarnegara[1)] 1907

Activity	Number of enterprises	Kecamatan
Coconut oil production	23	Rakit, Punggelan, Banjarnegara
Peanut oil production	30	Bawang
Copra drying	47	Rakit, Wonodadi
Coconut sugar production	76	Banjarmangu, Banjarnegara
Aren sugar production	87	Punggelan
Lime burning	one desa	Banjarnegara
Roofing tiles production	14	Banjarmangu, Rakit, Wonodadi
Stone carving	22	Sigaluh, Madukara
Bamboo plaiting	81	Bawang, Punggelan
Mat weaving	30	All lowland kecamatan
Brass shop	12	Banjarmangu
Gold & silver smithing	26	Banjarnegara, Rakit, Sigaluh
Forge	32	Sigaluh, Wonodadi, Rakit
Kris making	1	Wonodadi
Batik industry	350	All over the kabupaten
Embroidering	1	Banjarnegara

1) Kawedanan Purworejo-Klampok is not included, by then it was part of the Banyumas regency.

Source: Mindere Welvaartsverslagen 1907.

activities, like *batik* cloth production and gold and silver smithing are virtually extinct and had already disappeared in Banjarnegara in the thirties (Memorie van Overgave 1938). At the turn of the century dispersed production and low surplusses urged intermediary traders to organize the marketing of secondary activities, on which they had a tight grip. Regional and local *pasar* were the main trade channels for these commodities. This contrasts the present situation where some trade in secondary produce by-passes the *pasar* system.

At present, medium and large scale industry is rare in *kabupaten* Banjarnegara, but the town locates some: there is a medium-sized furniture factory, a brickproducer's association and in the more than. 100 employees-class a coconut oil factory. Apart from Banjarnegara town only Purworejo-Klampok is endowed with medium-scale industry. This chapter will end with a paragraph on the coconutoil factory to write the Banjarnegara history of large scale industry. At times there have been prospects, that it would add up to more than that. At the start of the century the imperative was noted for a tapioca factory in Banjarnegara to process regional cassava surpluses. And in the sixties the town was a candidate for a state-owned textile mill: it is the plant that is in Salatiga now. Besides two of Purworejo-Klampok's medium sized industries came into being in Banjarnegara: ceramic industry had a false start in Banjarnegara just before 1942 (Van Baal 1986) and the Chinese owned cigarette industry moved to Purworejo-Klampok in 1965, where it matured. In this chapter small scale industry will be dealt with first however, as it is much more important numerically. Two types of petty commodity industry receive special attention, for they make up the lot of Banjarnegara's town small scale industry; building material industry (including woodcraft) and foodprocessing, subject of paragraph 11.1 and 11.2 respectively.

11.1 BUILDING MATERIAL INDUSTRY AND WOODCRAFT

Banjarnegara's trade in building materials was reviewed in paragraph 10.3. At that place it was shown that some local industry was organized by wholesalers. A considerable part of the building material producers, however, has not lost independence. The town's building materials industry includes sanddiggers, brickmakers, bamboo-plaiters and floortile factories. Related to this type of activity is woodcraft: both carpenters and furniture factories. Table 11.4 shows how the enterprises interviewed classify according to structuring and form characteristics.

Brickmaking and sanddigging sites are found at that town's border. Just so for bamboo-plaiting, which is taken up in two

Table 11.4 Structuring and form characteristics of building material industries interviewed

Type of enterprise	Scale	Number of capitalist characteristics
Sanddigging	Petty	1
Bamboo-plaiting	Petty	1—3
Lumbersawing	Petty	2—4
Brickmaking	Petty-Corporate	2—5
Furniture-making		
Carpenter	Petty	2—3
Factory	Petty-Corporate	4—5
Floortile production	Petty-Corporate	4

isolated hamlets, that, though within the town limits, definitely have a rural outlook. Furniture craftsmen are ubiquitous. Furniture factories and floortile factories' dispersion is confined to the town's centre.

Bamboo-plaiters, sanddiggers and furniture carpenters are one man—one enterprise activities in Banjarnegara town. Other building material industries are employers. Thoma & Lempelius (1977) state that small scale industries' pays are low. So table 10.1 did show; wages at small scale industries are not on a par with construction work, and are even below what a petty trader earns. What is more, most small scale industries employ workers on piece work base only. But what do the bosses earn? Leaving out own-account workers, profit margins in small scale building materials industries seem to be worth the effort, so table 11.5 proves.

Organization forms differ among building material industries. Solo production like the non-wholesaler organized sanddigging, which is found at the Serayu River in Banjarnegara town, is most simple. A sanddigger will take sand and stones from the river and carry them with his carrying pole to his customer. Stones that are selected have a more or less fixed size: when split, the halves have

Table 11.5. Average monthly profit margins in building material industry

Floortile factories	Rp 260,000
Brickmaking industries	Rp 221,800
Furniture factories	Rp 480,000

to fit in a wall. Sand will be dried one day on the river bank to avoid unnecessary carrying. Sanddigging is not a favourite job amongst youngsters to take up. They prefer construction work, which is less coarse and invokes better returns.

Bamboo-plaiting has only a slightly more complex organization. Bamboo is purchased in the village and split, before it is plaited into mats. Such mats—there are different varieties—are used for ceilings, for covering floors or as walls in low budget houses. Sometimes a bamboo-plaiter has paid helpers. Mat weavers sell to building material wholesalers or to small contractors. Their bargaining position is bright compared to their colleagues in the second bamboo-plaiting hamlet, who specialize in making disposable baskets to be used for Banjarnegara fruit export. They get orders from a merchant and are not permitted to sell to other traders, unless at a higher price. Basket-weavers' remunerations are low compared to mat-weavers'.

In brickmaking there is more diversity. The brickmaking process is not very sophisticated in Banjarnegara. It involves moulding clay into the right shapes and then spreading some sand over the lumps to prevent them from sticking. Next, the bricks are piled and covered to protect them from rain. After the bricks have dried sufficiently in the sun, they are baked. Fuel-wood and labour are the most expensive inputs.

Organization alternatives in brick making have a wide range. At the one end a man taking up both production—even fetching the sand from the river himself—and marketing. At the other end an entrepreneur who confines to sales only, employing casual workers executing jobs piecework for him. In Banjarnegara a group of brothers, managing ten brickmaking sites in total, even cooperate as far as having the bricks baked at a central location. Baking is obviously the most expert and expensive part of the process. Like bamboo-plaiting and sanddigging, brickmaking incurs very elementary tools only, which costs do not outreach Rp 2000 per worker. Starting a brickmaking enterprise, however, involves other expenditures, that impede access for the lower income echelons, unless they have a suitable plot of land of their own. Leasing a clayey plot of *sawah* land requires that one is able to pay at least Rp 50.000 a year for rent. Usually after two years a piece of land is exhausted. Brickmaking enterprises expand or shrink according to the volume of capital the entrepreneur can dispose of.

Investments in floortile industry amount to even a great deal more. A hydraulic press is needed. This will cost at least Rp 500,000 for a secondhand one or Rp 2,000,000 for a new press. The major inputs are cement, trass and fine-grained sand, which is taken from the Merawu River or the Serayu River or even from outside the *kabupaten*. One floortile factory even had its own concession, on which it employed piecework sanddiggers. Because of the high investments, starting a floortile factory is priviliged to a happy few: well-to-do businessmen and (former) high-ranked civil officers, who have access to credit or family capital. Their investment will pay off, as could be seen from table 11.5. The nine Banjarnegara floortile factories provide casual labour opportunities, with low remunerations. Floortile factories supply contractors and building material wholesalers. Only one—a petty scale—factory interviewed stated that their major customers were private persons of higher income groups. Its tiles fetched a higher prize and were of better quality.

The last item of this paragraph is woodcraft, especially the production of furniture, which organization bears close resemblance to building trade. As in building trade there are two markets; one that constitutes of institutional orders and another made up of private customers. An order to make the inventory of an office or a school is seldom allotted to a petty scale enterprise; commonly a *CV* takes up the production of the furniture. Such a *CV* might operate as a building contractor too. The biggest Banjarnegara furniture factory employed 25 *tukang* at the time of survey. Its machinery was worth up to Rp9,600,000 and included an elaborate collection of electric tools. Such mechanization is absent in the non-institutional market. Among Banjarnegara people the furniture most popular nowadays is the iron frame type of chairs and benches with plastic covering or—more posh—wood-carved Jepara style furniture. However, in Banjarnegara there are no craftsmen skilled enough to do such carving. So this ornamented furniture is imported from the Jepara and Solo área as a whole or in parts, to be assembled in the town, as is done in one 10 employees enterprise that was interviewed. The fancy wood-carved furniture is very much in fashion among the civil servants. It is often bought on instalments, but most suppliers complain of payment troubles. Coarser, less decorative furniture is usually Banjarnegara made. Wooden counters, cupboards and all objects that have to match a customer's special wishes are made in petty-sized enterprises. Carpenters—some alternate woodcraft with employment as a construction worker—purchase all inputs themselves, or occasionally get timber from their customer. Daily returns fluctuate, but are in the Rp 1500 range. Thus they earn no more than those *tukang* employed in a furniture workshop. Such workshops might offer work to 4—5 carpenters. All materials are bought by the owner of the workshop, who is responsible for selling the furniture too. Like the solitary carpenter and the furniture factory, the workshops are orientated to local demand and working on order prevales for them too.

It strikes how building material industry resembles construction trade. No wonder the many crossovers. In building material industry too, institutional orders have the effect of favouring corporate sector enterprises and as soon as a manager can rely on such orders standardization and mechanization come in the scope in this industry.

In general labour conditions in building material industry are strenuous. Work is hard and remunerations are low. For those who are employed, occupation lasts as long as orders permit. In most activities there is an adverse influence of the rainy season. Bricks will not dry as fast for instance and wood-supply is irregular in the wet season. In sanddigging there is a seasonal handicap too; in the erosion-prone Serayu Uplands water is hardly retained and when rain starts to fall, the river soon flows too vehement to get the sand out, as all is covered by water. So on balance the dry season is more favourable for the building material branch. Fortunately this is the slack season of the agricultural calendar.

11.2 FOODPROCESSORS AND SMALL FOOD INDUSTRIES

Within Banjarnegara's modest-sized industry foodprocessing takes the foremost stand in absolute numbers. In the previous paragraph it was shown how within building material industry forms of organization differ. In foodprocessing, the options taken reflect a similar pluriformity. At the bottom end there are petty foodprocessors, mainly women, specialized in making one of the many dishes the Javanese cuisine consists of. Next in scale are small factories, like those making *tahu* or *krupuk*. At the final end of the scale in the Banjarnegara context, there is a coconut oil plant, subject of the next paragraph. Table 11.4 depicts how increasing scale coincides with the capitalist mode of production coming to the fore.

Foodprocessors number just short of 300 in Banjarnegara-town, likely even more for these very small-scale, home-type activities are liable to be underrepresented in our count of enterprises. For many women foodprocessing is the prime alternative to petty trade in making a living. Peluso (1982) showed how women switched to such occupations, when their children's age forced them to stay at home. It does not take too much effort to set up as a foodprocessor. Production concerns familiar recipees and the common kitchen utensils are used. Yet the equipment is a paramount and

Table 11.6. Structuring and form characteristics of food-industries interviewed

	Scale	Number of capitalist characteristics
Foodprocessors		
Tempe	Petty	0—1
Porridge	Petty	0—2
Snacks and meals	Petty	1—3
Small food factories		
Krupuk	Corporate	2—3
Kecap	Petty	3—4
Tahu	Petty	3—4
Ice cream	Petty-Corporate	3—4
Ice blocks	Corporate	4
Large scale industry		
Coconut oil	Corporate	6

constant source of expenditures, next to buying the ingredients. As many foodprocessors perpetually lack the money to purchase cast iron or brass pots and pans, they have to replace their aluminium kitchenware every one or two months.

There is an overwhelming variety of items prepared by the foodprocessors; sweets, snacks drinks up to ready-made meals. Some producers specialize in delicacies, consumed by the town's civil servants elite. Among the foodprocessors *tempe* producers are a major group. They are distinct from other enterprises in this size category, in that *tempe* is not a ready made consumable product, like porridge or snacks. *Tempe* can be made from almost anything put to ferment, but *tempe* made from soybeans is most common. On average a *tempe gedele* producer will use 3—5 kg soybeans a day, larger producers process 10 kg. The beans are soaked and boiled twice. The soybeans, now transformed to pulp, are cooled of and mixed with instant yeast. It is put into cut banana-leaves, that are closed with a bamboo string. These small sackets are left for one day, before they are sold. Most *tempe* processors sell to *warong* keepers or to vendors at the *pasar*, with whom permanent relations exist. Only a few processors retail their *tempe* themselves, covering one of the cheap places at the *pasar kota* for instance. Generally however quantities bought per customer are so small, that it would take a *tempe* processor a day to retail her daily output herself. *Warong* are an outlet to a host of petty food processors. Usually only those preparing ready-made meals, like porridge and *sate*, go out and try to find customers of their own. A porridge maker's route will be limited to the *desa* she lives in She might carry two kinds of porridge, two liter of each kind. Older porridge-vendors stay at home and sell to neighbours, who come to her home to fetch a plate of porridge. One porridge maker we met, however, made the jump, preparing much more porridge and employing a porter to carry the pans, while she did the selling. Such paid labour is exceptional in non-proletarianized foodprocessing. A son or a daughter might assist, but they are not on the pay roll. Profits are low in the branch and do not surpass those in hawking or petty pasar trade. Besides there is the risk of left-overs on bad days. Foodprocessorss cater for a very local and perishable demand.

Most foodprocessors will buy their inputs from hawkers or at the *pasar*, especially the fresh ones, or at a *warong*. Only some specialized items are bought at a *toko*. Two inputs are very crucial and should be mentioned. First are banana-leaves for wrapping up the foodstuff or to be used as a plate. Foodprocessors will take the leaves from their garden or buy them from farmers, who peddle leaves in *kampong*. Some foodprocessors complained of leaves being seasonally in short supply. Another crucial input is the wood used for fuel. Like lumber, fuelwood comes from the Southern Serayu Hills. Farmers transport their bushel of wood to town, taking breaks at fixed places. When during such a break they are approached by a potential customer, and a deal is made, they will follow him/her and deliver the load at his/her place. Nowadays one bushel costs Rp 500—600. Most wood is cut from gardens or illicitly taken from state forests, threatening their anti-erosion function. Erosion is a constant worry in the Serayu Hills. Some programs have been launched to combat these problems. The introduction of a fuel-efficient stove has been one of them. Some people argued that foodprocessors and small scale industries should be a target group in such a program, which we think is very just.

In small food industries, the second group distinghuished in table 11.6, wood is the foremost fuel too. Use to electricity or kerosene power is as yet limited. Among the *tahu* factories interviewed for instance, only one enterprise has begun to mechanize by installing a diesel-driven grinder for soybeans. Grinding is the first step in *tahu* production. In the semi-mechanized enterprise, the other steps are still done by manual labour. The soaked and grinded soybean-pulp is heated on a wood fire, before it is filtered. Afterwards it is put to settle, so the water can be taken off. The sediment is pressed dry to become *tahu*. The partial mechanization was paid for with a *K.M.K.P.*-loan. It gave this particular *tahu* enterprise an advantage over other producers, that stuck to human labour gri. The volume of soybeans processed daily does shows the difference: 200 kg to 60 kg. This increase in production was realized without workers being dismissed or attracted. Most *tahu*-industries employ some 3—5 labourers, who are paid piecework. Wages range Rp 750—1000 a day. The semi-mechanized factory is no different in this respect.

One significant difference between the mechanized and semi-mechanized enterprises interviewed, was their system of selling. The 200 kg enterprise only has traders for customers: Five *bakul* selling on commission drop in at the *tahu* factory every morning, the other half of the *tahu* output is brought to a number of *pasar*, where permanent trader-customers pay cash for the *tahu* bought. The 60 kg enterprise retailed the *tahu* itself; on a couple of *pasar* people from this family enterprise have a fixed place on the floor. *Tahu* entrepreneurs not only sell *tahu*, but sell the residue left after filtering the ground soybeans too. *Tempe undeg* is made from it, a cheap variety of fermented soybean cake. Petty *tempe undeg* processors will cluster near *tahu* factories. The residue is also sold for fish fodder.

The level of cooperation is quite high among *tahu* producers. In *desa* Karangtengah, where a number of *tahu* industries cluster, appointments are made on what to pay a labourer, which trader will be sold to and what price is to be reckoned. On an official plane there is even a state provoked organization, *Kopti*, to which *tempe* producers can subscribe too. Mostly medium-scale producers have done so. The *Kopti* however is still in statu nascendi. At the moment its major task is supplying small quantities of soybeans to its members for a reduced price.

Krupuk producers do not concert like that, even though most entrepreneurs have a common origin. Like the *tukang kredit*, most *krupuk* producers are Tasik Malaya people; there are some 10 in Banjarnegara. Most relate still strongly to Tasik Malaya, thus local spin-off is reduced. While *tahu* producers will buy their cast iron pans at a forge in Purbolinggo, *krupuk* producers will order thick aluminium ones in Tasik Malaya. *Krupuk* entrepreneurs interviewed, organized their own retail network, employing Tasik *krupuk* vendors. Such hawkers carry big containers to transport the fried *krupuk* to *warong*, *toko* and restaurants in town and at the countryside nearby. At such outlets the *krupuk* producer might have its own painted jar stationed, an exceptional instance of sales promotion. A *warong* earns Rp 1 per piece sold, and so a hawker does. As a hawker on commission might sell 1500—2000 pieces a day, his work pays off reasonably and no risks are involved.

One of the problems most pregnant in *krupuk* industry is finding labourers. Since the work demands some months of experience, the entrepreneur cannot employ just anyone. The troublesome task is operating the press; after a mix of tapioca and spices is made, it is put in a container, which has a number of holes. By putting some pressure on this container—there are various systems—, some of the paste comes out and is shaped by one swift stroke of the hand. This job requires considerable skill. Next the pieces are dried in the sun for three days, before they are fried on a stove and then swell up, thus rendering the famous light *krupuk*.

Krupuk enterprises are an example of corporate sector enterprises, dominated by pre-capitalist characteristics. Turnover and profits are high in the industry. All entrepreneurs questoined saved the money for setting up, while hawking in one of Java's big cities.

While *krupuk* industry is run by Tasik Malaya people and *tahu* and *tempe* are produced by semi-rural entrepreneurs, in ice production a distinct group can be discerned too, that we tentavily label petty bureaucratic entrepreneurs. Ice cream manufacturing is the scene of smaller scale producers taking over from corporate sector enterprises. The production of ice creams and ice blocks used for cooling has for decennia been the monopoly of a few Chinese owned plants. Quantities produced and prices were settled among them. In large cooling boxes, kept at low temperature by electric refrigerators ice was made. Thermoscans filled with ice creams were given to agents, who distributed them, even as far as the Kalibening district in the Northern Serayu Mountains. They passed through *warong* and children-peddlers, before all the stock was sold. This system was lubricated by commission. At the end of the day the remainder is returned and the quantity sold was paid to the producer.

Recently the tide has turned and one Chinese plant has already withdrawn from making ice creams. Ice creams are increasingly made by home-producers using a freezer. The lot of these producers are civil servants families. A civil servant's regular salary entitles him to a bank-loan, to be invested in a freezer. The major and critical input is electricity. As a household's wattage is limited, level of production is finite, unless they should relay on batteries or a generator. Ice cream production is a rewarding activity. Profits average Rp 3000 a day in the enterprises we interviewed, and repaying within one year the debt that is made at purchasing the freezer is no problem. Most petty ice cream producers exploit very cheap labour; children and servants assist the spouse-producer and 'wages' range Rp 150—250 daily. In retailing the home producers resemble ice factories, though due to the smaller output, intermediary agents can be skipped. *Warong* and hawkers sell on commission. A youngster, full time engaged in selling, can make Rp750 a day. The commission arrangement seems an asset for them. Compare their position to an independent *es dawet* vendor. *Es dawet* is a local speciality; an icy longdrink made of crumbled ice, biscuits, fruits and flavourings. Bad weather leaves an *es dawet* vendor at a heavy loss, for he cannot return his day's left-over, contrary to an ice-cream hawker engaged in a commision relationship.

It seems that patterns described for *krupuk, tahu* and ice manufacturing resemble those of other small scale food industry in Banjarnegara as well. Almost all of them orientate to a regional circulation at the most. Small scale food industries that export to outside the kabupaten are a rarity in the town. As in-town demand is varied, due to the presence of a substantive middle class, this leaves much scope to both petty scale food industries and foodprocessors. Food industry does not seem to be related to what is in supply locally, in contrast to agro-industry. So it is no wonder that a lot of the inputs are bought outside the *pasar* circuit, and come from *warong* (for foodprocessors) or from *toko* (for food industries especially). Sometimes however, when the major input is in abundant supply locally, for instance coconut sugar in case of *kecap* production, the enterprise will deal with village traders directly.

In Banjarnegara's building material industry too selling is confined to a local market. In contrast to food industries, these industries are tied to where the raw materials are found and cannot easily shift to where demand is highest. In both activities profit margins are attractive. Besides offering labour opportunities themselves, they provoke employment in trade. This applies to food industry in particular, since entities traded are small. Retailing is often taken up by a host of hawkers, that make a living of selling the manufactured food. Building material industry's multiplier will not be as large, for its customers are contractors or private builders, and seldom petty intermediaries.

11.3 THE COCONUT OIL FACTORY: LIVING HISTORY

In 1930 a coconutoil factory was established at the border of Banjarnegara town, in what used to be the chinese quarter. Ever since the history of Banjarnegara's large scale industry can be equated with the ups and downs of the coconutoil plant. All other attempts to start large scale industry have been shortlived in Banjarnegara.

At the plant coconut oil is made from copra. Copra is produced by numerous petty entrepreneurs. They process their own coconuts or purchase them—often with some advance money from copra traders. The copra producers, that were interviewed, process 250—5000 coconuts weekly, for 7—8 months a year. The other months the producers were engaged in agriculture. Generally returns are meagre. Family labour is common. Turning coconuts into copra is a time consuming process. The best nuts to be used are 12—13 months old. They are split in two before processing, the halves will be dried in the sun for one day before they are heated on a stove for a couple of hours. After the heating the husks can be taken off, to be used for fuel, and the flesh will be dried in the sun for another five days. By then it still contains 10—15% liquid. So, when the copra producers have sold their copra, the trader usually has to do some extra drying, as the factory does not accept copra with a moisture content of over 10%.

The factory is the sole user of copra in the *kabupaten*, but is not allowed to buy from farmers directly: intermediary traders cannot be by-passed. There are two sorts of copra traders in *kabupaten* Banjarnegara. First there are those 12 Javanese traders who, as a relict from a period when the copra cooperation flourished, are called *petugas koperasi* (cooperation officials). They have their office buildings from the cooperation and can borrow from its funds. The second group of traders, handling 70% of the *kabupaten's* copra, are three businessmen from Chinese descent. They are called—rather meaningless—*'rayon koperasi'*, for they do not enjoy any advantage of their linkage with the cooperation. Both type of traders are obliged to pay the cooperation costs of administration: Rp 2 per kg copra sold to the factory. The factory pays the Chinese merchants directly, but for some obscure reason *petugas* will paid through the cooperation's office.

Chinese have long been expelled from copra trade and their being a *rayon koperasi* seems a twist of fate. To prevent Chinese traders from reaping the benefits of coconut processing, so its manifesto says, the copra cooperation came into being in 1958. All copra trade in the *kabupaten* was relegated to the cooperation. Transport of coconuts out of the *kabupaten* was prohibited. Before 1958 coconuts were frequently exported to Pekalongan or Semarang, whenever the price for coconuts was higher than the copra price. The factory stipulated the price for copra by then. It bought *kabupaten* produced copra from chinese agents, who in turn were supplied by javanese traders. At that time, so the annual report of the cooperation states, local surplusses fell short of factory input needs and copra import became necessary. Neglect and diseases had reduced coconut harvests. When the factory was established in 1930 coconut yields were more abundant. Since the end of the nineteenth century copra had been one of Banjarnegara's export commodities. It seems that at that time it was purchased by Chinese merchants and brought to Gombong. As soon as the narrow gauge railway reached Banjarnegara, the merchants had the copra destined for Cilacap, to be sent abroad or to be processed in a Cilacap factory (SDS). The factory's initial establishment in Banjarnegara is explained by the high copra production in the Serayu Region at that time.

So in 1958 under the shield of the Military Commander, the monopoly of handling copra in the region was granted to the cooperation. It was not the cooperation's only privilege. Even more important was the compensation rule: for each quintal copra, that the cooperation delivered to the plant, it had to be returned 59 liter of coconut oil. One quintal copra renders 60—62 liter coconut oil on average, so the factory's profit margins were squeezed to the value of 1—3 liter oil per quintal copra and to selling the residue, which is used for fodder. By comparison, the market value of 100 kg copra nowadays equals 55.5 liter coconut oil. As long as the compensation rule lasted, the cooperation took up selling of coconut oil. It could settle the local retail price, on which the copra price to its members was based. The cooperation prospered. It employed 23 people and moved to a posh office in the town's centre. It owned four trucks. To its 2300 members it offered a number of insurances and they shared the cooperation's profits.

When the political climate changed after 1965, the cooperation's privileges were gradually lost. In 1968, first, the coconut export interdiction was relieved, a prelude of changes to come. In the seventies the coconut oil factory thought the time was ripe to break the unfavourable compensation rule. At that time even 85% of the factory's copra intake came from West Java and the Cilacap region. The factory took the next strategy; it offered its agents coconut oil on a bargain, in order to sell below the price the coconut cooperation got for the compensation coconut oil. At that time some Chinese merchants had entered local copra trade; they were offered the 100 kg copra = 59 liter coconut oil deal too. Coconut oil now being sold for a low price by others than the cooperation had the effect of stuffing the cooperation with oil. As the cooperation paid its member-copra driers with money earned by selling coconut oil, the situation got untenable as the cooperation became devoid of income. To avoid a crisis the the board of the cooperation had to go to the factory and ask for the compensation rule to be abolished, and be replaced by paying for the copra in cash, thus signing the cooperation's downfall. Why did the cooperation not lower prices at that time? It seems that a substantial part of the money, derived from selling coconut oil, disappeared into costs of organization; the organization was not reputated for its efficiency. Lowering the coconut oil prices would have pushed copra prices below what was felt reasonable to pay the members. Moreover, coconuts might be turned into other uses.

The last privilege, the marketing monopoly of copra, was lost in 1974. The *kabupaten* government then legalized what had become current practice: Chinese traders dealing in copra. The argument was that, Chinese could solve the shortage of copra supply in that year, as they are more skilled traders. They certainly are: they may combine copra trade with maintaining a *warong*. Farmers can repay their debts at the *warong* with copra. Chinese merchants are more generous with advance payments too. Both the Javanese *petugas koperasi* and the Chinese *rayon* do pay beforehand, but the Chinese often pay 100% in advance or will pay cash at least.

Its privileges being lost and Chinese merchants reentering trade, the cooperation was doomed to powerlessness. There are 90 members left, mainly copra traders. At present the cooperation survives on the Rp 2 each kg copra it still taxes and on the rent it recieves from letting a bank use the cooperation's onetime big office. Three clerks staff the cooperation, making statistics most of the day.

The coconut oil factory is a survivor too. Most of its machinery dates from back 1930. Only recently some diesel-motors have been replaced by imported electro-motors. Despite its museum-like outlook, the factory is run in an up to date way. In fact, it is one of two enterprises interviewed with a maximum of capitalist characteristics. The plant's shares are still owned by the kin of its three chinese founders. *'Sabda Guna'*, as the factory is called nowadays, distributes its coconut oil to agents in Purbolinggo, Banjarnegara, Wonosobo and Parakan. Normally it will process 300—400 ton copra monthly. The factory's capital reserve suffices to speculate, when copra and coconut oil prices fluctuate.

126 People are on *Sabda Guna's* pay-roll. It includes white collar workers—Chinese from Banjarnegara—, transport labourers and three shifts of factory labourers—the hub of them from semi-rural *desa* Karangtengah. Paternalism is rife at the plant: Blue collar workers wages are mainly turned out in foodstuff, the actual amount of rice, coconutoil and sugar depending on a worker's family-size.

Such is done to prevent labourers from wasting their wages on gambling. All 126 employees have a permanent contract. Even when copra supply declined to point zero, as happened at the time of the survey, workers were not dismissed. A couple of reasons accounted for the copra being virtually absent for 4 months. the outburts of the Gunungalung volcano in West Java caused a lot of trees there to expire. In fact the whole of Java was drought-stricken for a long time. The shortage of coconuts caused their price to surpass Rp 100. Export of coconuts out of the *kabupaten* became feasible. The price for copra had to follow, but could not follow as fast. As diagram 11.2 shows, the coconut oil factory even offered a price of Rp 360 per kg copra in May 1983. But since it takes 4—6 coconuts to make one kilogram, even this record price did not speed up copra production. Only coconuts from very isolated *desa* were processed, as copra is easier to transport than coconuts. Most coconuts however, were sent to big cities on West Java. One Banjarnegara lady coordinates the lot of this export. She gatheres the coconuts at *pasar* in *kecamatan* Punggelan, *kecamatan* Madukara and *kecamatan* Kaliwiro (*kabupaten* Wonosobo). At these instances she meets the 25 village traders, she had settled a price with and had paid in advance. Every day she sends a lorry of coconuts to West Java to be received by big merchants, that sell to petty traders. The lady's turn-over had staggered since the drought. Before, she used to send two loads a week to Pekalongan. The sudden export shows the periphere position of Banjarnegara in Java's marketing system. For four months local copra producers were out of work.

Though *Sabda Guna* will survive this slack period, there are structural problems, that threaten the factory. Recently coconut oil had to face increased competition of palm oil, which is a cheaper edible oil and contains less cholestrol. Most Javanese will prefer the taste of coconut oil however, but one cannot tell how long the plant will last on that. Banjarnegara's coconut oil has a particularly good fame, since the part of the copra input, that comes from the *kabupaten* (10%), is very fresh. Nevertheless, the copra supply from the *kabupaten* is going downhill: trees cut are not renewed and

Diagram 11.1. Copra production from the kabupaten processed by the coconutoil plant Sabda Guna and copra price offered: March 1982—May 1983

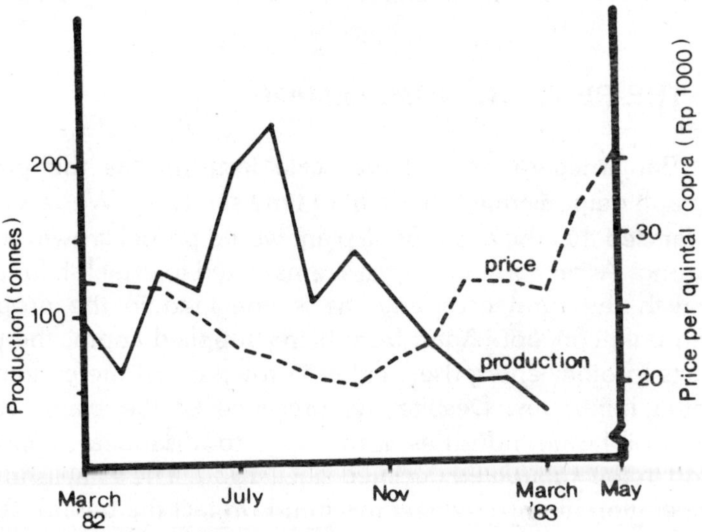

Source: Koperasi Kopra 'Cahyana'.

at the Mrica lake area many coconut palms will be drowned (Palte et al 1981). So the process of diminishing coconut harvests is still going on. Besides, the growing population consumes a growing portion of this produce too.

Sabda Guna is not the only coconut oil producer in Banjarnegara. There are some home producers of coconut oil too. A different process is used in these petty enterprises. The coconut flesh is grated and mixed with water to get a milky liquid (*santen*). This liquid is heated, so the oil will seperate. At present only one such petty produce can be found in Banjarnegára town. He processes 50—100 coconuts a day. His product is one-and-a-half times as expensive as the factory's. Customers are a select group of well-to-do, that appreciate the coconut oil's better taste. The waste of this process the petty commodity producer uses to make *tempe*. Before 1930, at times when copra prices were low, and in 1942—1950, when the coconut oil plant was dismantled, such home production was ubiquitous, but it was never fit to combat factory competition.

11.4 THE REAL EKONOMI LEMAH

Banjarnegara's sole large scale industry, as the previous paragraph demonstrated, has a hard time surviving. Whoever might have fancied that the coconut oil plant would propel growth is put in the wrong. As an agro-industry it seems suited to establish functional links with the rural economy, as is imagined in the propulsive growth pole concept. Apart from being supplied copra, the plant's contacts to other enterprises, either in town or on the countryside, are at a minimum. Despite the presence of the plant, causing coconut oil home industries at that time to disappear, copra production in the *kabupaten* declined since 1930. The establishment of a cooperation did not redirect this trend. In fact the period, that the cooperation ascended in power, coincided with some down years in copra supply. Diagram 11.2 is obvious. These failures also cast a sombre light on the small town rural motor concept.

Functional ties between petty commodity industries and countryside activities seem little more promising. In general petty commodity industries thrive on local demand or regional demand, resisting competition from outer *kabupaten* large scale industry only at the production of perishable and voluminous goods. Only few of them depend on regional supply of raw materials. Some industries however do use raw materials (primary commodities and home-industrial products) from the *kabupaten*.

Developing such enterprises seems an enthralling avenue. One example might be setting up *kecap* industries. A major input for processing *kecap* is coconut sugar. Particularly sugar that is wet, is suitable. As coconut and areng-sugar processing is a very widespread activity on Banjarnegara's countryside as map 11.1

Diagram 11.2. Annual copra production in kabupaten Banjarnegara, as handled by the copra cooperation: 1959—1982.

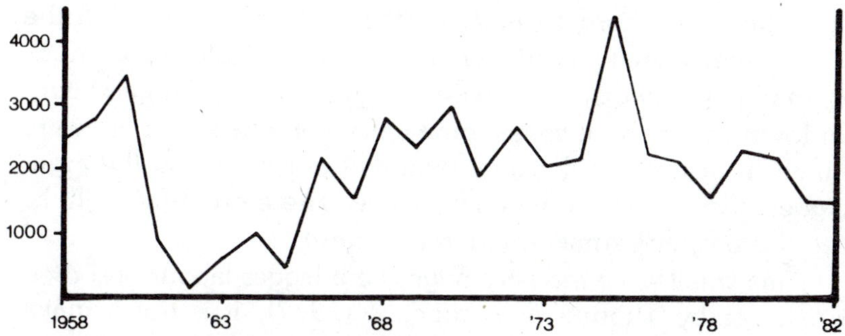

Source: Koperasi Kopra 'Cahyana'.

shows, it might serve as a base for a complex of *kecap* producers in Banjarnegara town. Another major input, soybeans, can be grown in Banjarnegara's vicinity too, without too much adaptation of cultivation. Since *kecap* is a non-perishable product, fetching a reasonable price, and is everywhere in high demand, export seems feasible. The process is quite simple and might be taken up in labour-intensive petty scale enterprises. One might conceive of a high quality product, first capturing the local market, supported by a local government funded promotion campaign. Another example of an agro-industry with a potential to develop mentioned in chapter 9 is *abon* industry.

In general stimulating small scale industry has the big adavantage of creating labour opportunities, both in industry and trade. For as the examples from the food industry show, small scale industry often has a regional circulation and is traded by petty local and regional circuit traders. Only the very small scale industries take up retailing themselves.

At present stimuli from the context are low. Small scale industries in practice seem boycotted from low interest credit schemes, designed though they are for the *'ekonomi lemah'*. Some clauses, like a security, are hard to meet by the petty producers and the world between a petty producer and a bank employee is much wider, than it is between the bank employee and the clientelist contractor for instance. Besides, as some entrepreneurs stated, industry is banned from town by local government policy, as, so the argument goes, they cause too much nuisance. Therefore they might be refused the proper permits (*hinderordonansi*).

Thus small scale industry might be a bigger labour absorber, than held for by Thomas & Lempelius (1977). It is not a major employer however. It might even be doubted whether small town unemployment will ever be relieved by it. The majority of the jobless concerns persons, that have finished secondary education. The low pay and coarse work at small scale industry is no alternative to them.

Chapter 12

SERVICE ENTERPRISES

This short chapter is dedicated to non governmental services. A wide diversity is encountered in Banjarnegara's non governmental service branch: barbers, brokers, a cinema and a Javanese opera, porters, prostitutes, repairshops, restaurants and transport enterprises are included. It is no use having them jammed in one category. Some enterprises even have such a casual character that there are problems labeling them an enterprise. Take broking of houses or second hand motorbikes for instance. By negotiating between buyer and seller, anonymous to each other, a person can make a lot of money; his is the difference between what the selling party has fixed as the bottom price and what the buying party is willing to pay, added with a percentage of the agreed sum. While some people specialize in this business, for most people broking is a very occasional occupation. Continuity is altogether lacking.

Rather than discussing several subs seperately, we will point at some trends in service enterprises. Some trends are similar to what goes on in industry and trade. Research in large conurbations did show the branch's function as a labour absorber. A number of occupations seems to be of the low skill, low capital kind, for which everyone qualifies. In a couple of them, however, in Banjarnegara entrance is barred to newcomers. Such has happened at the *pasar kota* in the porter's metier. Porters work in three groups, specializing respectively in rice, vegetables or fruit. They will take the one quintal-plus loads on their backs and carry them to where a *pasar* trader has his stall. As remunerations are Rp 100—200 per load, daily returns can be high: Rp 1500—2000 daily. Formerly organization used to be very strict among porters and profits were shared amongst all members of the group. Whoever entered profession had to pay a fee. Nowadays rules are less stringent. If someone wants to start as a porter however, he still has to ask permission of the other porters.

Such seclusion mechanisms also protect *manol* from competition. *Manol* operate at the minibus terminal behind the *pasar*. A *manol* will gather passengers and bring them to one of the minibuses waiting. The driver of the minibus is obliged to pay Rp 150—250 to the *manol* for filling up the minibus, whether or not passengers found their own way. A number of *manol* at the terminal are enlisted as members of the *SBAJR*, a trade union's division. As such *manol* are the only ones entitled to operate at the terminal and no new members are allowed, entrance to the trade is closed. An absurd situation has been the result. For non licensed *manol* operate at the *pasar* terminal too, being taxed the half of what they earn by licensed *manol*. It might be clear that working as a *manol* is a rough trade. Conflicts with drivers and between *manol* are frequent. Some *manol* have taken refuge to strategic points outside the terminal, where passengers board a minibus. At such informal terminals a *manol* will have to defend his claim by force. Drivers too try to pick up as many passengers as is possible outside the *pasar* terminal, circling the town, causing extra nuisance.

Minibus transport has grown explosively since 1974. At present the number of buses seems to outgrow the number of passengers, hence the fierce competition. The fast growth in minibuses has been explained as the effect of imitation; letting a minibus has proven a profitable investment and so many investers put their money in a minibus. There are some 800 minibus departures from the *pasar* terminal daily. Map 12.1 shows directions. Slight daily changes are caused by periodic markets. Besides

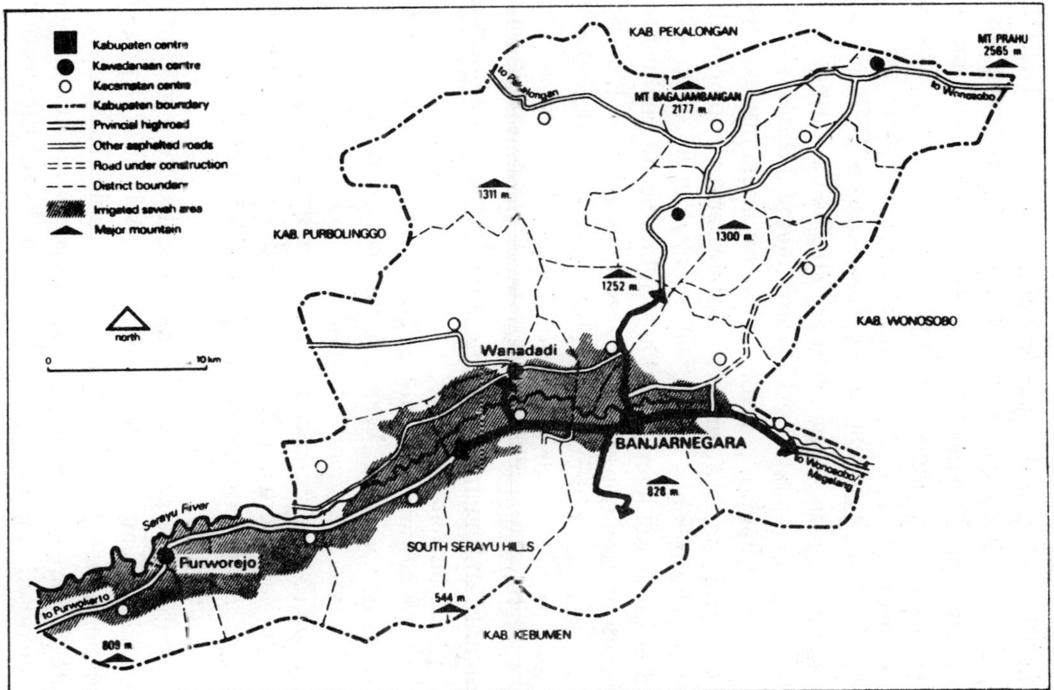

Map 12.1 Direction of departures and arrivals at the minibus terminal Banjarnegara

showing Banjarnegara as a knot on the Wonosobo—Purwokerto line, map 12.1 refers to Banjarnegara's service area. The minibus network often follows asphaltation of roads. Some of the gravelled feeder roads are explored by second hand minibuses, driven—despite their uniform haggard condition—by the owner. Such owner-drivers are uncommon in town. Most drivers are labourers. Of their daily net return, they keep a 15% share, one third of which is given to their helper. This helper cashes the fares and looks for passengers. The 15% arrangement is not waterproof. A minibus owner cannot control income on fares, nor expenses on petrol, *bea* and *manol's* services. So consensus replaces this arrangement. The minibus owner will usually get Rp 4000—7000 a day and a driver will keep Rp 2000—3000. Some minibus owners have already turned consensus into leasing contracts. Leasing contracts were already common in autobus transport and transport by a new type of diesel driven minibuses, that operate on the Wonosobo—Purwokerto line. Diesel driven minibuses gain increasing popularity among investers. These vehicles and the buses depart from a special terminal.

The development of motorized transport has been a blow to other forms of transport. Within town horse-cart transport is now devoid of future as a result of minibuses, taking passengers along their in-town route. Inter*kecamatan* commodity transport in the sixties—when roads were in dilapidated condition—was done by man-craft or by horse-cart on flat terrain. Minibuses and trucks have now completely taken over.

Another form of transport that benefited from road improvement is *becak* driving. The first pedicab arrived in Banjarnegara after the Independence Struggle. At present some 160 *becak* drivers populate the streets of town, some drivers being rural dwellers. It should be noted that 50% of Banjarnegara's *becak* drivers own their *becak,* which is a great deal more than in big cities. For those that hire their pedicab, rent is modest, compared to Jakarta or Yogyakarta: Rp 250 a day. A number of them is only casually engaged in *becak* driving and would not aspire a *becak* of their own.

For those not owning a pedicab, however, that have been making a living out of *becak* driving for years, a promising program was started by the *Y.P.S.E.*, a local participatory development organization. An association (*usaha bersama*) for pedicab drivers was initiated. A driver can hire a pedicab for a lower price at this association. Of his rent part is set aside for insurances and part for a borrowing fund and part for instalments. So after two year a driver has completed the pay of his *becak* and becomes owner. Another member can take his place following the same procedure. The *becak* drivers associated were asked to gather once a month at the home of one of them, to discuss problems. Solidarity and self-management was thus enhanced. The number of pedicabs, owned by the association, still falls short of the number of candidates, but other drivers can subscribe to the association too and by paying daily contribution are in the insurances and saving-borrowing scheme. Initiatives like the self-managed *becak* driver's association seem an excellent alternative to petty enterprises, that are excluded from most other programs.

So the transport sector reflect contrast and competition between petty and corporate sector. Repair—related intimately to transport—does too. A driver will always try to save expenses by fixing up his vehicle himself. If not, he will go to a repairshop. Car-repair in Banjarnegara is taken care of by a corporate sector garage. Although motorcar ownership is scarce outside town, one might pose the garage has a regional function. This enterprise has some electric equipment at its disposal like spray-guns, drills and a grinder. It employes 16 semi skilled workers on a semi permanent base. The garage's only rivals are petty mechanics. Such mechanics will hardly ever keep a stock of spare parts. Generally they are so capital-starved, that they have to ask for advance payments to buy the accesories needed. Some of the car mechanics interviewed will travel as far as Purwokerto to get them. A ditto pattern applies to motorbike repairmen, who number substantively more than car mechanics. An independent mechanic complained of the market being stuffed with new motorbikes, that need less fixing up.

Their occurence was partly caused by a newly started government program that enabled countryside primary school teachers to obtain a motorbike on attractive credit terms. Besides corporate sector motorbike dealers interfered by doing repair jobs.

In bicycle and *becak* repair corporate sector enterprises are absent. Petty transport is catered for by petty repair. The lower costs of bike parts enabled one repairman questioned, to have a complete set of accessories in store, which he fetched for cheap in Purwokerto. On average he spent Rp 150,000 monthly on spareparts. A colleague, who could not afford such expenditure, was supplied by a Banjarnegara hardware store. The pro of having some money in reserve are clear: it allows bicycle repairmen to circumvent the higher prices of the local retail network.

Intimate relations between petty enterprises of a different kind exist within foodvending. In many Javanese restaurants, snacks and dishes are served that are prepared by petty foodprocessors. In fact, to some foodprocessors such petty restaurants are a major outlet. The menu of rice and dishes, cooked by the restaurant proprietor, is completed by foodprocessor's products. The key to a restaurant's success is the friendly atmosphere it provides (Lasono, Suwandi & Lawen 1981). This contrasts to the sterile Chinese owned restaurants, that have at most the appeal of the modern. Such restaurants still number few in Banjarnegara town. Foodprocessors do not have a foothold in such enterprises. Apart from the home-made plates, food of the factory produced variety is offered.

Chapter 13

THE BANJARNEGARA PRODUCTION STRUCTURE

In this chapter the model outlined in chapter 4 is returned to. In the preceeding chapters the urban subsystem part of the model was used to classify enterprises within the small town production structure. Faced with an impressive pluriformity and the necessity to generalize about the interaction of different parts of the small town economy such classification is inevitable.

The model of chapter 4 has two dimensions in distinguishing enterprises. First a line is drawn between petty commodity sector and corporate sector using a multiple scale indicator, an enterprise is relegated to the corporate sector if one or more of three criteria are met: a turnover that surpasses Rp 5,000,000 monthly (85% of corporate enterprises did), a stock of capital goods valued at least Rp 5,000,000 (50% did) or a wage-list that includes 10 or more employees (30% did). If none of these criteria applies, an enterprise was classified as petty commodity sector. As a second dimension, since enterprises are marked by a mix of elements of the capitalist and pre-capitalist mode of production, the exact score of characteristics of the capitalist mode of production serves to differentiate within petty commodity sector and corporate sector.

The two dimensions—labeled form and structuring characteristics respectively—are not independent; in chapter 4 it was stated that the petty commodity sector has its roots in the pre-capitalist mode of production, while corporate sector enterprises are inclined to the capitalist mode of production. Opposite combinations of structuring and form characteristics occur as well. Taking the operationalizations explicited in table 4.2, both the trend and its exceptions stand out from diagram 13.1. The average number of capitalist characteristics for petty commodity sector and corporate sector is 2.6 and 3.7 respectively. Note however that it is a classification of enterprises surveyed and that our sample was a clustered one.

Diagram 13.1 Distribution of petty commodity and corporate sector enterprises interviewed to number of capitalist characteristics (percentages)

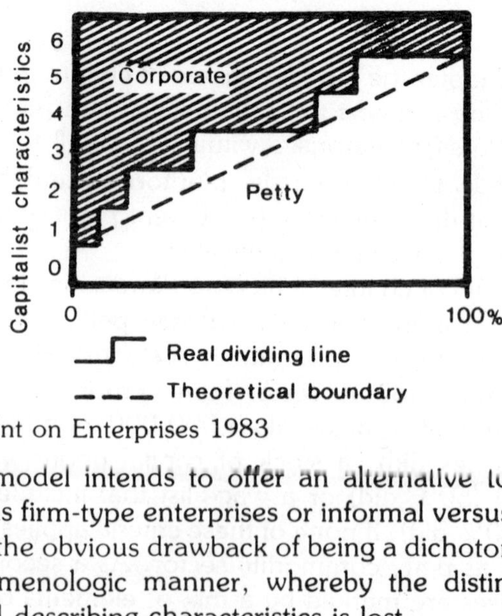

Source: Count on Enterprises 1983

The model intends to offer an alternative to concepts like bazaar versus firm-type enterprises or informal versus formal sector, that next to the obvious drawback of being a dichotomy, are defined in a phenomenologic manner, whereby the distinction between defining and describing characteristics is lost.

Below some generalized statements will be made on the petty commodity sector and the corporate sector and the modes of production. As thus the paragraph is a very abstract one. An effort is made to estimate the explanatory value of this sectoral classification to other divergences. The results should be interpreted with some caution however, since they were derived from a sample that by biasing some branches in the small town economy was not representative for the whole of it.

In paragraphs 13.2 and 13.3 the theme of interrelations within the production structure of the regional centre Banjarnegara is taken up. These paragraphs examine the most relevant links among enterprises within the same sector and between enterprises in seperate sectors. Paragraph 13.2 discusses interrelations in trade and services, paragraph 13.3 is concerned with interrelations in industry and construction.

13.1 PETTY COMMODITY AND CORPORATE SECTOR AND MODES OF PRODUCTION

In diagram 13.1 the correlation between mode of production and petty commodity sector versus corporate sector is visualized for the enterprises interviewed. It demonstrates that enterprises in the petty commodity sector and corporate sector alike are marked by a mix of capitalist and pre-capitalist elements. On average however corporate sector enterprises have a higher score of capitalist characteristics than petty commodity enterprises. It is instructive to check what particular elements of the capitalist and pre-capitalist mode of production apply to the petty commodity sector and hence, what elements discriminate between the sectors. Table 13.1 gives an overview of the distribution of corporate and petty commodity enterprises on indicators chosen to represent mode of production.

Pre-capitalist features in the petty commodity sector are the emphasis on labour instead of capital, the absent labour division and the infrequent use of credit (except for the short-term credit furnished by trading partners). Capitalist elements that prevale in the petty commodity sector are commercial orientation i.g. the purchasing of all inputs, a willingness to invest and the limited use of family labour. This latter attribute is partly due to the fact that a substantial number of petty commodity enterprises concerns own account workers. Yet strikingly still 28% of the petty commodity sector enterprises employs wage labourers, which is only slightly below the 35% that employs family workers.

Within the corporate sector family labour is returned to in 50% of the enterprises, whereas 76% in the sample has wage workers. Daily payments in stead of paying piecework is comparatively more common in the corporate sector (76%), than it is in the petty commodity sector (65%). Wages differ between the sectors as well; those employed in the corporate sector are paid one-and-a-half time as much as petty commondity sector wage labourers.

In addition to employing wage labour, the corporate sector is marked by other capitalist traits. It most enterprises there is a willingness to invest and a commercial orientation on the plane of inputs. Commercial orientation might be conceived of as producing

Table 13.1 Distribution of petty commodity sector and corporate sector enterprises on indicators of the modes of production (percentages)

		Petty Commodity Sector	Corporate Sector
Head of enterprises joins all lines of work	Yes (PreCap)	95	63
	No (Cap)	5	37
Non-paid family members employed	Yes (PreCap)	35	50
	No (Cap)	65	50
Wage labourers employed	No (PreCap)	72	24
	Yes (Cap)	28	76
Value of capital goods exceeds Rp 250.000/worker	No (PreCap)	95	59
	Yes (Cap)	5	41
Using formal or informal credit	No (PreCap)	93	87
	Yes (Cap)	7	13
Willingness to invest	No (PreCap)	43	23
	Yes (Cap)	57	77
Commercial orientation (purchasing all inputs)	No (PreCap)	13	4
	Yes (Cap)	87	96

for the market as well, but this indicator was not selected, since the definition of enterprises used throughout the survey—set down in the preface—includes their profit motive and thereby excludes subsistence production. Finally there are two capitalist structuring characteristics, that though they do not apply to a majority of corporate sector enterprises, do so to a considerable part of the sector. It concerns the division of tasks within the enterprises, operationalized as the the head of the enterprise being engaged with sales and organization only, and secondly the prevalence of capital-intensive ways of producing to labour-intensive ones. Rp 250.000 per worker occupied is taken as the dividing line for this latter indicator. Multiple regression analysis showed that these two indicators, next to use of paid labour explained most variance between petty commodity and corporate sector.

The findings on the capitalist penetration of the petty commodity sector resemble Van Dijk's (1982) observations on small scale enterprises in Salatiga town. He discovered a mix of pre-capitalist and capitalist elements in the management of small scale enterprises. Relevant pre-capitalist traits were the accent on labour instead of capital and the absence of labour division and capital formation. Commercial orientation (interpreted as working for the market), the minor importance of family labour vis-a-vis wage labour and the segregration between household and enterprise in general represented the capitalist mode of production. It should be noted however that most of these pre-capitalist features are not uncommon in corporate sector enterprises too. In general, the difference between the two sectors seems to be more a matter of tendencies than contrasts.

This segregretion of household and enterprise, noted by Van Dijk, does not apply to the Banjarnegara situation. Though the use of family labour is indeed rivalled by wage labour, many petty commodity sector enterprises take refuge to family resources in financing their venture and finding a place to work. Table 13.2 and 13.3 express so. Of those petty enterprises that have a permanent residence, a considerable portion takes up quarters in a part of the

Table 13.2 Source of initial investments in petty commodity and corporate sector enterprises (percentages)

	Private savings	Inheritance/ family money	Formal credit	Informal credit
Petty Commodity Sector	71	17	6	6
Corporate Sector	53	30	15	3

Table 13.3 Source of permanent working space for petty commodity and corporate sector enterprises (excluding pasar, percentages)

	Part of home	Inherited/ borrowed	Bought	Hired (plot or premises)
Petty Commodity Sector	21	35	13	31
Corporate Sector	5	29	33	33

the private dwelling or use inherited premises and next the initial investment to start business is often funded from private means or family capital.

Turning to family resources is not unique to the petty commodity sector. As table 13.2 indicates, paying for the initial expenditures with family money is even more common in the corporate sector, than it is in the petty commodity sector. It was already exemplified in chapter 7 by the Chinese custom to equip their kindred with a store of their own. Working place might stem from the family too; 29% of the corporate sector enterprises has inherited property to operate in. The part of the entrepreneurs that obtained their habitat by hiring or buying a plot or a building however is a great deal more.

It is interesting to compare the two sectors of the urban

subsystem briefly on other facets, under the reserve of the character of the sample. First, what we delimited as the petty commodity sector is reported by some scholars to be typified by great turbulence and everchanging interaction. The stereotype of easy access—and probably easy exit as well—contributes to this image, though some types of activities are sealed off by seclusion mechanisms. Yet on comparing corporate and petty commodity sector in Banjarnegara town, the latter do not seem to be less consolidated than corporate sector enterprises. Actually the average age of the petty commodity sector enterprises interviewed was 12.9 years (sic) and surmounted the mean of 11.1 years for corporate sector enterprises. Both figures are very high.

Turbulence, if there is turbulence in lethargic Banjarnegara, seems to fit in more with the corporate sector. To some extent the greater changeability in the corporate sector is explained by the opportunistic behaviour of the clientelist entrepreneur, an example of which is given in chapter 10. A prove of the greater turbulence is presented in table 13.4, reviewing how entrepreneurs perceived competition in their branch. It seems that within the corporate sector there are both more entrepreneurs that think of their branch as overcrowded and that think that it could allow extra entrants than in the petty commodity sector.

A second assumption to be commented upon is the use of local inputs. It has been argued that small scale enterprises use local resources more often. This quality was even included in the definition of the informal sector by the I.L.O. (1972).

Table 13.4 Perceptions of competition by petty commodity and corporate sector entrepreneurs (relative figures)

	New entrants possible	Enough participants	Too much competitors
Petty Commodity Sector	20	61	21
Corporate Sector	32	35	33

Table 13.5 Origin of major inputs to petty commodity and corporate sector enterprises (relative figures)

	Local	Non Local
Petty Commodity Sector	54	46
Corporate Sector	55	45

From this viewpoint table 13.5 denies the defining quality of such a characteristic. Although on the one hand, the selection of enterprises in the sample was distorted, for respondents were chosen within a number of branches in the small town economy, which has repercussions on the variance with respect to inputs used, on the other hand, the branches chosen represent the hub of the town's production structure. Table 13.5 demonstrates that the difference between petty commodity and corporate sector concerning the origins of inputs used is nihil. But though petty commodity enterprises do not use inputs from the *kabupaten* more often, they purchase from local suppliers more frequent. Most petty commodity sector enterprises are furnished by suppliers residing in town, unlike corporate sector enterprises. This hints at the wholesale function of Banjarnegara corporate sector enterprises in the local context. This theme of intersectoral supply is taken up in the next paragraphs, that deal with interrelations in trade and services, and construction and industry.

13.2 INTRASECTORAL AND INTERSECTORAL RELATIONS IN TRADE AND SERVICES

Enterprises interrelate in many ways. Art and substance of such interrelations are intriguing to study and often generalized statements are made. In these paragraphs the Banjarnegara context serves to comment on the complex character of economic interrelations and to evaluate some of these generalized statements.

Getting them organized is the credo of many a proposal to improve the fate of petty commodity enterprises. By collective buying and selling for instance or agreements on bottom prices petty commodity traders, that joined a cooperation, so it is argued, might solve practical problems and increase bargaining power. In some cases a third effect of such organization is defending the metier to newcomers. A striking example of this effect is the minibus terminal near *pasar kota*: non-union *manol* are exploited by unionists, who do not admit new members to their division of the *S.B.A.J.R.* Yet institutionalized cooperation is scarce in trade and services. Next to the *S.B.A.J.R.* a second exceptional example is a cooperative of second hand bicycle traders at *pasar* Ampera; this cooperative provides insurances to its members and is meant to erase the suspicion of fencing, usually attached to this type of trade. More often however non-official forms of cooperation solve the daily and structural problems of petty traders. Such informal agreements indeed are effective, as they suit the context of commerce, for too much obligations will hamper a trader to make a bargain at short notice.

The ad-hoc character of exchange relations is another often quoted issue. In Banjarnegara however it can be observed that to some extent market traders and hawkers avoid too many ad hoc acts of exchange and try to consolidate their venture by tieing customers; wholesalers at *pasar kota* try to tie patronizing traders and traders at minor *pasar* and hawkers try to tie private customers. Allowing delay payment is a key issue in securing such relations. As shortage of capital is the stereotype problem in trade, explicited at least by 30% of petty commodity traders interviewed, being delivered first and paying only afterwards is a common arrangement. It might even take the form of selling on commission, in which a trader is allowed to return unsold goods, and has the profit margins fixed by his supplier.

A substitute arrangement to allowing delay payments is granting trade discounts to the buying party on condition that the merchandise is paid cash. Thus some working capital of one's own allows higher profits to a trader, for one can apply for trade discount and in addition—as the example of the bicycle repairmen in chapter 12 illustrated—one is more free to choose one's supplier.

Trade discounts and the short term credit involved in permitting delay payment are often passed on from higher links in commodity circulation. Part of the retail trade in Banjarnegara concerns national circulation and the trade discounts or credit that a petty trader obtained from a Banjarnegara *toko* or *pasar* wholesaler are ultimately furnished by a wholesaler in Purwokerto, Semarang or some other Javanese city. Links in this circulation are a majority of the Banjarnegara *toko* and a minor part of the traders at *pasar kota*. Mostly corporate sector enterprises. They resell to private persons and petty commodity sector traders, that without exception have a lower score of capitalist elements: *warong*keepers, hawkers and *pasar* traders. The granting of delay payment or trade discount enables extra*kabupaten* wholesalers and, next, *toko* or *pasar* wholesalers to enlarge clientele. In this respect symbiosis seems an adequate term for the interlinkinbg of the petty commodity sector and the corporate sector in national commodity circulation.

In regional commodity circulation there is no such external source of trading capital. This regional circulation is represented by a majority of traders at *pasar kota* and a minority of *toko* in Banjarnegara town. If a regional circuit wholesaler offers short term credit to his customers, he has to provide it from his own means or ask the producer or trader, he was supplied by, to wait before getting paid.

Thus far the exchange of money and goods in the downward flow of commodities has been discussed. In marketing of primary commodities trading capital is a cardinal resource as well. In contrast to the pattern that is common in retail trade, where the selling party allows delay payment, in marketing the buying party by forwarding money to the suppliers injects capital to the branch. In retail trade receiving discount is a substitute for being permitted to pay afterwards. A parallel within marketing is the situation of peasants that, instead of engaging in a selling commitment await the harvest and sell themselves. Thus receiving a better price, as diagram 8.2 on the earnings of a clove crop illustrates.

Marketing of primary commodities is the arena where assumptions on the relations between rural and urban subsystem of the model in chapter 4 might be tested. Missen (1972) envisaged a peasant sector and—what we label—a petty commodity sector that were firmly interlaced. The petty commodity sector takes up the marketing of commercial surpluses produced by the peasant sector Part of the cash crops it transfers to corporate sector merchants, so diagram 4.2 suggests. The interrelation between petty comodity sector and peasant sector however is liable to change and the petty commodity circuit might be by-passed by the corporate sector, an underlying force of this change being the commercialization of peasant production, even to the point of peasants becoming commercial sector producers. Does this describe the Banjarnegara situation? Excluding local circulation, in which qualitate qua by-pass is impossible, some regional and national marketing flows were surveyed. Diagram 13.2, inspired by diagram 4.2, depicts some commodity flows.

Direct contacts between a farmer and a corporate sector merchant are seldom. This practice has some significance in vegetable and tobacco marketing in mono-cropped Wanayasa and Batur only. Usually intermediary traders interfere; petty *bakul* purchasing at the farmgate or at the village market. As a rule, these petty commodity *bakul* are rural dwellers, not townsmen. The *bakul* will sell to merchants that belong to the corporate sector: cattle exporters, rice-mill owners, vegetable traders and fruit merchants. This latter category of traders might reside in the regional centre, but this has become an exception rather than a rule, so it seems; most rice mill owners are better-off rural dwellers and cattle exporters origin from Purwokerto or West Java for the major part, which is where Banjarnegara's fattened stock is destined to. Even if the interface is a *pasar* in or near Banjarnegara town, merchants from the town are rivalled by corporate (and sometimes even petty commodity) traders

Diagram 13.2 Intrasectoral and intersectoral relations in trade in Banjarnegara

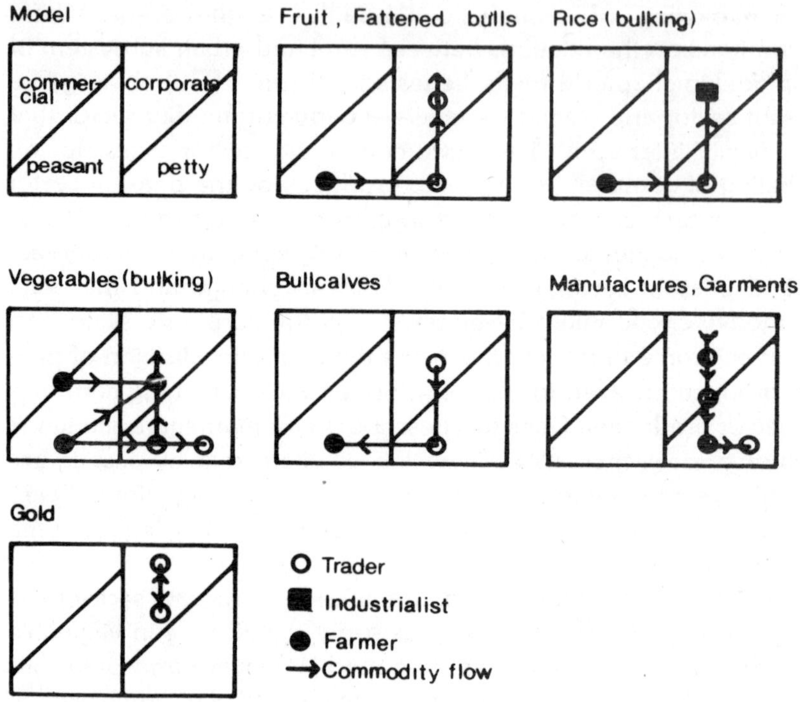

from other places. If one link in the marketing chain is about to be short-circuited, it is the corporate sector merchant that resides in the regional centre.

The corporate sector traders are the ones to infuse trading capital in the upward flow of agricultural surpluses. Capital needs are high in the bulking branch. Many peasants vexed by money shortage in the *paceclik* season are eager to sell their crop before it is mature. In the most extreme type of transactions, the *rampasan* arrangement in agro-forestry, they even agree to sell five to ten subsequent harvests. As a result the solvability of petty village traders is under pressure and the village traders have to turn to corporate sector merchants and ask for some payment in advance at their turn. So the poverty of the peasantry, manifest in their *paceclik* cash needs, puts petty traders at the mercy of corporate sector merchants. Since the latter, *tengkulak* or—in case of paddy—rice-mill owners, have access to bank loans, this gives them a clear advantage on petty *bakul*, who seldom manage to impress bank officials to equip them with cash before the harvesting season sets off. Alternatively, the fruit *tengkulak* might on their turn have contacted wholesalers in West Java and demanded some short-term credit.

Other arguments to arrange transactions beforehand are the circumvention of traditional harvest sharing methods, the insurance against harvest losses for the seller and diminishing the risk of being left with perishable merchandise for the buyer. This imperative has some meaning for *bakul* and—especially—corporate sector traders, that do not feel at ease on the distant markets they send to. It is even suggested that this uncertainty on distant markets contributes to the penetration of West Javanese merchants at *pasar* in Banjarnegara.

Not all peasants however sell beforehand. A substantial part of the peasants sells the crop after it is harvested, at the farmgate or bring it to a village market.

In livestock trade there is no short-term credit hierarchy from big city wholesalers to *tengkulak* to *bakul* and finally, to peasants. If a Banjarnegara livestock trader tries to obtain a bank loan, he will do so not because advancing money is necessary, but because paying cash incurs trade discounts in the first place and because, he has to wait delay payments from his clients in Purwokerto or West Java. The short-term credit to a peasant, common in fruit trade for instance, is replaced by a farmer agreeing to be paid only afterwards in livestock marketing. There might be three explanations for this difference. First, as a piece of livestock can be sold at any time, there is no *paceclik* season to a livestock owner. Secondly, livestock owners, especially cattle owners, do not belong to the lower income classes and have more to sustain on; thirdly often a bull or a goat is not owned by the peasant tending the animal, but by a well-to-do fellow villager who pays the maintaining peasant monthly or allow him to share in the profit. In general then, capital needs to a livestock trader are not as compelling as they are in fruit trade, rice trade or timber trade.

This paragraph started by pointing at voluntary, non formalized forms of cooperation. In chapter 4 it was noticed how competition between petty commodity enterprises was considered to be of a non-expulsive kind, contrary to competition between petty commodity and corporate enterprises. The manifold cooperation between petty traders seems to underscore this remark. Competition between petty traders is unmistakable, but it is not a step in a process, that in the end impels some petty traders to withdraw from trading. In some lines of trade obstacles have been created that have the effect of denying access to newcomers. The institutionalization at *pasar kota* is the most notorious case, and this obstacle was the result of government policy, not of traders' initiative. In general, as the case study on vegetable retail shows, the fine-grained interrelations enables many petty commodity traders to enter business.

Simultaneous occurence of competition and cooperation is not peculiar to petty trade only; within the corporate sector there is for instance agreement on the buying price and on the supplying *bakul* among Banjarnegara fruit merchants and also intensive coorporation within the *toko* branch, that sometimes expresses kinship ties.

A final question should be whether there is competition between petty commodity traders and corporate traders and if so, if it leads to the downfall of one of the actors. In as far as petty traders are a subordinate link to corporate traders in a regional or national commodity circulation as is documented at these pages, symbiosis should be the qualification. Sometimes every chain's scope is defined; confer gold trade. Yet on some fronts there is conflict between the circuits, tending to by-pass, as when petty commodity *bakul* sell to corporate sector wholesalers from outside *kabupaten* in stead of dealing with regional corporate sector merchants. Another example of conflict is the equivalence of *toko* traders (often corporate sector) and *pasar kota* wholesalers (sometimes corporate sector) in the distribution of manufactures, like garments. This competition is not accompanied by forms of cooperation, and the respective distributors attract customers at the expense of the rival sector. In this confrontation the *pasar* trader however is not necessarily the one who succumbs.

13.3 INTRASECTORAL AND INTERSECTORAL RELATIONS IN CONSTRUCTION AND INDUSTRY

Simultaneous competition and cooperation suggest high integration in the trade branches. In contrast, in construction the market is polarized. The first segment of the construction market, building private homes, is organized by the future residents themselves with the help of construction workers, whereas the more rewarding second segment, the government projects, is the stronghold of corporate sector contractors. This latter institutional market has been the scene of fast growth in the recent years. Licensed contractor companies almost doubled in number between 1982 and 1983. Imitative behaviour might be offered as a reason, but this imitation is not without reason for revenues are high in completing *proyek*. It attracted those people with the right finances to invest and contacts to use. One would expect competition to increase with the rising number of contractors. Competition however is a concept virtually alien to the contractor's business; the final decision on which contractor is allotted a promising order by the bureaucracy is not a matter of price calculated by the different appliants. Besides, on less rewarding projects there is consultancy between contractors, curtailing competition even further.

This polarization within construction is extended backwards; contractors have a different type of suppliers than private builders do. Contractors relate to corporate sector wholesalers usually for those inputs, that are bulky and in local supply. Suppliers in private housing construction on the other hand are of a petty commodity scale. The one exception to this segmentation concerns imported building materials with a high added value, which are sold by hardware stores to both contractors and private builders. Some contractors are wholesalers themselves and furnish fellow contractors with building inputs. Yet as the amount of work to a contractor fluctuates, most will avoid too much commitments. Machinery will be hired, not bought and construction workers are employed for the duration of a project only. Most contractors will refrain from consolidating business and avoid organizing building material supply themselves and order them at specialized wholesalers, that faced by a steady but ranging demand have them produced by piecework labourers or fetch them on request at independent enterprises. Thus it might be seen how the changing orders to corporate sector contractors postpones the proletaianization of construction workers and—indirectly—petty building material producers alike.

The other segment of the construction market's potential to employ workers in a permanent engagement is even less. As a matter of course private builders call in the help of construction workers only as long as the work on their home lasts. They might ask a senior *tukang* to supervise the construction and bring his team of workers, but these teams, called *stel*, disintegrate or attract extra *tukang*, when the job or individual commitments demand so.

The polarization in construction is not extended to the construction workers. Unlike what Van der Erve (1983) reports for Semarang city, *tukang* in Banjarnegara work intermittently in private housing construction and at government projects. Remuneration hardly differs between the two market segments. The concept of transfer of surplus is hard to operationalize, but if one would compare construction workers employed on a daily base at a contractor company to those working on the same conditions for a private builder, there seems to be no noteworthy difference between the two engagements. Only when a *tukang* is subcontracted a piece of work, instead of being paid for every day occupied, he can raise his returns. In addition it has to be noted that usually a *tukang's* remuneration is higher than what the contractor stated in his fake budget (*bouwsoom*) to the ordering bureaucracy.

This brief exposé of relations within the construction branch mentions a building material wholesaler organizing the production of building materials. Some other instances of traders organizing small scale industry might be recalled; the trader that controls bamboo weaving in the hamlet that specialized in baskets, who does not allow the weavers to sell to other traders at the same price that he receives his baskets at; and secondly, copra traders, both *petugas* and *rayon koperasi*, who regularly pay copra processors in advance, for these often lack the cash to purchase the coconuts to be dried. These cases could prompt one to think that things have not changed since the turn of the century, when—so the *Mindere Welvaartsverslagen* record—traders had a grip on secondary activities. However, the few examples just mentioned should be weighed against those many instances, in which small scale industries organize the distribution of their own produce.

Part of the petty commodity sector producers, especially those that are very small scale and tied to the local circuit, like prepared food processors, sell their output themselves. They go around peddling or have claimed a place at the market. Other petty commodity (sometimes already corporate scale) producers sell to *warong*keepers, hawkers or *pasar* traders. Resembling symbiotic relations between *toko* or *pasar* wholesalers and patronizing traders, the small scale industries allow their petty trader-clients to pay afterwards, at the end of the day or at the end of the week. A convincing example of organized distribution is *krupuk* trade. *Krupuk* producers grant short-term credit to *krupuk* hawkers and have even stationed jars, with the name of their enterprise painted on it, in the *warong* and restaurants the hawkers sell to. It seems that exerting a strong influence on the way the output is retailed is not confined to large scale, corporate sector industries like the coconut oil factory, that has his own network of agents too.

Resumingly, most petty industries and those industries that near a corporate scale sell to dependent petty commodity sector traders, or to consumers directly. If exceptions prove the rule, the rule is proven in building material industry, where some enterprises have their produce organized and channeled to corporate sector wholesalers or contractors.

Next the way the industrial enterprises are supplied should be shortly examined. Since agro-industries, but for the copra processors and the coconut oil plant, are absent in Banjarnegara town, relations with the peasant sector do not add up to much. Banjarnegara's small scale industries for the most part process imported materials, which they buy at local stores. Petty producers, like food-processors, numbering low in capitalist characteristics are served by petty scale *warong* mostly, while those industries that operate at the intersection of petty and corporate scale, like *tahu, krupuk* or floor-tile industries have their major input from *toko*. In diagram 13.3 these complex relations are summarized.

Like diagram 13.2, diagram 13.3 shows the oversimplified character of diagram 4.2, as corporate sector, petty commodity sector and peasant sector are not the monolitic block held for in that particular scheme. Some general lines however might be deduced.

Diagram 13.3 Intrasectoral and intersectoral relations in industry in Banjarnegara.

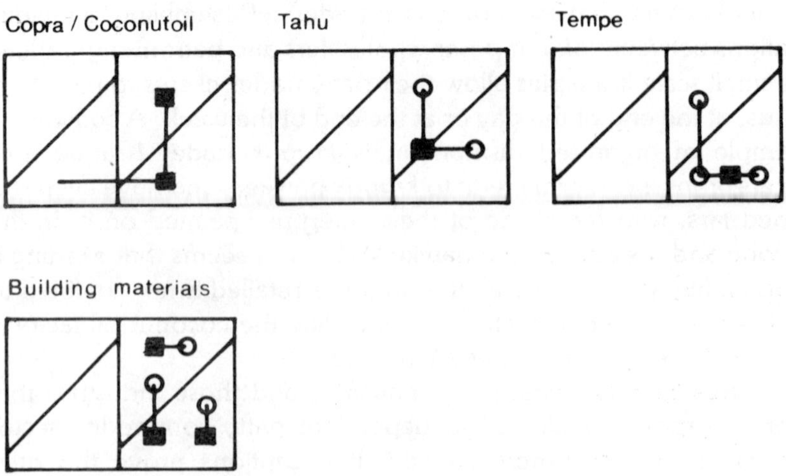

Commocities that origin from the peasant sector and that are destined for the corporate sector, whether in town or outside, are channeled trough the petty commodity sector. The total short circuiting of this link is still unusual. A considerable part of the petty commodity sector however has no link with peasant enterprises whatsoever. *Warong* and some small scale industry relates to corporate sector enterprises or to other petty commodity enterprises. These relations concern commodity flows and concommitant money flows only. Subcontracting links between corporate sector and petty commodity sector are exceptional in the small town Banjarnegara is.

With a final issue in this paragraph it is reviewed how small scale industries face one-another in Banjarnegara town. There are very few complaints on too much competition. In fact a lot of the enterpreneurs acknowledge the scope for new enterprises in their type of industry. In the next chapter we will return to the prospects for new small scale industry. The major rival in industry is not the fellow producer, but the import of manufactured items, through *pasar* and *toko* channels. In the past some industries were forced to expire by such extra*kabupaten* competition; *batik*-industry is an example in this respect.

Cooperation within the small scale industrial sector is not as extensive as it is in trade, though it is not unusual as the example of *tahu*-industry shows. Cooperation will often take a formalized structure, probably because it is harder to assemble producers than it is for traders to meet. Formalized cooperation has met variable success; the *KOPTI* has some prospects, but the copra producers cooperation was a clear failure.

Chapter 14

CONCLUSIONS FROM KOTA PENSIUN

This thesis intends to contribute to an understanding of the functioning of small towns in Indonesia, a subject that is as fashionable as it is unstudied in the last decade. We have narrowed down 'small towns in Indonesia' to Banjarnegara, a *kabupaten* town in Central Java, and we have translated 'functioning' into economic terms only. The production structure of Banjarnegara has been surveyed, with due regard to its hinterland contacts. Within the gamut of enterprises in Banjarnegara town we picked those branches, that to us seemed most important: retail, marketing, construction and industry. With a scheme drawn in chapter 4 and returned to in chapter 13 these branches have been analyzed.

In chapter 2 we discerned four small town concepts, on which—so it is posed—small town development might be modeled: propulsive growth pole, absorptive growth centre, rural motor and service centre. Some authors argue for a combination of these concepts. We now will reconsider these concepts and see how the findings of our survey on the Banjarnegara production structure fit in with them. Thus we will synthesize conclusions that have been reached per branch.

14.1 BANJARNEGARA AS A PROPULSIVE GROWTH POLE

The propulsive growth pole concept supposes that a condition for economic growth is contracting production efforts in one location. As its plot goes, a complex of interlinked enterprises should come into being, mutually benefiting from having their seat in the same location, and supported by human and physical infrastructure. Starter by eminence in this concept as applied to towns, is a large scale industry, that has a potential to develop contacts to economic undertakings in town and hinterland. Hinterland contact might be the initial reason for the industry to establish in town, and guarantees further spread as well.

In Banjarnegara there is one large scale industry, the coconut oil factory. It is in decline and though it is an agro-industry and indirectly relates to a host of rural copra processors, the effect it had on local copra production has not been an enhancing one. Copra production in the Serayu Valley has fallen; the factory used to sustain on regional supply, but nowadays, though the plant's capacity has not increased, copra from *kabupaten* Banjarnegara is only 10% of total input. Apart from some merchants, the plant does not have much forward contacts with Banjarnegara enterprises either, it supplies an occasional trader with coconut oil to retail or—exceptionally—to wholesale. What supporting infrastructure does the *Sabda Guna* plant relate to? Of course there is this copra cooperation, but the factory board used to consider it as a harass, and now it is considered up to nothing at all.

As the coconut oil plant does not catalyze economic growth in Banjarnegara, is any other branch capable of such spin-off? At present the boom branch in town is building industry. Contractor companies pop up, helping themselves to physical infrastructure projects from the *Inpres* budget. Their expansion is accompanied by a steady growth in private housing construction. As most inputs used in construction are bulky and thus incur high costs of transport, regional building material production and commerce has profited from the boom as well. Besides many construction workers are employed by it by now, both in town and on the countryside. It should be noted that building trade is not an export branch as it is addressed to local demand. Only two Banjarnegara contractors take up projects elsewhere, but on the other hand there are some eleven branch companies operating on the Banjarnegara market. Though construction trade does propel growth, it should be questioned how long this will continue and whether the effect is lasting. The boom is linked up with government orders and when they decline, which is not unlikely, construction trade and industry will collapse as well. The clientelist entrepreneur, that seized opportunities offered by *Inpres* funds, anyway does not resemble the ideal of the entrepreneur pur sang, that is willing and able to consolidate his venture at adverse circumstances.

Within the Banjarnegara production structure, there seems to be no activity that initiates propulsive growth. (Unless one considers the all-present government services as an economic sector. Alas, this was omitted in our research.) Small scale industries might be an alternative interpretation of the starter in the growth pole concept. At present most seem geared towards in-town demand, but there is a potential for petty agro-industries to develop, import substituting or export-oriented, as will be outlined in the next two paragraphs.

14.2 BANJARNEGARA AS AN ABSORPTIVE GROWTH CENTRE

In the absorptive growth centre concept, small towns are attached a role in redirecting metropole-ward migration. Rural migrants should be facilitated to settle in regional centres and town dwellers should be stopped to depart. If sufficient labour opportunities are provided, this goal is conceived an attainable one. The concept therefore focuses on the labour-absorptive branches within the small town production structure.

A first 'but' to be made is that unemployment in Banjarnegara town is to a large extent educated unemployment; youngsters, that have finished highschools like *S.M.P.*, *S.M.A.* and *S.M.E.A.*, whose ambition and whose parents' ambition generally is a white collar job. Most enterprises in town, especially those considered labour-absorptive do not qualify for them. Setting up an academy for accountancy—for example—, that enables them to get a good job (but outside town) would serve these highschool graduates better than developing small scale industry would. The character of regional un(der)employment that the absorptive growth pole is designed to solve is more difficult to appraise. Most likely, considering the unequal distribution of highschools and highschool students (cf. Ch 5), it will not be of an educated nature.

Tabel 14.1 gives a rough impression of labour absorption per branch. The estimates are based on multiplying the results of the questionnaires with results from the count on enterprises. It should be interpreted with care. The big employers seem to be retail trade, construction and small scale industry. We will briefly review the situation in the labour-intensive parts of these branches, where capital stock used per person employed is low. The petty commodity components of trade, construction and industry.

Small scale trade indeed is a major employer, especially the retail section, that is patterned by symbiosis and fragmentation as was commented in paragraphs 6.2, 7.2, 7.3 and 8.3. It has been shown that a good changes many hands before it reaches its final consumer. It seems an easy access section of the small town production structure, except for the general proglem of finding and tieing customers, which is frequently realized by allowing them to pay afterwards. Many women are able to make a living from petty trade. Retail trade however is not inflatable and infitum. At the *pasar kota* institutionalization, manifest in formal and informal claims to the sites, diminishes entry to new traders. Investments to establish at the *pasar kota* might be considerable, nearing what is needed to start a small *toko*. By-passing is another phenomenon, that causes jobs to disappear in the town's trade networks. In retail trade a first sign is the by-passing of wholesaling *toko*. By-passing is more familiar in

Table 14.1 Number of persons employed per branch in Banjarnegara

Trade	15.6%	Construction	15%
fruit	186	contractors	1504
vegetables	110	indep. craftsmen	856
clove	96	build. mat. trade	90
cattle	282		
rice	242		2450
cloth & garments	196		
other pasar trade	951	Industry	14.6%
ambulant	492	foodindustry	769
		build. mat. industry	158
	2550	other industry	1477
			2404
Shops	6.9%	Services	8.2%
toko	700	repair	402
warong	440	transport	454
		oth. serv.	490
	1140		
			1346
Agriculture	16.4%	Administration	8.4%
	2702		1383
Total	12592		

Unclassified 15% (estimated working population 16376)

Estimation based on employment figures per type of enterprise in the sample survey, weighed for sample fractions.

Source: Count on Enterprises, Census 1980, Monografi Desa 1983.

marketing. However, since the part of bulking trade that is channeled through town is controlled by a few merchants, the effect of bypassing will not so much be expressed in jobs lost, but diminish the rural motor potential in town, commented upon in the next paragraph.

What about small scale industry, the future labour absorber by assumption? At present its size is limited and labour opportunities offered are usually low-paid and strenuous, though they might fit in well with the agricultural calendar. Most small scale industry seems addressed to a diverse small town demand; take the numerous foodprocessors for instance. Still constraints are comparatively low and profits reasonable enough for more small scale industry to establish. Replacing the import of commodities by local produce seems one strategy. Upgrading regional export another. In this respect we have argued for *abon* and *kecap* industry to establish in Banjarnegara: technology is available; there seems to be a steady market for these products and regional inputs can be used. Such industries could have their locus in town. It demands however that the *kabupaten* government changes its attitude towards small scale industry, for nowadays it is thought of something that can hardly be tolerated in peaceful and clean Banjarnegara.

14.3 BANJARNEGARA SERVING ACCELERATED RURAL DEVELOPMENT

The rural motor concept depicts a town, whose enterprises and institutions support productive activities in the hinterland. The providing of rural enterprises with inputs, that are not at hand in the *desa* is meant by it. The location of subsidiary activities and processing industries, that require a hinterland above a certain threshold size. Thus it can concern credit or agricultural inputs like fertilizer or high yielding seeds; tools or raw materials for home industries. A wider interpretation includes the upgrading or marketing both of cashcrops and products from home industry. Although into what direction rural resources have to be developed is yet open to debate, we now will briefly summarize how Banjarnegara enterprises relate to the rural production structure. Governmental services were not surveyed in this respect.

Within the Banjarnegara production structure there are only few enterprises, that specifically equip peasants and rural home producers with inputs necessary. One major group are cattle traders, that import calves from East and Central Java, thus supporting fattening activities in the northern districts of *kabupaten* Banjarnegara. Next one might point at some agencies, distributing fertilizers. Other input will pass the town's shop and market channels as well, but though diversity is large, their quantity is not substantial. A trend to be noted is that rural producers in Java do not depend on the regional town to get what they need. Road infrastructure is adequate for distribution not to follow a long chain of central places. It does not matter whether a depot is located in town or near the highway somewhere out of town. Besides, as can be seen from *K.U.D.* organization, decentralization to *kecamatan* centres undercuts Banjarnegara's role as a supplier of agricultural inputs.

On marketing: in the bulking of rural produce Banjarnegara neither seems essential as a staple town. Generally peasants would not be devoid of a marketing outlet, if there was no Banjarnegara town. As is outlined in chapter 8, vegetable export and, to a lesser extent, clove export avoids Banjarnegara trade networks. In marketing of *salak*, *petai* and *cengkol* and in marketing of cattle, the town is still a major node. We have suggested that such is correlated to the dispersed occurence of these export products, which makes collecting and sending from the village inefficient for surpluses are too small. The previous examples are regional commodities, that enter a national commodity circulation. In the regional commodity circulation, the role of Banjarnegara neither is clear-cut. We reviewed rice marketing, which by-passes Banjarnegara town; the *pasar* is a minor transit for the upland districts only. In cattle trade on the other hand, *pasar* Petambakan, a few miles outside town, has some weight in the regional circulation of cows and waterbuffaloes, though goat trade is not particularly focused on this cattle market.

Agro-industries are another case to fit in the rural motor

concept. By upgrading local produce, they can enhance its position on the national market. In the previous paragraph it was stated that such industries number few in the town, but that they merit more attention; *abon* and *kecap* industry were mentioned. Another agro-industry is the corporate sector coconut oil plant, supplemented by a copra producer's cooperation; its history as an agro-industry was disappointing however.

14.4 BANJARNEGARA AS A SERVICE CENTRE

Finally we examine Banjarnegara's performance as a service centre. The issue at stake in this concept is that everyone should have access to facilities. Usually the concept is translated in terms of government services, like health care, extension, education and government credit for example. In chapter 5 it is tentatively evaluated how the town's institutions serve the hinterland. As the *kabupaten* capital, Banjarnegara has attracted the hub of facilities in the *kabupaten*. We surveyed origin of pupils at the state highschool (*S.M.A. Negeri*), inpatients at the town's hospital and debtors at the three government banks in town. Though these institutions do not have equivalents in the *kabupaten*—there are some alternatives, but of a different quality—, they are patronized by town-dwellers mostly. Of students at the *S.M.A. Negeri*, 48% have their parents living in town. 52% of in-patients at the hospital are townsfolk. For credit facilities at the banks the picture is less distorted: 22% of debtors at the *B.R.I.*, *B.P.D.* and *B.P.P.D.* in town reside in Banjarnegara. It looks like the situation is remote from equal access to all people in the *kabupaten*.

Does the same pattern hold true for Banjarnegara enterprises? Banjarnegara *toko* sell a host of items, that are not available anywhere else in the *kabupaten*, except for Purworejo Klampok maybe: motorbikes, minibuses, handcarved furniture, glasses, newspapers. Selling such luxury items is often taken as a standard for discerning higher order centres, that serve a wide hinterland. We argued that though rural dwellers make up part of the clientele to such *toko*, there might be an alternative reason for the concentration of luxury shops in town, which is its being a local pocket of wealth. In many *toko* urban customers probably by far outnumber rural customers.

Banjarnegara *toko* still serve rural dwellers however, but indirectly. Some shops wholesale to traders, that sell in *kecamatan* near Banjarnegara town. Using words like circulation and circuit once again; the small town *toko* act as the regional distribution circuit in a national commodity circulation. Part of the traders at *pasar kota* do act likewise. Besides, *pasar kota* and *pasar* Petambakan stand firm as the regional circuit in a regional commodity circulation, as is shown in paragraphes on vegetable retail and trade in draught animals. Very roughly the service area of the town's trade institutions is confined to the southeastern part of the *kabupaten* (*kawedanan* Banjarnegara). But even at this domain, by-pass by agents from big city wholesalers undercuts the service centre function of Banjarnegara town. Good accessibility has been considered a prerequisite in the service centre concept, but it ia a prerequisite for by-pass too. Moreover, similar to what was discussed in the previous paragraph, decentralization of services—*toko* arising in villages—diminishes Banjarnegara town's potential in this respect.

Finally, we judged the serviceability of contractor companies. Nucleated in town, they take up projects scattered over the *kabupaten*. Accesibility restraints work the other way around here. As projects in remote and mountainous area's incur high transport costs, even so much for their distance from Banjarnegara town as for road conditions and the absence of building material industry up north, profit margins are squeezed and such projects are not preferred. These projects are only taken up, if they are compensated by a project in an area, that allows low transport costs and high gains.

In chapter two the overview of small town concepts was concluded with remarking, that crossovers are often urged for. So be it: many types of activities fit in more than one concept; agro-industries might both absorb labour and improve marketing opportunities for rural produce. Most branches within the small town production structure are ascribed one or more functions. But the opposite might be true as well. There might be severe conflict between concepts. An example: *toko* might represent the service centre aspect of a small town; at the same time they will kill perspectives for small scale industries by introducing competitive products. Such conflicts have been dealt with in chapter 13.

All in all present Banjarnegara falls short of planning concepts —which is not altogether surprising since that is what planning concepts are made for—. Worse however, for most concepts prospects are gloomy. Rural motor and service centre potentials are threatened by by-pass and decentralization of facilities. Long term propulsive growth seems far off, since the continuing success of the building boom is doubtful. Labour absorptive growth is more promising, table 2.1 already hinted at it, but need a different attitude from local policy makers.

In this thesis we discussed the viability of small town development by surveying the production structure of one regional centre, Banjarnegara. The desirability of such development has not been reviewed. It should be noted that the major social problems are not located in small towns. Developing small towns thus is only justified, if it helps non town dwellers. Whether concentrating development effort in small towns is the best avenue then, is open to debate, the outcome of which is partly answered by the viability of the small town concepts mentioned. The Banjarnegara picture does not justify too much optimism in this respect. Additional research, as is done in the Small Town Research Project, in towns less apt to be surnamed *kota pensiun* should support or reverse this view.

REFERENCES

Armstrong, P & T. McGee (1968), Revolutionary Change and the Third World City: A theory of urban involution, in: Civilizations, Vol. 18, No. 3, pp 353—76.

Baal, J. van (1986), Ontglipt Verleden; tot 1947: Indisch bestuursambtenaar in vrede en oorlog, Wever, Franeker.

Bandjarnegara (1922), Kaart Afdeelingshoofdplaats, schaal 1:2500.

Blankhart, S (1922), Urbanization in Indonesia; A quantitative review, Institute for Geographical Studies and Urban and Regional Planning, Vrije Universiteit Amsterdam.

Breman, J (1976), Een Dualistisch Arbeidsbestel? Een kritische beschouwing van het begrip 'de informele sector', Van Gennep Rotterdam.

Brunsveld, T (1983), A profile of the Tahu and Tempe Sector: Cases from Bekasi, West-Jakarta and Tanggerang, paper delivered to the WUOO workshop on Indonesian Towns, October 27—29, Leiden.

Burger, D.H. (1975), Sociaal-Economische Geschiedenis van Indonesia, Amsterdam.

Burger, D.H. (1939), De Ontsluiting van Java's Binnenland voor het Handelsverkeer, Veenman, Wageningen.

Carlier, C (1980), Een Onderzoek naar enkele Sociaal-Geografische Processen in Verband met Erosie in het Serayu-dal, Unpublished M.A-thesis, State University Of Utrecht.

Castles, L (1967), Religion, Politics and Economic Behaviour in Java: The Kudus cigarette industry, Cultural Report Series No 15, Southeast Asia Studies, Yale University.

Chandler, G (1981), Market Traders and the Sale of Clothing in

Rural Java, Centre of Southeast Asian Studies, working paper no 25, Monash University, Melbourne.

Cohen, M., J. English & M. Brookfield (1977), Functional Diversity at the base of the Urban System in Peninsular Malaysia, Journal of Tropical Geography, 1977, pp 12—25.

Collier, W (1978), Food Problems, Unemployment and the Green Revolution in Rural Java, Prisma, March 1978, pp 38—52.

Dapice, D & D. Snodgrass (1979), Employment in Manufacturing 1970—77: a comment, in: B.I.E.S., Vol 15, No 3, pp 127—31.

Dewey, A (1962), Peasant Marketing on Java, Glencoe Free Press, Illinois.

Dick, H.W. (1978), Indonesian Prahu's and Chinese Junks: Some issues of definition and policy in informal sector studies, in: J.P. Rimmer, D. Drakakis-Smith & T. McGee, (eds.), Food, Shelter and Transport in Southeast Asia and the Pacific, Australian National University, Canberra, pp 237—256.

Dike, A.A. (1979), Some Misconceptions of African Urbanism, in: S. El-Shakhs & R. Obudho (eds.) Development of Urban Systems in Africa, Praeger, New York.

Dijk, M.P. van (1982), Some Impressions of the Informal Sector of Salatiga (Indonesia), Universitas Satya Wacana—Vrije Universiteit, Salatiga-Amsterdam.

Erve, H van de (1983), The Diversity of Workrelationships in Construction in an Indonesian City: A case study of Semarang, paper delivered to the WUOO workshop on Indonesian Towns, October 27—29, Leiden.

Forbes, D.K (1981), Petty Commodity Production and Underdevelopment; The case of peddlers and trishaw drivers in Ujung Pandang, Indonesia, Progress and Planning, Vol 16, 1981.

Friedmann, J & M. Douglass (1976), Agropolitan Development: Towards a new Strategy for Regional Planning in Asia, in: UNCRD, Growth Pole Strategy and Regional Development Planning in Asia, Nagoya.

Geertz, C (1963), Peddlers and Prince; Social change and economic modernization in two Indonesian towns, University of Chicago Press, Chicago and London.

Geertz, C (1965), The Social History of an Indonesian Town, MIT Press, Cambridge, Massachussets.

Giebbels, L.J. (1983), Jabotabek, paper delivered to the WUOO workshop on Indonesian Towns, October 25—27, Leiden.

Grant Anderson, A (1980), The Rural Market in West Java, in: Economic Development and Cultural Change, Vol 28, No 4, pp 753—778.

Hadi, Hariri (1984), Kecamatan town can stem the invasion of large cities, in: Prisma, No. 32, pp 50—54.

Hansen, N.M. (1978), Growth Strategies and Human Settlement Systems in Developing Countries, in: Fuchen Lo & Kamal Salih (eds.), Growth Pole Strategy and Regional Development, UNCRD, Nagoya.

Hansen, N.M. (1981), Development from Above, in: W. Stohr & D. Taylor (eds.), Development from Above or Below, John Wiley & Sons, Chichester.

Hulst, H.G.F. (1938), Memorie van overgave van Banyumas 1938, Bijdragen tot het mailrapport, 192/1938.

Hunink, R. & J. Stoffers (1984), Mixed and Forest Gardens on Central Java; An analysis of socio-economic factors influencing the choice between different types of landuse, Diskussiestukken van de vakgroep S.G.O., No 29, Utrecht.

International Labour Office (1972), Employment, Incomes and Equality: a strategy for increasing productive employment in Kenya, Geneva.

Iula/Aiilsg (1983), Problems and Prospects of Alternative Growth Centers, workshop report, March 17—28, 1983, Bombay.

Jong, de, W.; J.G.L. Palte & F. van Steenbergen (1983), The Role of Banjarnegara as a Small Regional Centre in Central Java, in: The Indonesian Journal of Geography, Vol. 13, pp 37—52.

Kahn, J. (1975), Economic Scale and the Cycle of Petty Commodity Production in West Sumatra, in: M. Bloch (ed.), Marxist

Analyses and Social Anthropology, Malaby Press, London, pp 137—158.

Kantor Statistik Kabupaten Banjarnegara (1978, 1980), Banjarnegara Dalam Angka, Banjarnegara.

Kantor Statistik Kabupaten Purbolinggo (1981), Wonosobo Dalam Angka, Purbolinggo.

Kantor Statistik Kabupaten Wonosobo (1980), Wonosobo Dalam Angka, Wonosobo.

Kartahardja, A (1979), The National Policy on Human Settlement in the Third REPELITA (1979—1984); Some thoughts for its formulation, in: Masalah Bangunan, Vol 24, No 1.

Killing, A. (1928), Het Middenstandskredietwezen in Nederland en Indie; Prea-advies voor het congres der middenstandsvereniging "Batavia", Bandung.

Lasono, C.; F.M. Suwandi & T. Lawen (1981), Delapan Kisah Nyata Bagaimana Merintis Usaha, Bina Swadaya, Jakarta.

Lebrun, O. & C. Gerry (1975), Petty Producers and Capitalism, in: Review of African Political Economy, Vol. 3, pp 20—32.

Lo, Fu-Chen & Kamal Salih (1976), Growth Poles and Regional Policy in Open Dualistic Economies: Western theory and Asian reality, in: UNCRD, Growth Pole Strategy and Regional Development Planning in Asia, proceeding of the seminar on industrialization strategies and the growth pole approach to regional planning and development: the Asian experience, Nagoya, Japan, 4—13 November 1975, Geneva.

Mai, U. (1983), Small Town Markets and the Urban Economy in Kabupaten Minahasa (North Sulawesi, Indonesia), paper presented at the fourth Bieleveld colloquium on Southeast Asia: Urbanization in Southeast Asia, University of Bieleveld, January 7—8, 1983.

McCawley, P. & M. Tait (1979), New Data on Employment in Manufacturing 1970—77, in: B.I.E.S., vol 15, No. 1, pp 125—136.

McCawley, P. & M. Tait (1979), Employment in Manufacturing

1970—77: A Reply in: B.I.E.S., vol 15, No. 3, pp 132—144.

McTaggart, W.D. & D. Stormont (1975), Urbanization Concepts in the Restructuring of Indonesia, in: Journal of Tropical Geography, Vol 41, pp. 34—44.

Milone, P.D. (1966), Urban Areas in Indonesia: administrative and census concepts, Institute of International Studies, University of California, Berkeley.

Mindere Welvaartsverslagen (1907), Onderzoek naar de Mindere Welvaart der Inlandsche Bevolking op Java en Madura.

Mitsuo, Nakamura (1976), The Crescent Rises over the Banyan Tree, Cornell University, Ann Arbor.

Monografi Desa (1982), Statistik Kecamatan, Banjarnegara.

Mourmans, W. (1981), Het Dualisme Begrip in de Analyse van Ontwikkeling, CASP, Rotterdam.

Muhaimin, Y.A. (1983), Politics, Businessmen and the Indonesian Middle Class, Prisma, No. 30, pp 22—23.

Nibbering, J.W. & A. Schrevel (1982), The Role of Additional Activities in Rural Java; A case study of two villages in the Malang regency, Diskussiestukken van de vakgroep S.G.O., No 17, Utrecht.

Nijkamp, B. & D. Peeters (1984), Migratie en Rurale Werkgelegenheid: Een onderzoek naar transmigratie in ruraal Central-Java, Indonesie, Unpublished M.A.-thesis, Utrecht.

Palmier, L.H. (1960), Social Status and Power in Java, University of London, Athlone Press, London.

Palte, J.; Suhardjo; Tukiran; Murtono & Wuryanto (1981), Socio-economic Structures and Developments in the Rural Uplands Surrounding the Upper Serayu River (Central Java), NUFFIC Socio-economic Input Project, Yogyakarta-Utrecht.

Peluso, N.L. (1982), Occupational Mobility and the Economic Role of Rural Women; a case study of women working outside agriculture in two villages in Sleman, Yogyakarta, Population Studies Centre, Universitas Gadjah Mada, Yogyakarta.

Program Kerja Tahun Anggaran 1983/1984 (1983), Bupati Kepala Daerah Tingkat II Banjarnegara, Banjarnegara.

Robison, R. (1978), Towards a Class Analysis of the Indonesian Military Bureaucratic State, in: Indonesia, Vol 25, pp 17—39.

Roepke, J. (1979), Entrepreneurship and Economic Development in Indonesia, in: Prisma, No 13, June 1979, pp 51—66.

Rondinelli, D.A. & K. Ruddle (1978), Urbanization and Rural Development, a spatial policy for equitable growth, Praeger, New York.

Rondinelli, D.A. (1983), Secondary Cities in Developing Countries; Policies for diffusing urbanization, Sage, Beverly Hills.

Rozestraaten, v.D. (1983), Greater Bandung Development, paper presented at the WUOO workshop on Indonesian Towns, October 25—27, Leiden.

Santos, M. (1977), Spatial Dialectics: The two circuits of the urban economy in underdeveloped countries, in: Antipode, 1977, pp 49—60.

Sardi, J. (1983), Peranan Kota Kecil dalam pengembangan pedesaan, in: Ekonomi dan Keuangan, Vol 31, pp 147—161.

S.D.S.: Serajoedal Stoomtrammaatschappij Archives,

J. Hillen (1898), Nota van een Reis van Banjarnegara naar Karangkobar, Batoer, Dieng, Wonosobo, Parakan en Ngadirejo van 5—17 november 1898.

W. Oltmans (190/), Rapport Betreffende een Studiereis in het Achterland der Serajoedal Stoomtrammaatschappij.

J.v. Delden (1896), Nota over den Serajoedal Stoomtram.

W. Morpey (1917), Verslag van een Dienstreis naar Batoer, 20—23 juni 1917.

Sensus Penduduk (1971, 1980), Biro Pusat Statistik, Jakarta.

Sethuraman, S.V.S. (1976), Jakarta: urban development and employment, ILO, Geneva.

Stohr, W. & D.F. Taylor (1981), Development from Above or Below, John Wiley & Sons, Chichester.

Sugijanto, S. & B.T. Sugijanto (1975), Urban Areas in Indonesia as Development Catalysts, Prisma, 1975, Vol 2, No 3.

Sutherland, H. (1978), The Making of Bureaucratic Elite; the colonial transformation of the Javanese priyayi, Heinemann, Singapore.

Tan, Giok-San (1963), The Chinese of Sukabumi, Cornell University, Ithaca.

Taylor, D.F. (1978), Role and Function of Lower Order Centres in Rural Development, In.: Lo, Fu-Chen, Rural Urban Relation and Regional Development, UNCRD, Nagoya.

Thoma, G. & C. Lempelius (1977), Heim- und Kleinindustrie in Zentral Java, Forschungsauftrag des Bundesministers fur Wirtschaftliche Zusammenarbeit, München.

Titus, M. (1982), Social-Spatial Consequences of the Integration of the Serayu region (Central Java) into the Colonial System, In: O.v.d. Muyzenberg, P. Streefland & W. Wolters, (eds.), Focus on the Region in Asia, CASP Rotterdam.

Titus, M.; F.v. Steenbergen & W. De Jong (1986) Exploratory Notes on the Economic Structure and Role of Small Urban Centres in the Serayu Valley Region, in: Nas. P., (ed.), The Indonesian City. KITLV, Foris, Dordrecht.

Un-Escap (1979), Guidelines for Rural Centre Planning, UN, New York.

Universitas Satya Wacana (1975), Kotamadya Salatiga; Suatu Laporan Survey tentang Keadaan Sosial-Ekonomi dan Pembangunan Daerah, Salatiga.

Unnevehr, L.J. (1984), Transport Costs, Tariffs and the Influence of World Markets On Indonesian Domestic Cassava Prices, in: B.I.E.S., Vol 20, No 1.

Witton, R.A. (1969), The Development of Cities in Java: a Preliminary Empirical Analysis, in: Southeast Journal for Sociology, Vol 2, pp 62—80.

Wolters, W. (1983), Local Level Processes Leading to Agrarian Differentiation; The case of desa Watulawang in Central Java, paper delivered to The Agrarian Differentiation Workshop,

East-West Center, Honolulu, Hawaii, December 14—20, 1983.

Wolters, W. (1984), The Interface Between Agriculture and Trade in Connection with State Polities: A Central Java case study, paper for the fifth Bieleveld colloquium on Southeast Asia.

Wong, S.T. & K.M. Saigol (1984), Comparison of the economic impacts of six growth centers on their surrounding rural areas in Asia, in: Environment and Planning A, Vol. 16, pp. 81—94.

GLOSSARY

Assistent resident	:	highest administrative rank in the colonial administration at the regency level.
Alun-alun	:	central square in front of the regent's dwelling.
BIMAS	:	Bimbingan Masal: agricultural modernization program.
BPPD	:	Bank Pasar Pemerintah Daerah: regional development bank.
BRI	:	Bank Rakyat Indonesia: people's bank of Indonesia.
Dinas Perindustrian	:	department of industry.
Dinas Perdagangan	:	department of trade.
Dinas Pertanian	:	department of agriculture.
DPU	:	Dinas Pekerjaan Umum: provincial department of public works.
DPUK	:	Dinas Pekerjaan Umum Kabupaten: regency level department of public works.
DOLOG	:	Depot Logistik: state logistical depot.
Duku	:	kind of fruit.
Durian	:	kind of fruit.
Ekonomi lemah	:	economically weak sector.
FBSI	:	Federasi Buruh Seluruh Indonesia: trade union.
Gabah	:	threshed, unhulled rice.
Hwe	:	chinese rotating credit system.
Inpres	:	presidential decree.
Jamu	:	traditional medicine.

Jengkol	:	kind of fruit.
Kabupaten	:	regency.
Kawedanan	:	administrative level below kabupaten (now defunct).
Kecamatan	:	sub-district.
Kelurahan	:	urban desa-level administrative unit.
KIK	:	Kredit Investasi Kecil: credit program for small scale investment by enterprises.
KK	:	Kredit Kelayakan: credit program to relief temporary shortage of working capital in completing government orders.
KMKP	:	Kredit Modal Permanen: credit program that furnishes working capital to small scale enterprises.
Puskesmas	:	Pusat Kesehatan Masyarakat: public health centre.
Pendopo	:	roofed, unwalled structure used for official meetings and ceremonies.
Petai	:	bean-like tree crop.
Pribumi	:	private.
Priyayi	:	person of noble descent.
Rencana Induk Kota	:	regency town master plan.
Repelita	:	Rencana Pembangunan Lima Tahun: five year national development plan.
Rukun Tetangga	:	lowest administrative unit encompassing one neighbourhood.
Rupiah	:	Indonesian currency; at the time of the questionnaires 1 US Dollar = Rp 800.
Salak	:	kind of fruit.
Sawi	:	chinese cabbage.
Sensus Penduduk	:	population census.
Sensus Pertanian	:	agricultural census.
Sensus Perindustrian	:	industrial census.
Serajoedal Stoom-trammaatschappij	:	Serayuvalley Tramway Company.
Timbangan	:	scales.

Tukang	: craftsman; this term is used for all sorts of professions, that do not need very intricate skills.
Waringin	: banyan tree.